Crab Cake page 79

Plum Sauce

Root
#1
ny
Chico

1 C plum jam

1 cider Vinger

teap. grated onion

$\frac{1}{4}$ t ground allspice

$\frac{1}{4}$ t ground ginger

Combine all ingin Saucepan: Heat.
slowly stir Constantly to boiling coal

Plum Souce #
2 $\frac{1}{2}$ Pound firm, ripe Plums
3 $\frac{1}{2}$ cup granulated Suger

rinse plums + remove pits. finely chop or force plum throu
food chopper to make 4 cups. place plums in a 4 quart pot;
stir in sugar until well blended. Let stand 1 hour
wash 4 $\frac{1}{2}$ pt jars, Keep Hot until needed. prepare lids as Manu-
facturer directs.   over

Bring plum mixture to boil over med heat
stirring frequently Continue cooking, uncovered
and stirring occasionally, until thickened about
20 mi.

Ladle hot jam into 1 hot jar at a time
leaving ¼ in head space. Wipe jar rim with
clean damp cloth, Attach Lid, fill and close
remain jars 1 Process in a boiling-water
Canner for 10 mi (15 mi at 1.000 to 6000 feet;
20 mi above 6000 feet)

Black Beans with Lettuce + Tomatoes.

2 Tbacon Bits or 2 slice of Bacon cut
in ½ peaces. 1- Large Red bell pepper Cut into
2 x ¼-in- strips. (2 cloves of Garlic mince) ⅓ C
(Canned tomatoes Sauce)(1 Table spoon of
Canned Chipotle chilies in addo sauces)
1 Tablespoon of fresh Lime Juice.
1- 15 oz Can black beans Drained, Salt + pepper
1- Small head of Roman Lettuce Chop about 4 cups
2- Med tomatoes ¼ C chop red onion

Cook Bacon in heavy skilet untel Chris
Pour of fat, Add Bell pepper, garlic,
to Skelit, and fry over med Heat 1 mi
Add To tomatoes sauce chipotle chilies
and lime juice Bring to Boil stir
frequently. Mix in Beans season with
Salt + pepper. Transfer to a Bowel
Mix in Bacon, Luttue, tomatoes,
Onion, Serve warm or at loom temperature.

American
Home Cooking
Beer Batter

Soak Trout in Lemion Juice
Beat 2 Egg yoke with Beer _ Salt + Pepper
add 3 oz of flour mix until Smove
Jet it thiken.
Beat Egg white Salt fold in to
Beer Batter.

American
Home Cooking

Nika Hazelton

THE VIKING PRESS · NEW YORK

Printed in the United States of America

For
Harold Hazelton
with
love and thanks

ACKNOWLEDGMENTS

*For helping me with this book, I want to thank
Marjorie Blanchard, Martha Durham, Letty
Warner, and most especially Nona Clarke.*

Contents

American
Home Cooking

Introduction

This book, as its title shows, is about American home cooking. It is an attempt to bring back the dishes that make people say, "How well I remember . . ."—the food people cooked and ate with pleasure before American home cooking was vulgarized by synthetic and convenience foods or scared into inept reproductions of foreign cuisines. Of course, many of the dishes in the book are still being cooked, and cooked more and more since home cooking is coming back into its own, possibly because so many of us wish for a simpler, healthier life.

This book is not a survey of America's past and present food habits, nor is it a comprehensive collection of regional dishes. Both these subjects have been treated by many writers but by none as superbly as by Waverly Root and Richard de Rochemont in their *Eating in America, a History,* or by James Beard in his *American Cookery.* As I said, the book is about the food that was cooked at home, recipes which in many cases are standard ones but which I judge best of their kind or to which individual cooks, including myself, have added their own touches. Obviously, it was impossible to include all the dishes people are nostalgic about, depending on their ethnic and regional backgrounds. Thus this book, like all cookbooks, reflects the tastes of the author (myself) and the people who have liked my food.

Basically, the character of America's traditional home cooking is English–northern European. Especially English; roast beef, potatoes, pies, and cakes are still national favorites, cooked in pretty much the same old English way.

It is interesting that no foreign cuisine has ever remained the same in America. Italians in Italy don't eat spaghetti with meatballs or as a side dish; the Chinese in China don't know chop suey, nor do Mexicans a Texas chili con carne. The salt cod of the Portuguese has found its American expression in codfish balls, and the spices of the Far East have become bland in the curried dishes of the South, such as Country Captain. The cooking of New Orleans is far spicier than its French parent, but soul food is milder than African food. I also wonder whether the foreign cuisines taught in the recent proliferation of cooking schools will change the everyday cooking habits of the students. Will they do the chopping and mincing and slow cooking of inexpensive foods as is done in France? (No wonder the food processor that makes short work of the first two was invented there.) Will they make the *sofritto*, the minced mixture of fat, onion, garlic, and herbs that is the beginning of so many Italian dishes? Will they really search out the variety of chili peppers that are typical of Mexican cooking? Will they stuff vegetables as in Near Eastern cooking? I don't know, but I am inclined to think that, by and large, foreign food remains special-occasion food and in a crunch, most people revert to the likes of steak, baked potatoes, and pie. Or meatloaf, as the case may be.

Everybody knows how the food of the native Indians has influenced America's present food. But not much is said about the way the ever-shifting frontier created purely American food habits. I am thinking of the quick hot breads that are strictly American. These can be made in a skillet, like the kettle a basic cooking instrument of the frontier, or in a simple oven standing in the embers of the open hearth. These breads don't need the slow working of yeasts nor the built-in baking oven which is the sign and symbol of settled communities.

To the frontiersman, who in order to survive had to catch fish and game and cook it himself out in the wilds, we owe the national passion for cooking out-of-doors. Even in times when only women cooked, men did not find it demeaning to cook outdoors over a wood fire.

By and large, the national American taste has always been largely for soft, sweetish foods, chowders, quick breads, stews, beans, and overdone vegetables, noodles, and rice—crunchy vegetables and pasta *al dente* are recent innovations. And of course for endless pies and cakes (Americans are not pudding eaters like the English)—all foods that are basically childish and offer easy gratification. I once conducted a survey on the kind of food people like to cry into, and invariably the food was soft and bland. No one wanted to chew on a carrot or a piece of meat.

Much has been written about the Great American Sweet Tooth and its deleterious effects; it has been with us since the early settlers. I think this may not only be due to the fact that the taste for sweetness is an innate one (we like something sweet even after a satisfying meal) but also traceable to England and northern Europe, sources of our food habits, where cold, damp climates called for quick-energy foods like sugar, especially before the days of modern heating, warmer clothing, and better nutrition. We all enjoy these benefits now, but our tastes are still for sugar in its original form, molasses, maple, honey, jam, cereals containing it, ice cream, sodas, cookies, nuts, chewing gum, and the innumerable snacks that are part of American food habits. In no other country in the world has sugar crept into foods it has no place in, such as salad dressings, canned foods, baby foods, and breads—to make them more palatable, the manufacturers say. However, there is hope for the teeth and health of at least some Americans. Young parents of the health food generation are more careful about feeding sugar to their children in candies, soft drinks, and desserts. But, alas, many parents feed their children quantities of Granola, which is loaded with sugar of one kind or another, under the impression that though honey or raisins may contain sugars, they are healthy sugars.

Traditionally, American seasonings have been bland, with the exception of some minority foods such as those of the Mexicans, Poles, and Italians who still practice Old World cooking habits. The

blandness of American home cooking is very evident in the old
chicken recipes and it may be due to the fact that in days gone by
food could well afford to be underseasoned. The basic ingredients
were fresh and flavorful to a degree almost unknown to us and
needed none or only a little of the herbs and spices that traditionally mask poorer foods. The number of such seasonings was
small; herbs like sage, mint, and parsley and spices like nutmeg,
cloves, and cinnamon were used again and again, possibly because
of the homogeneity of early American society, whose members all
liked the same flavors in their food.

Even today, homey American cooking is cautious as to seasonings; I have seen recipes in small-town newspapers (especially
in the Midwest) that suggest the use of half a bayleaf in a stew
with 1½ pounds of meat or 1 teaspoon of parsley in a tomato sauce.
Stronger seasonings, with the increased use of herbs and spices,
seem to date mainly from the Second World War, when large num-
bers of Americans came for the first time in close contact with European and other foreign foods; they now stand for sophistication.
Modern food needs heavier seasoning because it has so often very
little flavor; I am thinking of the assembly-line chickens, the hor-
mone-fed beef, the half-ripe or overripe vegetables that come from
afar, and the indifferent fruit, all looks and practically no taste. I
have also noticed that frequently even newly bought dried herbs
and spices are by no means full-flavored. They sat too long on the
shelves of their market; even unopened, spices lose much of their
zing with age. In practice, this means that you have to add more
dried herbs or spices than are specified by the recipe to get a desired flavor, not as good as is provided by a fresh dried herb or
spice but better than no flavor. With herbs, I like to have the flavor
of one prevail in a dish and regret the attitude that if one herb is
good, three are better.

Over the years, the American diet has become much lighter:
we have turned from starchy to protein and vegetable foods. Reasons for this are the shift from active to sedentary occupations, better housing, heating, and clothing (when you're cold you crave
richer, heavier foods); better health and nutrition; the great all-
American sport of dieting; and more sophisticated food tastes. Pros-
perity has enabled people to eat more meat and fewer potatoes,
and the cholesterol and other scares have induced a certain number

to cut down on fats. Here again the influence of the health food movement must be stressed.

About American regional cooking, now being leveled out by modern food technology and communication: always excluding that of ethnic groups, I think the only true and really different regional cooking in America was and is that of the Creoles of Louisiana. Southern cooking (other than Creole cooking) is certainly different from that of New England, but the differences are largely a matter of nuances, such as the preference for white cornmeal over yellow for hot breads—the hot breads are still there. They are also a matter of available raw materials, which taste different but are used in the same manner, such as sweet potatoes in the South as against northern white potatoes.

Midwestern and Far-Western cooking are offspring of their Eastern forerunners, making use of local foods such as game and produce, but still stressing sweet, soft, starchy dishes. All American cookbooks have large sections of cakes, pies, and breads compared to those in French or Italian cookbooks, but none have more than Midwestern ones. Perhaps this is because the Midwest is wheat-growing country and the home base of the enormous flour companies; one has only to think of the influence of the popular Betty Crocker cookbooks and the Pillsbury Annual Bake-Offs.

To develop a regional way of cooking, a region has to be settled by a homogenous group of people, or by people who have meshed their different origins. When this latter process has taken place, California will have a true regional cuisine rather than single typical dishes based on local foods such as its seafood and vegetables. It strikes me that cities like New York and states like California, where there is a constant influx of new people, are far more open to foreign influences. In California, the influence is oriental, in New York continental, and in both places people take an inordinate interest in cooking, as well as in cooking schools and cookbooks.

But over the years, as has happened everywhere, American life and American food have become standardized. Mass-produced foods, national supermarket chains, national brands, and recipes in national magazines and newspapers have largely eliminated regional differences. On the other hand, the cooking mania that is sweeping the country has produced an interest in foreign and exotic cooking that is unknown in Europe. This is not only an upper-class interest; supermarket magazines such as *Family Circle* and *Woman's Day* are constantly (and often successfully) telling people how to make quite sophisticated foreign dishes from what is available on the shelves of their supermarket clients. American cooks are adventurous and I think most Americans will eat something they don't know at least once. Not so Europeans, as anyone who has tried to serve sweet potatoes or okra to a Frenchman or an Italian, knows to her/his sorrow; the language heard on such occasions cannot be reproduced in a family book like this one. Interestingly, the Americanization of Europe has affected the way foods are produced (freezing, packaging, assembly-line chickens, and so on) but not the way they are cooked. Italians still don't like anything but Italian food, the French prefer their own, and so do the Spaniards and the Scandinavians. Only the English, maligned as they are for their cooking, seem to show some interest in American foods, notably fast foods. As far as I know, there are no books on American cooking in France, England, Germany, and Italy, whereas in America there are many books on the cooking of those countries.

I think the diet of educated Americans is much more varied than that of their European counterparts. The chief reason for this, besides Americans' interest in foreign countries, is that educated American cooks (and the women still do most of our cooking) are expected to cook things that no French, German, or Italian cook would tackle. Can you see a French woman in Lille making a Greek spinach pie with phyllo sheets, or an Italian woman in Pisa cooking Chinese style, or a German one making Mexican food? But American women are expected to be international cooks—besides being, all in one body, wives, mistresses, mothers, chauffeurs, gardeners, charity workers, athletes, and professional breadwinners. What seems odd to me is that they want to and are proud to be as omniscient and omnipotent as possible. Perhaps Women's Lib will change all this.

Food in today's America has become very much a matter of class. (Of course, the rich and educated in every country have always eaten differently from the rest of the population, if only in a more refined preparation of the same foods.) American working-class people make far more use of convenience foods and don't go in for carefully cooked-from-scratch dishes in expensively decorated kitchens. What to do with convenience foods, how to combine them into something different, is the primary interest of the majority of Americans; we only have to think of the stream of recipes sent out by Campbell Soups for the use of their products—notably mushroom soup—in sauces and stews and so-called gourmet casseroles. Whereas the kulturny, status-symbol-conscious crowd fill more and more cooking schools, like groupies surrounding a pop star. As a matter of fact, most cooking-school teachers do produce themselves as leaders, as stars, as ultimate authorities. These higher cooking interests require a certain amount of education, leisure, and money, while most people are content with the recipe offerings of newspapers, ads, the back of packages, and possibly the wedding present cookbook.

Either way, it seems to me that good old home cooking has been forgotten. The convenience-food crowd has no time, and the fancy-food crowd wants instant spectaculars. But there are a lot of people in between who are able and willing to devote some of their time to cooking everyday foods properly. These are the people who bake their own breads, cakes, and cookies, who make their own pies, who neither overcook their vegetables nor have to stir-fry them only; who use convenience foods when it is convenient— canned consommé, bouillon cubes, canned tomatoes in winter, baked beans for two, and so on—doctoring them up as needed.

Another factor contributing to our changing food attitudes is the circumstance that families no longer eat all their meals together, as they once did as a matter of course. Breakfast and lunch are no longer joint meals. Even the daily family dinner is no longer taken for granted, what with all family members pursuing their individual interests. Working fathers and/or mothers come home late, teenagers have their sports and activities, housewives their groups, and the tyranny of television rules that certain programs have to be watched, meal time or not. The solution for all these different eating times, according to the people who have to cope with them day in, day out, is short-order cooking with convenience foods.

Then there are the ever more numerous fast-food restaurants, providing foods that children love and giving the cook a break from the kitchen. Also, they are reasonably priced: where else can a family eat dinner without going broke?

What is interesting to see is the relation between home cooking and restaurants. As people cook less and worse at home, restaurants fall largely into two categories: high-priced places where the food is good but unaffordable for almost everybody and affordable places where the food is at best indifferent. In a city like New York, I have found that a decent meal decently priced is almost invariably an ethnic meal—Greek, Chinese, Lebanese, and so forth.

Throughout America, women's, grandmothers', schoolchildren's, hospital, and church groups put out their own little cookbooks to raise money. Many of these books are excellent. But why is the food in their towns so poor? Anybody who travels through the United States knows that, by and large, breakfasts and steak dinners are the only edible meals in the average small or even medium-sized American town. I also wonder how many of the people who belong to gourmet societies, who buy high-flown cookbooks and go to cooking schools, will send back a dish that is not properly done in a fancy restaurant. It seems odd that when there were fewer cookbooks and little or none of the current preoccupation with food, food was much better. In other words, less theory and more practice; whatever the books say, you don't become an excellent cook overnight.

I like to cook and to eat well, and I feel that I owe my family proper meals. But I don't like spending my whole life in the kitchen. In this book, I hope to prove that it is possible to produce good food without everlasting fussing. I've put in recipes that I've been asked for many times—such as the various chocolate cakes—and recipes for simple things that everyone knows and almost everyone forgets. The choice is a personal one, as I said earlier, but I wish I could have catered to everybody's nostalgia. I also did not feel it necessary to include dishes that are easily found in standard cookbooks—basic meats, vegetables, sweets, and so on.

Nor have I included recipes for baking bread, except for some quick hot breads. There are many books now on the market which deal with the subject of bread baking at length (as it should be dealt with). The renewed interest in home baking is a hopeful sign that home cooking is coming back.

As for my own way of cooking. I shop largely in my neighborhood supermarket because American supermarkets are fine places to find even foreign foods, such as olive oil, chilis, teas, jams, canned foods, and others. Supermarket food has been called plastic, and some of it is, but one can avoid that. Besides, any food is what you make of it. And how on earth could Americans, our millions, be provided with food except in supermarkets, which offer a choice and save time and money. Though supermarket produce has improved over the last few years, I still prefer to buy fresh vegetables and fruits in a vegetable market, but grapefruit, oranges, onions, pototoes, and similar staples are perfectly good in supermarkets. My supermarket also sells perfectly acceptable chickens and everyday meats like bacon, sausages, ground round of beef, and pork chops. Better meats, so to speak—veal, roasts, ham, liver, kidney, and such—are better bought at a butcher's.

I seldom shop in health food stores, finding them too expensive and not always truthful: I buy there only special products, such as certain soy sauces, sea salt, and grains. As for their vegetables and fruits—naturally with some exceptions—I don't think that they compare with the produce of a good vegetable and fruit stand, except in the height of summer, when health food store tomatoes and other locally grown produce can be better—and much more expensive. But I certainly don't knock the health food movement. On the contrary, I admire it for having brought about better food habits, regardless of some excesses.

Since all American fowl and meat are too fat, I cut off all visible fat and remove chicken skins. I cook from scratch and don't use such prepared foods as breaded shrimp, sauced-up vegetables, frozen cakes and pies, but I occasionally use frozen pie crust as a base, because nobody I know ever eats the crust of a pie. I use some canned foods, like tomatoes, chilis, beans (it is not worth cooking up a mess of beans for two and I now cook regularly only for my husband and myself). I use, when pressed, clear chicken bouillon and bouillon cubes—the imported Swiss ones, since there is a world of difference between them and the American ones. I use such frozen vegetables as peas, lima beans, corn, and okra when the fresh are out of season or of poor quality. I use frozen raspberries and strawberries when I must, but always I try my utmost to eat seasonal foods. I use olive oil for cooking, and I use butter because butter tastes better and because I don't like what I read in the fine print on margarine packages (and on the packages of artificial dairy or egg products). The chemicals may be the same, but I prefer to take mine from nature. There is no need to fear butter in small quantities; it does not have to be smeared on bread or to drench foods. Besides, I also use non-sticking frying pans which cut down or eliminate fats. But I think that a little fat is needed in making scrambled eggs, in home-frying potatoes, or in beans and other legumes. The flour specified in recipes is invariably sifted first and then measured. I use large eggs, and when something is specified as minced, I mean just that—chopped very, very fine. I am not particularly fond of sauces, nor is my husband; we prefer cooking juices (degreased when necessary). Since the metric system has not yet crept into American cooking, baking times are given in degrees Fahrenheit and weights in pounds and ounces.

Finally, why should I, foreign-born and bred, write about American home cooking? Because that's what I have cooked, well over two-thirds of my life, for an American husband and sons who, except for spaghetti, don't really like any other food.

Appetizers,
Hors d'Oeuvres,
and Sandwiches

DEVILED ALMONDS

Southern

This method is good for either a small or a large number of almonds.

almonds
salad oil
salt
cayenne pepper

Pour boiling water over the almonds and let stand for a few minutes. Drain a few at a time and pinch off the brown skins. Dry the blanched almonds on a clean kitchen towel, making sure they are really dry. In a heavy frying pan, heat 1 or 2 teaspoons salad oil. The amount depends on the size of the pan, but there should be no more than a thin film—just enough to prevent almonds from scorching. Over medium heat, fry the almonds until they are beginning to get golden brown. Shake the pan constantly to prevent sticking, or stir with a fork. Drain almonds on paper towels, and while they are still hot, sprinkle with salt and cayenne pepper to taste. It is best to serve the almonds hot, in a heated wooden or china bowl.

ANCHOVY CANAPÉS

All-American

This may well be the granddaddy of all canapés, but it is practical and always well liked.

hard-cooked eggs, shelled
thin-sliced or regular sliced firm white or brown bread
sweet butter, at room temperature
mayonnaise
canned anchovy fillets (the kind that are rolled and have
    a caper in the middle), drained
parsley

Before slicing all the eggs, slice one to use as a guide in cutting bread. The best way to get even slices is to use an egg slicer, the gadget that puts the hard-cooked egg into a well and slices it with 10 thin wires. Reserve the end slices for egg salad. Select the largest egg slice. Cut the crusts off the bread, and cut the bread slices into rounds slightly larger than the egg slice. Butter each round and spread lightly with mayonnaise. Top each round with an egg slice and top the egg slice with a rolled anchovy. Place on a platter and decorate with parsley sprigs. Refrigerate before using.

Note:
The eggs need not be salted since anchovy and mayonnaise are salty.

HOT BISCUITS WITH STUFFING

From a Chicago hostess

½ recipe or 1 recipe biscuit dough (page 199), depending on how many of these small biscuits you want
butter, at room temperature
deviled ham or pâté de foie gras or foie-gras mousse

Make biscuit dough according to directions. Roll out and cut
into small 1- to 1½-inch rounds. Bake according to directions, but
check oven at intervals since smaller biscuits will bake more
quickly than standard-sized ones. When the biscuits are done, split
them quickly and butter them. Stuff each biscuit with about 1
teaspoon deviled ham, pâté, or mousse. Serve in a dish lined with a
napkin to keep biscuits hot. Work swiftly, as the biscuits should be
served as hot as possible.

6–12 SERVINGS

STUFFING FOR CELERY

All-American

1 bunch celery

Wash the celery, drain, and dry. Separate the stalks, remove
the tough ones (use for soups and stews), and if necessary, peel off
strings. Trim the stalks and cut into 3-inch lengths. Fill half of the
length (about 1½ inches) with stuffing. Refrigerate before serving.

STUFFING I
¼ pound (about 1 cup) crumbled blue cheese, at room
temperature
2 tablespoons butter, at room temperature
⅓ cup finely chopped salted almonds or salted peanuts

Combine ingredients and blend until creamy.

STUFFING II

1 3-ounce package cream cheese
2 tablespoons heavy cream
1 to 1½ tablespoons anchovy paste
   salt
   freshly ground pepper

Combine the cream cheese, heavy cream, and anchovy paste and blend until creamy. Taste. Add a little salt if necessary, and add pepper.

6–12 SERVINGS

PIQUANT HORS D'OEUVRE SHRIMPS

From a Virginia hostess

½ pound small shrimp (about 18–20 shrimp), cooked
   and shelled
½ cup water
2 tablespoons butter
   salt
   freshly ground pepper
   Tabasco to taste
4 tablespoons white vinegar or cider vinegar (do not use
   wine vinegar), or vinegar to taste
   lettuce leaves

Put the shrimp into a heavy saucepan. Add the water, butter, a little salt, pepper, and Tabasco. Cook over low heat, shaking the pan frequently to prevent sticking, for about 3–4 minutes or until the shrimp are thoroughly heated through. Add the vinegar and shake the pan to mix. Cook, shaking the pan frequently, for 3–4 minutes longer or until the shrimp have absorbed the flavor of the vinegar. Taste and if necessary add more salt, pepper, and Tabasco.

Chill the shrimp in the liquid. At serving time, drain and place o
platter lined with lettuce leaves. Spear each shrimp with a toothpick for easy eating.

6–8 SERVINGS

CHERRY TOMATOES AND
SMOKED OYSTERS

From New Orleans

*It is preferable to use the tiny smoked oysters (about 40
in a 3-ounce can), but if they are not available, drain large
smoked oysters and cut them in half.*

40 cherry tomatoes
    salt
 1 3-ounce can smoked oysters, drained

Cut each cherry tomato down to within ¼ inch of the base.
Spread apart and sprinkle with a pinch of salt. Slip an oyster into
each tomato.

40 SERVINGS

REVITALIZED POTATO CHIPS
OR CORN CHIPS

All-American

Place large whole potato chips or corn chips on a heat-proof
platter presentable for serving. Sprinkle with grated sharp Cheddar
or grated Parmesan or grated Pecorino cheese. At serving time, heat
the broiler, and broil chips just long enough to melt the cheese.
Serve hot from the platter.

CHUTNEY DIP

All-American

This is especially good as a dip for cooked shrimp or for tiny, drained canned red beets, or with spears of Belgian endive.

1¼ cups mayonnaise
  2 tablespoons heavy cream
  2 tablespoons sour cream
  ⅓ cup thick chutney, finely chopped

Combine all the ingredients and mix well. If too thick, add a little more heavy cream, 1 teaspoon at a time, for desired consistency.

MAKES ABOUT 1¾ CUPS

THE GREAT ALL-AMERICAN CLAM–CREAM CHEESE DIP

Make this as clammy as your heart desires.

  2 3-ounce packages cream cheese, softened
  1 tablespoon onion juice
  1 large garlic clove, mashed
  2 tablespoons mayonnaise, or
    ¼ cup heavy cream
  ½ to 1 cup drained minced clams
    salt
    freshly ground pepper
    dash Tabasco

Combine the cream cheese, onion juice, garlic, and mayonnaise or heavy cream and blend them by hand or in a food processor until fluffy. By hand, blend in the clams. Taste for saltiness (clams may be salty) and add salt, pepper, and Tabasco. Mix well and beat until very soft. If mixture is too thick, stir in another table-spoon mayonnaise or cream. Serve with potato chips, raw vegeta-bles, or pretzel sticks. Or spread on crisp crackers, topping each spread cracker with a tiny bit of fresh parsley or dill weed.

MAKES ABOUT 1¼ CUPS

CREAM CHEESE–WATERCRESS DIP

Inspired by the Yale Club Spread

    8 ounces cream cheese
    2 tablespoons milk
 ⅓ to ½ cup chopped watercress leaves
       grated horseradish to taste (drain bottled horseradish
       very thoroughly)
       salt
       freshly ground pepper

With an electric beater, beat the cream cheese and milk until smooth. Stir in the watercress and horseradish and blend well. Season with salt and pepper to taste. Serve on crackers.

MAKES ABOUT 1⅓ CUPS

SIMPLE LOW-CALORIE COTTAGE-CHEESE DIP

All-American

1 cup low-calorie cottage cheese or regular cottage cheese
salt
dash of Tabasco or cayenne pepper to taste
1 2-ounce jar red caviar

Combine the cottage cheese, a little salt, and the Tabasco or cayenne in a bowl or in a blender or food processor. Beat until smooth. Stir half of the caviar into the mixture. Spoon into a little bowl or serving dish and sprinkle with the remaining caviar. Place in the middle of a serving platter and surround with raw vegetables crisped in water; good choices are carrot and celery sticks, small cauliflowerets, strips of zucchini and cucumber, small cherry tomatoes, fennel (finocchio) slices, and radishes.

MAKES ABOUT 1 CUP

MALAXÉ

From a French hostess in New York City

½ cup butter, at room temperature
½ cup mashed Roquefort or blue cheese
2 tablespoons cognac, Calvados, Armagnac, or any
   good-quality California or Spanish brandy

Combine the butter, cheese, and brandy in a food processor and process until smooth. Or beat ingredients by hand until smooth and creamy. Spread on rounds of Melba toast or pumpernickel.

VARIATION:
Spread about ¼ teaspoon of the mixture on half of a large

shelled walnut or pecan and top with another half, sandwich
fashion.

MAKES ABOUT 1 CUP

QUICK CHICKEN-LIVER SPREAD

From California

*I save chicken livers from my various chicken dishes and
freeze them. Then I make this spread when I need one in a
hurry—this is a more-or-less dish.*

      2 tablespoons butter
      1 medium onion, minced
      ½ pound chicken livers, trimmed and cut into pieces
      ⅓ cup sherry
        salt
        freshly ground pepper
        dash Tabasco
      2 tablespoons brandy or bourbon

Heat the butter in a deep frying pan. Cook the onion until
soft and golden. Add the chicken livers and all the other ingredients. Simmer over low heat without a cover for about 15–20 minutes. Then purée in a blender or food processor or force through a
sieve. If too thick to spread, stir in a little sherry or brandy, 1 tablespoon at a time. If too thin, return to frying pan and cook over medium heat, stirring constantly, for 2–4 minutes or until thickened.
Cool. Spread on toast or crackers.

MAKES ABOUT 1 CUP

CHICKEN-LIVER PÂTÉ IN THE SHAPE OF A PINEAPPLE

From New York

This is a very decorative pâté, yet it is easy to make. You will need a good-looking top from a fresh pineapple and pimiento-stuffed olives for the look.

1 fresh pineapple with unblemished thick foliage
2 cups (1 pound) butter
2 pounds chicken livers
2 medium onions, cut into quarters
1 teaspoon curry powder
¼ teaspoon Tabasco
¼ teaspoon salt
¼ teaspoon freshly ground pepper
⅛ teaspoon allspice
4 tablespoons brandy
1½ to 2 cups sliced pimiento-stuffed olives

Cut the foliage off the pineapple and reserve, saving the pineapple itself for another use. Heat 1 cup of the butter in a saucepan. Add the chicken livers, onions, curry powder, Tabasco, salt, pepper, allspice, and 2 tablespoons of the brandy. Cook covered over medium heat, stirring frequently, for about 7–8 minutes. Turn mixture into a food processor or blender. Blend until smooth. If cold, return to saucepan and heat over low heat, but do not boil. Stir in the remaining butter and brandy. Chill mixture. Mold into pineapple shape and place on a serving platter. Cover with neat rows of slices of pimiento-stuffed olives; slices should touch one another. Cap with the pineapple foliage.

MAKES ABOUT 5 CUPS

JEWISH CHOPPED CHICKEN LIVER

From New York City

Bobby Hertzberg, who gave me the recipe, claims that this—the best chopped liver I ever ate—"is the absolute definitive Jewish chopped liver (though no one will agree. Everyone has his own. Still, mine is best)."

½ cup chicken fat (chicken fat is essential)
2 large Spanish onions, chopped medium fine
½ pound chicken livers (if large, cut in half)
2 hard-cooked eggs, cut in quarters
1 teaspoon salt
⅓ teaspoon freshly ground pepper
   thinly sliced white radishes

Heat the chicken fat in a heavy frying pan. Add the onions. Cook, stirring constantly, until onions are golden brown. With a slotted spoon, transfer onions to wooden chopping bowl or food processor bowl. Add the chicken livers to the frying pan. Cook, stirring all the time, over moderate-high heat for about 3–5 minutes, until browned on outside but still pink inside. Livers should be medium rare; do not overcook. Add livers and pan juices to the bowl containing the onions. Add the eggs, salt, and pepper and mix well. Chop with a rounded chopper until fine, but not too fine and not puréed—mixture needs texture. If using food processor, switch on-off 5–7 times. Turn into a serving bowl and refrigerate covered. Return to room temperature before using on plain crackers, matzohs, or thin-sliced seeded rye. If desired, serve with the traditional thinly sliced white radish garnish.

Notes:

The mixture must be chopped in a bowl; it is too loose to chop on a board.

Heretically, I have made this with ⅓ cup chicken fat and 2 large ordinary onions, and it was good.

In some parts of the country, it may not be possible to buy

chicken fat that is already rendered. If none is at hand, the skin and fat from 1 frying chicken, cut up and cooked very very slowly over low heat, will give approximately ½ cup of rendered chicken fat. Strain the hot fat through a fine strainer to remove the "grieben," or cracklings, and use the grieben in biscuits.

MAKES 2 CUPS

LIVERWURST SANDWICH SPREAD

All-American

approximately ½ cup liverwurst
3 tablespoons chili sauce
¼ cup finely chopped olives
½ teaspoon minced onion
buttered pumpernickel

Mash the liverwurst with a fork and beat with the chili sauce, olives, and onion. Or combine in a food processor and blend until smooth. Spread on buttered pumpernickel.

MAKES ABOUT ¾ CUP

EGGS À LA RUSSE

All-American

The Russian dressing that goes over the eggs may also be used as a dip for crisp raw vegetables.

RUSSIAN DRESSING

1 cup mayonnaise
¼ cup chili sauce
1 tablespoon grated onion
1 large garlic clove, mashed
2 tablespoons finely chopped pimiento-stuffed olives or
   pitted black olives
1 tablespoon minced parsley
   Tabasco to taste (optional)

1 head Boston lettuce
6 hard-cooked eggs, peeled and halved lengthwise
1 tablespoon drained capers (chop if large)

To make the dressing, combine all the ingredients and mix
well. Remove any blemished leaves from the lettuce. Separate the
remaining leaves and wash them. Dry them individually with paper
towels. Line a platter with the lettuce leaves. Place the eggs, cut
side down, on the lettuce. Pour the dressing over the eggs. Sprinkle
with the capers. Chill for about ½ to 1 hour before serving.

6 SERVINGS

BAKED-BEAN SANDWICHES

From New England

1 cup undrained baked beans, homemade or canned
¼ cup reserved bean juice or enough to moisten, or
   ¼ cup apple sauce
2 tablespoons piccalilli
   salt
   freshly ground pepper
4 slices cold cuts, leftover meat, or cheese
4 slices buttered bread

Drain the beans and reserve juice. Mash beans and stir in
enough of the bean juice or apple sauce for the proper spreading

consistency. Stir in the piccalilli, salt, and pepper. Place a slice of meat or cheese on one slice buttered bread. Cover with half the bean mixture and top with another slice of meat or cheese and another slice of buttered bread. Repeat with remaining bread.

VARIATION:

This simple-minded sandwich can be varied, I am told, deliciously, with chili sauce, minced onion, or onion slices in lieu of the piccalilli or—and why not—along with the piccalilli.

2 SANDWICHES

EGG-AND-HAM-SALAD SANDWICHES

All-American

2 hard-cooked eggs
½ cup ground cooked ham, preferably smoked ham
1 teaspoon grated or minced onion
1 tablespoon minced celery (optional)
⅓ cup homemade mayonnaise
4 slices bread, lightly buttered

Chop the eggs fine. Combine with the ham, onion, celery (if used), and mayonnaise. Mix well. Spread between buttered bread slices.

VARIATION:

Use ½ cup ground cooked chicken instead of ham and add 2 tablespoons minced pickle to filling.

2 SANDWICHES

SUBMARINE SANDWICH

All-American

*Descended from the elegant Oyster Loaf, offered by way-
ward gentlemen to pacify the little woman at home, and
cousin to the miscellaneously filled Po'Boy of New Orleans
at the turn of the century and to the present-day Hero.*

    4 pieces Italian bread (long loaf), each about 8
      inches long
    4 tablespoons mayonnaise
  2-4 tablespoons prepared mustard
    1 tablespoon salad oil
    1 tablespoon wine vinegar
    1 small garlic clove, mashed
    4 large lettuce leaves, washed and dried
    6 ounces sliced Italian salami
    6 ounces sliced American cheese
    6 ounces cooked sliced ham
    6 ounces sliced provolone cheese

Cut bread pieces in halves horizontally. Spread mayonnaise
on one half and mustard on the other half of each piece. Combine
the salad oil, vinegar, and garlic and mix well. Dip the lettuce
leaves into the mixture and shake off excess. Place lettuce leaves on
mayonnaise-covered half of each half slice, and top with salami,
American cheese, ham, and provolone. Cover with the mustard-
covered half slices and cut each in half diagonally.

4 SANDWICHES

Soups, Chowders, and Gumbos

CHICKEN BROTH

All-American

This is a basic broth, to be used for soups and whenever chicken broth or bouillon is called for in a recipe. Refrigerate covered for 4 to 5 days, or freeze.

3–4   pounds chicken parts—wings, backs, necks, gizzards
  2   cups chopped celery, white part and leaves
  1   medium onion, chopped
  1   large carrot, chopped
  ½   cup parsley leaves
  1   tablespoon salt
  6   peppercorns
  7   cups boiling water

CHICKEN CORN SOUP

Remove all visible fat from the chicken parts, b...
skins. Place chicken in a large kettle. Add all the remain...
ents; the boiling water seals in the flavor of the chicken...
be used for other dishes. Bring to the boiling point. Lower heat to
very low and skim. Cover the kettle and simmer over low heat for
1–2 hours, skimming as needed. Strain the soup through a colander
into a bowl. Place in refrigerator to settle the fat by chilling; when
the fat is solid, remove it and throw it away. (Or remove the fat
from the hot broth by first spooning off as much as possible and
then blotting up the remainder with paper towels.) Scrape the veg-
tables off the chicken pieces and remove and discard all skin,
bones, and remaining fat. Use the meat for Chicken Corn Soup
(see following recipe) or other dishes.

MAKES ABOUT 6 CUPS

CHICKEN CORN SOUP

Traditional in Pennsylvania Dutch country

*A soup for hungry people and a full meal for less hungry
ones. When I make Jambalaya (page 65), I use backs,
wings, necks, and gizzards to make broth (see preceding
recipe) and use the broth and the chicken meat for this
soup. Though the original recipe does not call for it, I
think the soup is improved by adding either a couple of
dashes of Tabasco or 1–2 tablespoons fresh lemon juice to
the finished soup.*

6 cups well-flavored chicken broth, free of fat
½ teaspoon saffron
2 cups shredded cooked chicken
1 cup fresh or frozen corn kernels
1 cup egg noodles, broken into pieces
2 hard-cooked eggs, chopped
   salt
   freshly ground pepper
2 tablespoons minced parsley

Heat the chicken broth in a soup kettle and stir in the saffron. Bring to the boiling point and lower heat. Add the chicken and the corn. Bring the soup again to the boiling point and add the noodles. Cook over low-to-medium heat for about 10 minutes or until the noodles are tender. Remove from heat and add the eggs. Taste and, if necessary, add a little salt and pepper. Stir in the parsley and serve hot.

Note:

This is a more-or-less dish, that can be made less thick by using less corn and fewer noodles or thicker by adding more of either or both. However, it is not meant to be a thin soup.

4–5 SERVINGS

FRESH TOMATO SOUP

All-American

Easy, and no canned tomato soup equals it.

- 2 tablespoons butter
- 1 large onion, thinly sliced
- ¼ cup minced celery
- 2 tablespoons minced carrot
- 6 large ripe tomatoes, peeled and coarsely chopped
- 6 cups chicken bouillon or water
- ½ teaspoon dried thyme
- 2 tablespoons uncooked rice
  salt
  freshly ground pepper
- ¼ cup minced parsley

In a heavy saucepan combine the butter, onion, celery, carrot, and 2 tablespoons of the chicken bouillon or water. Simmer covered over low heat, stirring frequently, for about 10–15 minutes or until the vegetables are soft. Do not brown. Add the tomatoes and the rest of the bouillon or water. Cook covered over low heat, stirring occasionally, for 15 minutes or until tomatoes have cooked to a pulp. Purée in a food processor or blender or strain through a food mill. Return to saucepan and add the thyme and rice. Cook covered over medium heat for about 10 minutes or until rice is soft. Check seasoning; bouillon may be salty. Add salt, if needed, and pepper. Sprinkle with parsley. Serve hot.

Note:

The amount of juice in tomatoes is unpredictable. If the soup looks too thick, add a little more water, 2 tablespoons at a time. The soup is excellent chilled; in this case, omit the rice.

4–6 SERVINGS

HOT OR CHILLED
CREAM OF ALMOND SOUP

From Southern California

1½   cups whole blanched almonds, finely ground in
       blender or food processor (about 2½ cups ground)
  6   cups homemade or canned chicken bouillon
  1   small onion, or 2 large shallots, minced
  2   bay leaves
  3   tablespoons butter
  2   tablespoons flour
  1   cup milk
  1   cup heavy cream
 ⅛   teaspoon ground cardamom or mace
       salt
       freshly ground white pepper

Combine the almonds, chicken bouillon, onion or shallots, and bay leaves in a saucepan. Bring to boiling point, lower heat to lowest possible, and simmer covered for 30 minutes. Remove bay leaves and keep soup warm. In another saucepan, over low heat,

heat the butter and stir in the flour. Cook, stirring constantly, for 2 minutes; do not let brown. Add milk and cook, stirring all the time, until thickened and smooth. Stir this mixture into the almond soup and blend thoroughly. Cook over low heat, stirring constantly, for about 5 minutes. Remove from heat and stir in cream, cardamom, salt (be careful not to oversalt, as bouillon may be salty), and pepper. Return to heat and heat through, but do not boil. Serve hot or chilled, with watercress sandwich fingers.

6 SERVINGS

PEANUT SOUP

From Virginia

This soup, unlike most peanut soups, uses real peanuts rather than peanut butter; this makes it fresher-tasting.

> 1 pound shelled dry-roasted peanuts
> 6 cups chicken bouillon
> ¼ cup minced onion
> 1 tablespoon cornstarch
> 2 cups half-and-half, or 1 cup milk and 1 cup heavy
> cream, mixed
> salt
> freshly ground pepper
> Tabasco to taste
> ¼ cup minced chives or parsley
> 6 tablespoons chopped salted peanuts

Grind the dry-roasted peanuts in a food processor, or, a few at a time, in a blender. Do not overgrind or overblend, or the peanuts will be pasty. Heat the bouillon in a large saucepan. Add the ground peanuts and the onion. Bring to boiling point. Reduce heat to low, and simmer without a cover for about 30 minutes. Stir frequently. Turn into a food processor or blender and purée, or strain through a food mill. Return to saucepan. Stir the cornstarch into the half-and-half of milk and cream. Bring soup back to boiling point and stir in the cornstarch mixture. Stir constantly to avoid lumping. Reduce heat to very low and cook for 10 minutes. Season with salt, pepper, and Tabasco. Sprinkle with chives or parsley before serving. Top each serving with a tablespoon of chopped salted peanuts.

6 SERVINGS

CHEESE SOUP

From Vermont

Use a sharp Vermont or New York State Cheddar.

    4 tablespoons butter
    2 cups finely chopped onions
    4 tablespoons flour
    4 cups beef stock or canned beef bouillon
    2 cups milk
       salt
       freshly ground black pepper
⅛–¼ teaspoon cayenne pepper
    2 cups (½ pound) freshly grated or shredded sharp
       Cheddar cheese

Heat the butter in a soup kettle. Add the onions. Cook over medium-low heat, stirring constantly, for about 5 minutes or until onions are very soft; do not brown them. Stir in the flour. Cook, stirring all the time, for 3–4 minutes; do not brown. Gradually stir in the beef stock or bouillon. Cook covered over low heat, stirring frequently, for 10 minutes. Add milk, salt, black pepper, and cayenne; go easy on salt because the cheese will be salty. Bring to the boiling point. Reduce heat to very low and stir in the cheese. Cook, stirring constantly, until cheese is melted and soup very hot. Serve immediately, in heated bowls.

6 SERVINGS

PUMPKIN SOUP

From New England

     1 quart milk
     2 tablespoons butter
    ⅓ cup flour
     2 cups cooked fresh or canned mashed pumpkin
       (see note)
       salt
       freshly ground pepper
    ½ teaspoon ground nutmeg, or ¼ teaspoon Tabasco
     2 tablespoons minced chives

Heat the milk. Knead the butter and flour together with the tips of your fingers. Drop mixture in pea-size pieces into the hot milk, beating well after each addition. Cook until smooth and thickened. Stir in pumpkin, salt, pepper, and nutmeg or Tabasco. Cook over low heat, stirring constantly, until thickened and very hot. Sprinkle with chives and serve immediately.

Note:

To make mashed pumpkin from fresh pumpkin, cut pumpkin into 2- or 3-inch chunks or strips and peel. Place in a large saucepan and add enough boiling water to cover pumpkin pieces and come up 3 to 4 inches above them. Cover saucepan and boil over low heat for about 20–30 minutes or until very tender. Drain and mash. Cool before using.

4–6 SERVINGS

OLD-FASHIONED
VEGETABLE SOUP

All-American

You can add any vegetables at hand and make the soup as thick and varied as you wish. It is quicker to chop the vegetables, but very much nicer if they are diced.

3	pounds beef shin with meat
10–12	cups water
½	cup diced onion
¼	cup diced celery or to taste
¼	cup diced carrot or to taste
¼	cup diced turnip
¼	cup diced green pepper or to taste
¼	cup broken green beans or to taste
¼	cup peas or to taste
½	cup lima beans
1	cup canned tomatoes or fresh tomatoes, chopped
¼	cup chopped parsley
½	teaspoon dried thyme
	salt
	freshly ground pepper

Put the meat into a large soup kettle and add the water. Bring to boiling point. Simmer covered, over low heat for 2 hours or until meat falls from the bone. Drain into a bowl. Remove and reserve meat. Chill broth until fat rises to the top; remove fat and pour broth back into soup kettle. Bring to boiling point. Cut meat from bones and cut into small pieces. Add meat and all remaining ingredients to broth. Simmer covered until vegetables are tender; timing is not important.

MAKES ABOUT 2½ QUARTS

THICK BARLEY SOUP

From North Dakota

*This came from a farmer's wife of Finnish descent, via her
California son who skis and cooks.*

     3 tablespoons butter
     ½ cup medium barley
     1 large onion, minced
     1 celery stalk, minced
     1 large carrot, minced
     1 tablespoon flour
     8 cups hot chicken or beef bouillon
        salt
        freshly ground pepper
     1 cup light or heavy cream
     ¼ cup minced dill

Heat the butter in a large heavy saucepan or soup kettle.
Add the barley, onion, celery, and carrot. Cook over medium heat,
stirring constantly, for about 5 minutes, or until barley is golden
and vegetables are getting soft. Stir in the flour and cook for 1 more
minute. Stir in the hot bouillon. Simmer, covered, over low heat for
about 30 minutes or until barley is tender. Season with salt and
pepper. Just before serving, stir in the cream and heat through but
do not boil. Sprinkle with minced dill.

   6 SERVINGS

FAMOUS U.S. SENATE
BEAN SOUP

From Washington, D.C.

Beloved by our lawmakers.

1 pound marrow beans
3 quarts cold water
3 medium potatoes, cooked, peeled, and mashed
6 celery stalks, chopped fine
2 medium onions, minced
2 garlic cloves, minced
¼ cup chopped parsley
2 pounds ham hock
  salt
  freshly ground pepper

Soak the beans in water overnight. Drain and place in a
large saucepan. In enough fresh water to come 2 inches above the
beans, cook until tender; if necessary, add a little more water.
Drain. Add the 3 quarts cold water, the potatoes, celery, onion, garlic, and parsley, and mix well. Add the ham hock. Season with salt
if needed (ham hock may be salty) and pepper. Bring to boiling
point and lower heat. Simmer covered for about 2 hours, stirring
frequently. Remove ham hock and take meat off bones. Dice meat
and return to soup. Serve hot, with garlic bread.

MAKES ABOUT 2 QUARTS

BLACK-BEAN SOUP

All-American

Although it used to be necessary to soak dried beans over-
night before using them in a recipe (and although many
cookbooks still call for this technique), this is a needless
waste of time. The beans soften and swell just as nicely in

the quick-soaking method described here. You can buy black beans in any Latin-American market if your supermarket doesn't have them; no other bean will do for this recipe.

Never salt beans until they are cooked tender; salt added during cooking toughens them.

Madeira can be used instead of dry white or red wine.

1 pound (2¼ cups) dried black beans
2⅓ quarts water
1 meaty ham hock, or 1 pound smoked ham, or 1 pound slab bacon
2 large onions, chopped
2 garlic cloves, chopped
1 celery stalk, chopped
1 small carrot, chopped
1 teaspoon dried thyme or oregano
freshly ground pepper
salt
½ to 1 cup dry white or red wine
1 cup tomato sauce
1 lemon, thinly sliced, seeds removed
sour cream

Pick over and wash the beans. Drain. Combine beans and water in a large kettle. Bring to boiling point, cook for 2 minutes, and remove from heat. Cover and let stand at room temperature for 2 hours. Add the ham hock or other meat, onions, garlic, celery, carrot, and thyme or oregano. Bring to boiling point, lower heat to very low, and simmer covered for 2 hours or until beans are soft. Remove ham hock, if used, cut off meat, and dice it; if using other meats, dice them. Reserve meat, together with about 1 cup of the cooked beans. Taste soup and season with pepper; add salt if needed (the meats may be salty). Purée the soup in a blender or food processor or through a food mill. Return to kettle and stir in the wine and tomato sauce. Cook for 15 more minutes. Return reserved meat and beans to soup and heat through thoroughly. Turn into a tureen and float lemon slices on top of soup. Allow 1 lemon slice to each individual serving. Pass sour cream to spoon with each serving.

8 SERVINGS

YELLOW PEA SOUP
WITH ALLSPICE

From Michigan

As my Michigan-born husband remembers it.

1 pork butt, weighing approximately 2 pounds
3 quarts water
2 tablespoons bacon fat or meat drippings
2 medium onions, finely chopped
1 medium carrot, finely chopped
1 celery stalk, finely chopped
1 pound yellow split peas, picked over and washed
 salt
 freshly ground pepper
¼ teaspoon ground allspice (or to taste)

Put the pork butt and the water in a large kettle. Simmer covered over low heat for about 1½ hours or until tender. Remove pork butt and reserve. Skim off fat from broth. Pour broth into a bowl and reserve. In the same kettle, heat the bacon fat, or drippings. Add the onions, carrot, and celery. Cook, stirring constantly, for about 3 minutes. Return broth to kettle and add the peas, salt, if needed (broth may be salty), pepper, and allspice. Simmer covered over low heat for about 1 hour. Meanwhile, dice pork butt. Add to soup and cook 30–60 minutes longer. Serve very hot.

6–8 SERVINGS

LOBSTER STEW

From New England

The classic lobster stew is very plain, to let the goodness of the pure lobster taste come through. However, at least to me, a dash of cayenne or Tabasco improves it. This recipe works also for 1 pound shrimp, cooked and shelled.

½ cup butter
1 pound cooked lobster meat, flaked
4 cups milk
2 cups heavy cream
salt
freshly ground white pepper
cayenne or Tabasco to taste (optional)
½ teaspoon paprika

In a saucepan large enough to hold all the ingredients, heat the butter. Add the lobster meat and cook over medium heat, stirring constantly, for 3 minutes. Turn off heat and cover saucepan. Combine milk and cream and bring to scalding. Pour over lobster. Season lightly with salt and pepper and with cayenne or Tabasco if desired. Sprinkle with paprika and mix well. Cool. Refrigerate covered for at least 4 hours or overnight. At serving time, turn into double-boiler top and heat over boiling water to just the boiling point, but do not boil. Serve hot, with crackers.

2–3 SERVINGS

OYSTER STEW

From New England

The Worcestershire sauce gives a little zip to a bland dish, but purists may want to omit it.

3 cups milk
1 cup heavy cream
2 cups (1 pint) shucked oysters (if large, cut in half), with their liquor
salt
1 teaspoon Worcestershire sauce
4 tablespoons butter, cut into pieces and at room temperature
freshly ground pepper

Combine the milk and cream in a heavy saucepan or in the top of a double boiler. Heat but do not scald or boil; this is best done in a double-boiler top over boiling water. Turn the oysters and their liquor into a small saucepan. Heat over low heat, bringing almost but not quite to boiling, only until the oysters begin to curl at the edges. Do not let cook or oysters will toughen. Remove from heat and with a slotted spoon transfer oysters to a bowl and re- serve. Add the oyster liquor to the milk mixture and simmer to- gether but do not boil. Add a little salt and stir in the Worces- tershire sauce. Add oysters and heat thoroughly but do not boil. Stir in the butter and keep over heat only until butter has almost completely melted. Serve in heated soup bowls with a sprinkling of pepper.

Note:
This sounds complicated but it is not. The essential thing is not to boil the stew but simmer it until very hot.

4 SERVINGS

CREAMY SHRIMP SOUP

From North Carolina

3 cups milk
1 cup heavy cream
1 tablespoon flour
2 egg yolks
  grated rind of ½ lemon
  juice of 1 lemon
¼ teaspoon ground mace
⅛ teaspoon Tabasco
  salt
  freshly ground white pepper
1 pound cooked shelled shrimp, or 2 cups cooked shelled
  shrimp, broken, not cut, into pieces
⅓ cup sherry

Pour the milk and cream into the top of a double boiler. Take out 3 tablespoons of mixture and blend with the flour to a smooth paste. Heat milk mixture to scalding and stir in flour paste. Cook, stirring constantly, until smooth and thickened. Place over boiling water. Cook for 5–10 minutes. Beat the egg yolks thoroughly in a small bowl. Stir in the lemon rind, lemon juice, mace, and Tabasco. Gradually stir egg mixture into milk, stirring constantly to avoid lumping. Season with salt and pepper. Add the shrimp and mix well. Cook, stirring frequently, until soup is very hot. Stir in sherry and cook for 2 more minutes. Serve immediately in heated soup cups or small bowls.

4 SERVINGS

NEW ENGLAND CLAM CHOWDER

Chowders are thick soups, taking their name from the French chaudière, *a stew pot. Whether they are made of fish or vegetables (corn chowder), salt pork is obligatory, and so are onions, potatoes, and milk or cream. New England Clam Chowder is the best known, made with small variations in different places; in Boston, the soup is thickened with flour and almost smooth. Like all old colonial dishes, this is a more-or-less affair. As they used to say, you just add some more water or milk to your chowder to accommodate unexpected guests. It is essential that the potatoes be cut small, or you'll be eating a potato stew.*

 1 quart shucked hard-shell or soft-shell clams, or 2–3 10½-ounce cans minced clams
 ¼ pound salt pork, blanched, cut into ¼-inch cubes, rind removed
 1 large onion, diced
3–4 medium potatoes, cut in ½-inch dice
1½ cups boiling water
 2 cups liquor from shucked or drained clams, supplemented if necessary with bottled clam juice or water

> 2 cups half-and-half or light cream or milk, or 1 cup
>   milk and 1 cup heavy cream
>   salt
>   freshly ground pepper
> 1 tablespoon butter

Drain the clams; strain the liquid and reserve. If using fresh clams, cut off and discard heads, if any, and rinse clams quickly under running cold water to remove any sand and bits of shell. Chop coarsely and reserve. Put pork into a large heavy saucepan or kettle. Cook over low heat until well rendered, but do not burn. Take out the crisp pork bits and reserve. Drain off all but 3 tablespoons of fat. Add the onion and cook over low heat, stirring constantly, for about 5 minutes or until soft and golden. Add the potatoes and the boiling water and cook for about 5–8 minutes or until potatoes are almost soft. Add the chopped clams and cook for 5 more minutes. Remove from heat. Measure the reserved clam liquid and if necessary add bottled clam juice or water to make 2 cups. Heat in a small saucepan. Scald the half-and-half or milk and cream in a larger saucepan. Stir the clam juice into it. Stir the mixture into the clam-potato mixture. Stir to mix. Season with salt and pepper. Skim off any excess fat that might be floating on top. Just before serving, add the reserved pork bits and stir in the butter. Serve immediately, or keep hot, but not boiling, in the top of a double boiler over simmering water. The chowder is better if flavors are allowed to blend for 15 minutes to 1 hour. Better still, refrigerate and heat and serve the next day.

Note:
Some old recipes thicken chowder with plain unsalted crackers, soaked in cold milk and placed in each bowl. I think it is better to pass unsalted crackers separately.

Note:
To blanch salt pork (or bacon), cover with boiling water and let stand 2–3 minutes. Drain before using.

5–6 SERVINGS

MANHATTAN CLAM CHOWDER

From New York, Rhode Island, Connecticut

Essentially, this is a vegetable soup with clams. Some versions use corn, carrots, and turnip, but all have tomatoes. If the other vegetables are wanted in the soup, dice them and cook in boiling water to cover until almost but not quite tender. Add to soup with clams.

¼ pound salt pork, blanched, cut into ¼-inch cubes, rind removed
2 medium onions, diced
½ cup diced celery
3 cups diced potatoes (½-inch dice)
3 cups boiling water
2 cups fresh or canned tomatoes, chopped and with juice
salt
freshly ground pepper
¼ teaspoon dried thyme
1 pint shucked large or quahog chowder clams, chopped, with liquid
dash cayenne or Tabasco

Put the pork cubes into a large heavy saucepan or kettle. Cook over low heat until well rendered, but do not burn pork cubes; they should be white. Pour off all but 2–3 tablespoons of fat. Reserve pork cubes. Add the onion and celery. Cook, stirring constantly, until soft and golden; do not brown. Add the potatoes and boiling water. Simmer covered over low heat until potatoes are almost tender. Add the tomatoes, salt, pepper, and thyme. Cook for 5 more minutes. Add the clams and their liquid. Stir to mix well. If too thick, add a little more hot water, ¼ cup at a time. Season with cayenne or Tabasco to taste. Simmer covered over very low heat for 15 more minutes. Serve hot.

4–5 SERVINGS

WHOLE-FISH CHOWDER

From Maine

As with all chowders, you can use a little more fish, a little less water, fewer or more potatoes—it doesn't matter.

4–5 pounds whole haddock or cod, cleaned but with head
        and tail left
   2 quarts water
   1 teaspoon salt
4–6 whole peppercorns
4–5 medium boiling potatoes (about 1½ pounds),
        peeled and cut into ½-inch pieces
   ⅔ cup diced blanched salt pork or bacon (see
        preceding recipe)
   1 large onion, minced
   2 tablespoons flour
   1 teaspoon Worcestershire sauce
   2 cups half-and-half or light cream
   4 tablespoons butter, softened

Place the fish in a large kettle; if fish is too large, cut in half. Add the water, salt, and peppercorns. Bring to boiling point and lower heat. Simmer without a cover for 1 hour. Remove fish from broth. Strain broth and reserve. Remove head, tail, skin, and bones from fish and let fish cool. Cut fish into bite-sized pieces. Cook the diced potatoes in the fish broth until they are almost but not quite tender. Drain, and reserve potatoes and broth separately. In a heavy frying pan over low heat, cook the salt pork or bacon until crisp and golden. Add the onion and cook for 3–4 minutes or until soft. Stir in the flour and Worcestershire sauce. Over low heat, stirring constantly, cook until flour is golden brown. Bring the reserved fish broth to boiling point, lower heat, and stir in the salt pork–onion mixture. Simmer for 15 minutes or longer. About 20 minutes before serving time, add fish, potatoes, and half-and-half or cream to fish broth. Heat thoroughly but do not boil. Stir in butter and heat until butter is melted. Serve hot, with pilot crackers.

Note:

To make ahead of time, cook the fish and potatoes; make the salt pork–onion mixture and stir into fish broth. Keep refrigerated until needed. Then heat broth, add fish, potatoes, and half-and-half or cream, and heat through, then stir in butter.

6–8 SERVINGS

Gumbos

✧

Gumbos—thick soups or thin stews depending how you look at them—are truly and originally American dishes, and wonderful ones at that. They are usually associated with the Creole cookery of New Orleans and the rest of Louisiana, but they are also made in other states of the Deep South. These highly flavored dishes may contain chicken, rabbit, shrimp, oysters, crabs, singly or in combination, and they are thickened with either okra or filé powder. Okra gave gumbo its name, which is the African word for that vegetable; all gumbos are influenced by African cooking. Filé powder is made from dried powdered sassafras leaves, discovered as a thickener by the local Choctaw Indians. Both okra and filé powder give gumbos their characteristic texture; as a rule, they are not used together in the same dish. Many gumbos have as a base a French roux, a mixture of flour and oil or butter cooked to a rich brown which gives a specific texture and smoky flavor. But not all gumbos have a roux, though generally there is an initial browning—of, let us say, the chicken. Once filé powder is added to a cooked gumbo it must never boil again or the dish will be stringy; if necessary it can be kept warm over hot water. Gumbo is always served with boiled rice. Two or three tablespoons of fluffy boiled rice are placed in each soup plate or bowl and the gumbo is spooned over the rice. The gumbo and rice are never cooked together.

For gumbo lovers I recommend one of the very finest regional American cookbooks, *The Original Picayune Creole Cook Book* (New Orleans, La.: The Times-Picayune Publishing Co.).

Gumbos are true folk cookery, made from whatever was at hand, depending on the cook's individuality. Some gumbos include tomatoes, others don't, modern gumbos may have corn or lima beans—but the spicy, herby, hot flavor and the specific gumbo texture from the okra or filé powder remain.

I invariably make gumbos for foreign visitors and anybody to whom I want to show the best of American cooking—and invariably people love them.

CHICKEN GUMBO

From New Orleans

Like all thick soups or stews, gumbos can be thicker or thinner depending on whether they are used as a soup or a main dish. For a thinner gumbo, add more chicken broth or water—or, if you have any, the water left from cooking shrimp. The traditional way of making chicken gumbo lands the chicken pieces with their bones in the soup plate, where they are hard to manage, but this recipe avoids this, without affecting the flavor of the gumbo. I also skin the chicken because I don't like the fatty skin of the bird.

    1 4-pound chicken, cut into pieces
       salt
       freshly ground pepper
  ½ cup flour
    4 tablespoons butter, lard, or bacon fat
2–3 quarts chicken bouillon, water, or shrimp water
       (in which shrimp were cooked—see above)
  ½ pound lean ham, preferably smoked ham, diced
  ½ cup minced onion
  ½ cup minced green pepper
    1 bay leaf
  ½ teaspoon dried thyme
  ½ teaspoon hot red pepper flakes

1 dozen shucked oysters, with liquid, and/or
   ½ pound crabmeat (optional)
2–3 tablespoons filé powder
   boiled rice

Skin the chicken pieces and remove all fat. Rub with salt and pepper. Coat with half the flour. Heat 2 tablespoons of the butter or other fat in a frying pan. Over high heat, quickly brown the chicken pieces. Transfer to a large saucepan or soup kettle and add the chicken bouillon, water, or shrimp water. Bring to boiling point and reduce heat to low. Simmer covered for about 20 minutes or until pieces are almost tender; chicken will be cooked further. Remove chicken pieces from broth and let cool enough to handle. Reserve broth in kettle. Bone the chicken and cut into bite-sized pieces, but do not make pieces too small. In the same frying pan, heat the remaining butter or other fat. Stir in the remaining flour and cook, stirring constantly, until medium brown. Add the ham and the chicken pieces. Cover and cook over low heat for about 5–10 minutes. Add the onion and pepper and cook for 2–3 more minutes. Add contents of frying pan to the broth in the kettle. Add the bay leaf, thyme, and pepper flakes. Bring to boiling point, turn heat to low, and simmer covered for 30–60 minutes. Add the oysters and/or crabmeat (if used) 10 minutes before gumbo is ready. Remove gumbo from heat and stir in the filé powder, beginning with 2 tablespoons and adding more if necessary to thicken to taste. Serve with boiled rice.

Note:
Sometimes I add 1–2 cups lima beans (fresh or frozen) and 1 cup fresh, frozen, or canned corn kernels. This is not traditional, but it tastes good.

6–8 SERVINGS

SHRIMP GUMBO

    2 tablespoons lard, butter, bacon grease, or salad oil
    2 tablespoons flour
    1 cup minced onion
    ⅓ cup minced sweet green pepper
    2 garlic cloves, minced
    3 cups canned tomatoes, with their liquid
    1 pound fresh okra sliced, or 2 10-ounce packages
        frozen sliced okra
    2 bay leaves
    ½ teaspoon dried thyme
      salt
      freshly ground pepper
    ¼ teaspoon Tabasco or to taste
    2 pounds shelled raw shrimp or 2 pounds shelled
        frozen shrimp, thawed and drained
        hot water

Heat the fat in a large frying pan. Stir in the flour and cook over low heat, stirring constantly, until flour is medium brown. Add the onion, green pepper, and garlic. Cook, stirring constantly, until onion is soft. Stir in the tomatoes, okra, bay leaves, thyme, salt, pepper, and Tabasco. Bring to boiling point and lower heat. Simmer covered for about 30 minutes, stirring frequently. Add shrimp and cook for 10 more minutes. If soup is too thick, thin with hot water to desired consistency.

4–6 SERVINGS

Eggs, Cheese, Rice, and Pasta

MRS. HOPKINSON'S
EGG-AND-CHUTNEY CASSEROLE

From Boston

Mrs. Tom Hopkinson, wife of the painter and kindest of friends, was one of Boston's great hostesses and famous for her delicious and original food. She served this casserole for lunch and I remember her saying that it was better to make several separate casseroles rather than to double or triple the recipe. The basic proportions are, in this order: 1 inch fried onions, 1 inch well-drained boiled rice, ¼ inch chutney, 4 eggs; the whole covered with a sauce which can be curry, tomato, or chili; I think curry best. I also prefer to use a mild chutney rather than a very hot one. If the chutney comes in large pieces, they should be chopped.

6 tablespoons butter
2 large or 3 medium-sized onions, finely chopped
1 cup raw rice, cooked according to directions to
    make approximately 3 cups cooked rice
1 cup chutney
2 tablespoons flour
1½ cups milk
    salt
    freshly ground pepper
1 to 2 teaspoons curry powder, or to taste
½ cup light or heavy cream
4 small or medium eggs

Generously butter a 1½-quart deep baking dish. Heat 3 table-spoons of the butter in a heavy frying pan. Add the onions and cook, stirring constantly, until soft and golden; do not scorch. Reserving frying pan, transfer onions to a baking dish, distributing them evenly. Top with an even layer of rice. Top rice with a layer of chutney. Set aside. In a small saucepan, heat 2 more tablespoons of the butter. Stir in the flour and cook, stirring constantly, for 1–2 minutes. Add the milk. Cook over low heat, stirring constantly, until sauce is smooth and thickened. Season with salt and pepper. Reserve. In the frying pan in which onions were cooked, heat the remaining 1 tablespoon butter. Stir in the curry. Cook over low heat, stirring constantly, for 2–3 minutes to release curry flavor. Stir the sauce into the curry and mix well. Stir the cream into the mixture and cook over low heat, stirring constantly, until well heated through.

With the back of a spoon, make 4 depressions in the onion-rice-chutney mixture. Drop 1 egg into each depression. Spoon sauce over the whole top of the casserole. Bake in a preheated moderate oven (350°F) for about 25–30 minutes, or until eggs are set. Serve hot, with corn bread, and a salad.

Note:
Do not use large eggs; they have too much white to set properly. It is hard to know just when eggs are set; I sort of poke around, gently.

4 SERVINGS

CREAMED EGGS

From New England and the Midwest

This dish is nice for light meals and a good way of using up all those dyed hard-cooked Easter eggs.

      4 tablespoons butter
      3 medium onions, thinly sliced
      3 tablespoons flour
      2 cups light cream or milk, heated
        salt
        freshly ground pepper
     ⅛ teaspoon ground nutmeg, or 1 teaspoon prepared
        mustard
   6–8 hard-cooked eggs, shelled and thicky sliced
     ½ cup heavy cream, whipped (optional)
        hot toast or corn bread

Heat the butter in a heavy saucepan. Add the onions and cook over low heat, stirring constantly, for about 5–10 minutes or until the onions are very soft but still white. Stir in the flour. Gradually stir in the hot cream or milk. Season with salt, pepper, and nutmeg or mustard. Cook over lowest possible heat, stirring frequently, for 7–10 more minutes. (The long cooking removes the taste of raw flour.) Add the eggs and heat through without boiling. Fold in the whipped cream (if used) just before serving. Serve in a heated serving dish or heated individual ramekins. Pass toast or corn bread.

4 SERVINGS

EGG SALAD

All-American

     6 hard-cooked eggs, peeled and coarsely chopped
     1 tablespoon minced onion
     1 tablespoon minced celery
  1–2 tablespoons minced sweet pickle
     1 tablespoon pickle juice
        salt
        freshly ground pepper
    ¼ cup mayonnaise

Combine all ingredients in a bowl and mix well. Chill for 2–4 hours before using. If using for sandwiches, spread on white or whole-wheat bread lined with washed and dried lettuce leaves, and top salad with thin slices of radishes and/or onions.

MAKES 1½ CUPS

EASY CHEESE SOUFFLÉ

From a Washington, D.C., hostess

If you need more soufflé, do not double the recipe and make a larger soufflé. Repeat the recipe and make two small soufflés. Grated Swiss and Parmesan make a lighter soufflé than one that contains Cheddar.

     2 eggs
    ⅔ cup heavy cream
    ¾ cup grated Swiss cheese
    ¾ cup grated Parmesan cheese
        salt (optional)
        freshly ground pepper
        dash Tabasco

Preheat oven to 450°. Lightly beat eggs and beat together

with cream. Stir in Swiss and Parmesan cheeses, mixing well. Taste mixture for saltiness; if necessary add a little more salt. Add the pepper and Tabasco. Pour into a 1-quart baking dish. Bake for about 25 minutes or until golden brown. Soufflé will puff up during latter part of cooking time. Serve immediately.

2–3 SERVINGS

QUICHE LORRAINE

Of French origin, Quiche Lorraine has become a fashionable All-American dish, popular for light lunches, suppers, or cocktail snacks. It is essential to use a deep 9-inch pie dish or the quiche will slop over into the oven. If you're in any doubt about the size of your pie dish, stand it on a cookie sheet while baking.

1 9-inch pastry shell, unbaked
   dried beans or raw rice
6 ounces (1½ cups) grated Swiss or Gruyère cheese
8 slices crisp bacon, crumbled
3 eggs
1 cup heavy cream and ½ cup milk, or 1½ cups
   light cream
¾ teaspoon salt
¼ teaspoon freshly ground pepper
⅛ teaspoon cayenne pepper or Tabasco
½ teaspoon dry mustard (optional)

Preheat oven to hot (425°). Prick bottom and sides of pastry shell with a fork. Line shell with waxed paper and fill with dried beans or uncooked rice. Place in a deep 9-inch pie dish and bake for about 5 minutes or until firm but not browned. Remove paper and filling and cool. Sprinkle with the cheese and bacon, distributing them evenly over pastry shell. Beat together the remaining ingredients and pour into pastry shell. Bake for about 10 minutes at 425°, then reduce oven heat to moderate (350°) and bake for 15 more minutes or until firm. Test for doneness—the quiche is done when a knife inserted just off center comes out clean. Cool for about 5 minutes before cutting into wedges. Serve from the pie dish.

6 SERVINGS

RINKTUM TIDDY CHEESE RAREBIT

All-American

An American offspring of the classic English Welsh Rabbit (rarebit is the American spelling) which substitutes tomatoes for the beer or ale of the original, possibly to please teetotaling cheese lovers. This pleasant, nourishing dish used to and may still be the joy of Scouts, dormitory feasts, and ladies' luncheons—I have found it to be a good brunch or supper dish.

   1 tablespoon butter
   1 very small onion, minced
   2 cups canned tomatoes, well drained
   1 teaspoon salt
¼ teaspoon freshly ground pepper
   1 teaspoon sugar
   2 cups (½ pound) shredded American cheese
   1 egg, beaten
     buttered toast

Heat the butter in a heavy saucepan. Add the onion and cook, stirring constantly, until onion is soft. Do not scorch. Add the tomatoes, salt, pepper, and sugar. Cook over low heat, stirring frequently, for about 5 minutes or until tomatoes have cooked into pulp. Add the cheese. Cook, stirring constantly, until cheese is melted. Stir in the beaten egg and remove from heat. Stir for 1 minute longer. Serve over hot buttered toast.

3–4 SERVINGS

GRITS AND CHEESE
CASSEROLE

From Texas

*Good as a main lunch dish or as accompaniment for roast
or grilled meats.*

> 5 cups water
> 1 teaspoon salt
> 1 cup grits
> ½ cup butter (1 stick), cut into pieces
> 2 cups (½ pound) grated sharp cheese
> 3 eggs, well beaten
> ⅛ teaspoon Tabasco or to taste

In a heavy saucepan or in the top of a large double boiler
(leave the bottom aside for the moment), bring water to boiling
point and add salt. Slowly stir in the grits, stirring after each addition to prevent lumping. Return to boiling point. Turn heat to low.
Cover and cook slowly on direct heat or, if double-boiler top is
used, over boiling water for about 25 minutes, stirring frequently.
Remove from heat and stir in the butter and cheese. Cool to lukewarm and stir in the eggs and Tabasco. Turn into a generously buttered 1½-quart casserole. Bake in a preheated moderate oven (350°)
for about 30–40 minutes or until golden brown. Serve hot. Leftovers
may be sliced and fried in butter until crisp.

VARIATION:

You can also use 1 cup grits cooked according to package directions. Simply add butter, cheese, eggs, and Tabasco as indicated,
and proceed with the recipe.

4–6 SERVINGS

SYLVIA'S RICE AND
SOUR-CREAM CHILI CASSEROLE

From New Mexico

A lunch or supper main dish.

¾ pound jack cheese or mild Cheddar cheese
2 cups sour cream
½ cup finely chopped and seeded green chili peppers
4 cups cooked but still firm rice
  salt
  freshly ground pepper
½ cup grated Cheddar cheese

Cut the jack or mild Cheddar cheese into ¼-inch strips. Mix together the sour cream and chilis. Season the rice with salt and pepper. Generously butter a 1½-quart casserole. Add half the rice, top with the sour-cream mixture, and top this with cheese strips. Top with the remaining rice, smoothing it down. Cook in a preheated moderate oven (350°) for 25 minutes. Sprinkle with grated Cheddar and cook for 5 minutes longer or until cheese is melted and bubbly.

VARIATION:

For a different flavor, this casserole may be made with whole cooked hominy.

6 SERVINGS

MEXICAN RICE

From the Southwest

This and the following recipe are interesting accompaniments for meat dishes.

    2 tablespoons salad oil
    1 medium onion, minced
    1 garlic clove, minced
    1 cup raw regular rice
    2 medium-sized tomatoes, peeled and chopped,
      or ⅔ cup drained canned tomatoes
    1 teaspoon chili powder or to taste (optional)
      salt
      freshly ground pepper
    2 cups beef bouillon

Heat the oil in a heavy saucepan. Add the onion and garlic.
Cook, stirring constantly, for about 4–5 minutes or until soft. Add
the rice. Cook over medium heat, stirring constantly, until rice is
golden. Add the tomatoes, chili powder (if used), a little salt and
pepper, and 1½ cups of the beef bouillon. Bring to boiling point and
lower heat to low. Cover and simmer for about 25 minutes or until
rice is tender and liquid has been absorbed. Stir occasionally and
check for moisture; if necessary, add the remaining ½ cup bouillon,
2 tablespoons at a time.

4–6 SERVINGS

SAGE RICE

From New Mexico

*Chopped pecans or walnuts can be substituted for the
pine nuts.*

    3 cups chicken bouillon
 1½ cups long grain rice
    2 teaspoons dried sage, or 2 tablespoons chopped fresh
      sage leaves, or to taste
      salt
      freshly ground pepper
    3 tablespoons butter
  ½ cup pine nuts (pignon or pignolia)
    2 tablespoons minced parsley

Combine the chicken bouillon, rice, and sage in a heavy saucepan. Bring to boiling point and reduce heat to very low. Add salt if necessary (bouillon may be salty) and pepper. Simmer covered for about 15 minutes or until rice is tender but not mushy. Heat the butter in a small frying pan. Add the pine nuts and cook, stirring constantly, for about 2 minutes or until barely golden. Stir the butter and pine nuts into rice and sprinkle with parsley. Serve hot.

4–5 SERVINGS

SUPERIOR MACARONI AND CHEESE

All-American

M and C is either very, very good, as in this recipe, or unspeakably horrid, as far too many of us remember from our school and college days. People groping for the higher aspects of food should remember that dear old American M and C is simply the French Macaroni à la Béchamel, a beloved first course. A good-quality Cheddar, yellow or white, is essential.

    2 cups (8 ounces) elbow macaroni
    3 tablespoons butter
    ¼ cup minced onions
    3 tablespoons flour
      salt
      freshly ground pepper
      cayenne to taste
    1 cup milk or light cream
    ½ cup dry white wine
    2 cups grated sharp Cheddar (½ pound)

Cook the macaroni in plenty of rapidly boiling salted water until not quite tender. (It will be cooked again and must not become mushy.) Drain and reserve. Heat the butter. Add the onions.

Cook over low heat, stirring constantly, until onions are soft but still white. Stir in the flour, salt, pepper, and cayenne. Cook for about 2 more minutes. Gradually stir in the milk or cream and wine. Cook, stirring all the time, until sauce is smooth and thick. Stir in the cheese. Cook until cheese is melted. Mix together the macaroni and the cheese sauce. Turn into a generously buttered 1½-quart casserole. Bake in a preheated moderate oven (350°) for 20 minutes or until heated all the way through and golden brown on top.

Note:
Buttered fresh leaf spinach (page 172) is good with this.

4–6 SERVINGS

EDDIE HERTZBERG'S
NOODLE PUDDING

From New York

½ pound medium noodles, homemade or store-bought
6 tablespoons butter
  salt
  freshly ground pepper
2 cups creamed cottage cheese
2 cups sour cream

Cook the noodles in plenty of rapidly boiling salted water until almost but not quite tender. Drain. Turn noodles into a generously buttered 1½-quart baking dish. Toss with 4 tablespoons of the butter, salt, and plenty of pepper. Stir in the cottage cheese and sour cream and mix well. Dot with the remaining 2 tablespoons butter. Cook in a preheated moderate oven (350°) for about 30 minutes or until golden brown and bubbly.

4–6 SERVINGS

Chicken, Meat, and Game

Chicken

ROAST STUFFED CAPON

    1 6- to 8-pound capon, ready to cook
    ½ lemon
       salt
       freshly ground pepper
       stuffing (see following recipe)
       about ½ pound butter at room temperature
    ¼ pound melted butter

Preheat oven to moderate (375°). Wipe the bird with a damp towel. Rub the cavity with the cut lemon and sprinkle with salt and pepper. Stuff loosely; stuffing swells during cooking. Secure cavity with small poultry skewers or sew with needle and thread. Rub butter lavishly all over the bird. Place the bird on its side on a rack in a shallow roasting pan. Baste frequently with melted butter. After 30 minutes, turn bird to other side, basting with butter. After 30 minutes more turn bird on its back. All-over roasting time is 20–25 minutes to the pound, basting frequently with remaining melted butter and pan juices. Transfer the bird to a hot platter. Turn off oven and keep for about 10 minutes before carving. Serve with pan juices on the side.

Note:

Any stuffing that does not go into the bird may be put into a small baking dish and dotted with butter. Cover with foil and put into oven 30 minutes before capon is done. Remove foil and serve from the dish.

6–8 SERVINGS

MRS. VAILL'S
CORN-BREAD STUFFING

From New York

This quantity will stuff a 6- to 8-pound capon or turkey.

- 6 cups crumbled yellow corn bread
- ¾ cup chicken or turkey stock
- 7 tablespoons butter
- 2 cups finely chopped onions
- 1 cup finely chopped celery
- ½ pound small button mushrooms, caps only (halve or quarter large mushroom caps)
- 1 turkey liver, or 2–4 chicken livers, chopped fine
- ¼ cup sherry or Madeira

¼ cup minced parsley
½ teaspoon ground thyme
   salt
   freshly ground pepper

Turn corn bread into a large bowl and crumble again. Stir in the chicken or turkey stock. Heat 4 tablespoons of the butter in a heavy frying pan. Add onion and celery and cook, stirring constantly, until soft. Add to bowl. In the same frying pan, heat 2 tablespoons of the butter and cook mushrooms in it for 3–4 minutes. Add mushrooms and their liquid to bowl. Heat remaining 1 tablespoon butter in the same frying pan and cook the livers in it for 2 minutes, or only until pink. Add to bowl. Stir sherry or Madeira into frying pan and scrape up all the bits clinging to bottom and sides of pan. Cook for about 2–3 minutes or until wine is reduced by about half. Add the wine, parsley, and thyme to the bowl and stir to mix thoroughly. Add a little salt (corn bread is salted) and pepper and mix again. Stuffing should be fluffy and crumbly and not too moist, as the bird's moisture will be added to it during cooking. Stuff bird loosely just before roasting.

Note:
If there is any leftover stuffing, use for Stuffed Chicken Breasts (see following recipe). Or put it in a buttered pie pan or baking dish, add a few tablespoons stock or broth, dot with a little butter, and cover with aluminum foil. Bake along with bird during the last 30 minutes cooking time.

MAKES ABOUT 8 CUPS

STUFFED CHICKEN BREASTS

From Kentucky

The practical way of making this rather elegant dish is to use leftover ham and leftover corn-bread stuffing. In other words, plan your leftovers.

6 small whole boned chicken breasts
6 slices country (Smithfield-type) ham (about 8–10 ounces)
12 tablespoons (¾ cup) Corn-Bread Stuffing (see preceding recipe)
6 tablespoons sherry
6 tablespoons butter
1 teaspoon paprika
⅓ cup melted butter

Place the chicken breasts between 2 pieces of waxed paper. With the back of a saucer or the flat side of a cleaver flatten the breasts out, but do not pound them. Open up breasts skin side down. On one side of each breast place 1 slice ham. Top with 2 tablespoons stuffing and sprinkle stuffing with 1 tablespoon sherry. Fold the other part of chicken breast over ham and stuffing as in making a sandwich. Secure sides with toothpicks. Place in one layer in a baking dish just large enough to fit the chicken pieces and sprinkle with paprika. Dot each piece with 1 tablespoon butter. Bake in a preheated hot oven (400°) for about 35–40 minutes, basting frequently with the melted butter. Serve hot.

6 SERVINGS

OLD-FASHIONED PLAIN CHICKEN FRICASSEE

From New England and the Midwest

An 1860 recipe. Since today's chickens have a super-fat skin, I take it off, as I take off all other fat. In this recipe, it is essential that all fat be taken off, or the broth, used for the sauce or gravy, will have to be tediously degreased. Note that, for the gravy, the broth, which already contains butter, is simply thickened with flour rather than being made into a standard white sauce.

1 3½- to 4-pound chicken, cut into quarters
   salt
   pepper
1 teaspoon dried thyme
½ cup (1 stick) butter
3 cups water
1 small onion
3–4 tablespoons flour (depending on how thick a
   gravy is wanted)
½ cup light or heavy cream
   biscuits or buttered noodles

Remove all fat and skin from chicken and cut off wing tips. Wash and dry chicken pieces and rub with salt, pepper, and thyme. Place in a heavy casserole. Add the butter (this will make a flavorful dish), water, and onion. Bring to boiling point. Turn heat to low. Simmer covered for 30 minutes or until chicken is tender. Transfer chicken to a serving dish, spoon a few tablespoons of broth over it to keep it moist, and keep warm in a low oven. Remove the onion from the broth and measure 1½ cups broth into a saucepan. Combine flour and cream to a smooth paste and stir into broth. Cook over low heat, stirring constantly, preferably with a wire whip to avoid all lumping, for about 3–4 minutes, or until sauce is smooth and raw flour taste has cooked out. Check and if necessary correct seasoning. Pour sauce over chicken and serve hot over hot biscuits or hot buttered noodles.

Note:

An agreeable modern touch is to squeeze the juice of ½ lemon into the cooked sauce.

I find it impossible to give totally accurate measurements in the amount of water used to cook the chicken. It depends on the size of the saucepan and also on the chicken's moisture content. For maximum flavor, the chicken should be cooked in a small amount of water.

4 SERVINGS

CHICKEN PIE

All-American

      1 4- to 5-pound stewing chicken
        boiling water
      2 celery stalks, with green leafy tops cut up
      2 bay leaves
      1 tablespoon salt
      6 small yellow onions, or 12 small white onions
        Baking-Powder Sweet-Milk Biscuits (page 199)
      6 tablespoons butter
      6 tablespoons flour
      1 cup bouillon from the kettle
   1⅓ cups light cream or milk
        freshly ground pepper
      ⅛ teaspoon mace
      3 tablespoons sherry
      ⅛ teaspoon dried thyme or tarragon
        milk

Put chicken into a kettle large enough to hold all the ingredients easily. Add boiling water to come halfway up the chicken. Add celery, bay leaves, and 1 tablespoon salt. Bring to boiling point and lower heat. Simmer, covered, for 1½ to 3 hours, until the cooking liquid has become a rich bouillon and a fork can easily be stuck into a leg. Add the onions during the last 20 minutes cooking time, or cook them separately in water to cover until tender but not mushy. Remove cooked chicken and onions from bouillon and cool. Skim fat off bouillon and strain or, if at all possible, chill bouillon and skim off all risen fat. Measure 1 cup bouillon and reserve; use remaining bouillon for soup. Make Baking-Powder Sweet-Milk Biscuits, cut with small glass or biscuit cutter, and chill. Or use frozen baking-powder biscuits. Remove all skin, bones, gristle, and any remaining fat from chicken. Cut meat into large pieces. Generously butter a 2-quart baking dish. Layer chicken pieces and onions in dish. Heat the butter in a heavy saucepan. Stir in the flour and cook, stirring, 2 minutes. Stir in the reserved 1 cup bouillon and the cream or milk. Cook, stirring constantly, for 3–4 minutes or until smooth and thickened. Taste sauce and if necessary add a little salt.

Add pepper, mace, sherry, and thyme or tarragon, and blend. Pour sauce over chicken. Top with biscuits. Brush biscuit tops with milk. Bake in a preheated hot oven (425°) for about 15–20 minutes or until golden brown.

Note:

If you have any leftover ham, cut about ½ cup of ham strips and add to chicken.

4–6 SERVINGS

JAMBALAYA

From New Orleans

Jambalaya, cousin to the Spanish paella, is a rice and meat dish that can be simple, with one or two meats (pork, sausage, ham), or as festive, as the following dish. Unless I roast a chicken, when a crisp skin is desirable, I remove all the skin and fat in my chicken cookery; this makes for shorter cooking times. Chicken skin is very fat (a fact) and horrid (my opinion). When I make this Jambalaya, I use only the good meaty parts of the chickens (legs, breasts), reserving the wings, backs, necks, gizzards, etc., for making Chicken Broth (page 26) and shredding the meat for Chicken Corn Soup (page 27). Jambalaya is a more-or-less dish, you'll notice, and one not worth making for only a few people. It is a good party dish.

3 3- to 4-pound chickens, cut into serving pieces
  flour
4 tablespoons lard, salad oil, or bacon fat
3 cups chopped onions
2 cups seeded chopped green or red sweet pepper
2 bunches scallions trimmed and thinly sliced
2 garlic cloves, minced
½ cup minced parsley
½ pound lean baked ham, cut into ½-inch dice

1½ pounds lean pork, cut into ½-inch cubes and all fat
     trimmed off
  1 pound Polish sausages or sweet or hot Italian sausages
     (about 6)
  3 teaspoons salt (approximately)
  1 teaspoon freshly ground pepper
  ½ teaspoon Tabasco (or to taste)
  4 bay leaves, crushed
  1 teaspoon dried thyme (or to taste)
  ¼ teaspoon ground allspice
1½ cups raw long-grain rice
  3 cups hot chicken broth or water

Use a 7- or 8-quart casserole or kettle. Separate the chicken
pieces into legs and breasts; if the breasts are whole, cut them into
halves. (Reserve backs, wings, etc., for other uses.) Remove and
discard the skin and all fat from the chicken legs and breasts. Dip
the pieces lightly into flour and shake off excess flour. Heat the lard
or other fat in the casserole. Over high heat, quickly brown the
chicken pieces on all sides. Turn them frequently, using tongs or
two spoons so as not to pierce the meat. Transfer the browned
chicken pieces to a platter and keep warm. Add the onions, green
or red peppers, scallions, garlic, parsley, ham, and pork to the casserole. Lower heat to medium. Cook, stirring very frequently, for
about 10-15 minutes or until the vegetables and meats are
browned. Cut the sausages into ½-inch slices and add them to the
casserole. Stir in the salt, pepper, Tabasco, bay leaves, thyme, and
allspice. Cook, stirring constantly, for about 3-4 minutes. Return
the chicken pieces to the casserole. Add the rice and the hot broth
or hot water. With a fork, stir gently to mix the ingredients. Over
high heat, bring to the boiling point. Lower heat immediately to
very low (if needed, use an asbestos pad) and cover the casserole.
Cook for about 20 minutes, stirring occasionally, until the chicken is
almost cooked through and the rice almost tender. Uncover the casserole and cook for 10 more minutes or until the rice is dried, stirring from time to time; it may be necessary to raise the heat to medium. Serve at once.

6-8 SERVINGS

BRUNSWICK STEW

A dish of Indian origin, associated with the early cookery of Georgia, Kentucky, and Tennessee. It was originally made with squirrel, raccoon, or opossum, but as the years tamed the wilderness, chicken and domestic rabbit took the place of the wild creatures.

 2 3-pound frying chickens, cut into pieces, or 6 pounds
   rabbit (if frozen, thawed)
   salt
   freshly ground pepper
   flour
 6 tablespoons butter
 2 small onions, minced
 1 sweet green pepper, seeded and minced
 2½ cups canned tomatoes, undrained (1 No. 2 can)
 ¼ cup chopped parsley
 ½ teaspoon ground thyme
 2 cups whole kernel corn cut from the cob, or frozen
   corn, thawed
 2 cups shelled lima beans or frozen lima beans, thawed

Trim all the loose fat off the chicken or rabbit. Rub the pieces with salt and pepper and coat them on all sides with flour. Heat butter in a frying pan and brown the pieces in it. Transfer to a casserole (skin side up, if chicken). Cook the onions and green pepper in the same frying pan, until they are soft but not heavily browned. Add the tomatoes, parsley, and thyme. Bring to the boiling point and pour sauce over the casserole. Simmer covered over low heat, stirring frequently with a fork, until the meat is almost tender—anywhere from 15 to 20 minutes. Add the corn and lima beans and cook for 5–7 more minutes or until the vegetables are cooked and the meat tender.

5–6 SERVINGS

Thoughts on Fried Chicken

There are many ways to fry a chicken and every good fried-chicken cook is convinced hers/his is best. I will list some of the possibilities so that readers may experiment: They may dip the cut-up chicken first in either water, milk, buttermilk, or even cream; or they may salt the chicken pieces and refrigerate them overnight, then blot them dry of the accumulated juices before peppering, flouring, and frying them. The dipped chicken pieces may be coated with flour only or with flour mixed with grated cheese or with cracker crumbs, or breadcrumbs, and then fried. Or else, they can be dipped in a batter, or, after the initial flouring, dipped in egg and then in cracker crumbs or breadcrumbs.

The chicken pieces can be pan- or deep-fried in lard, bacon fat, butter, vegetable shortening, or salad oil or olive oil, or in a combination of fats. A mixture is necessary when butter is used since butter burns more quickly than the oil with which it is usually mixed. It is essential that the frying fat be fresh and sweet, since stale fat is plain awful in smell and flavor. It is also essential to have the fat always at the right temperature, which is around 375° on a frying thermometer or when a cube of bread will turn golden brown in about 60 seconds. Let the fat heat up again between batches. I'm not mad for appliances but I must admit that an electric deep-fryer is a great help for any deep-frying because it automatically keeps a steady temperature. White and dark chicken meat cook differently, the dark taking longer. It is therefore advisable to cook pieces of the same color together or to use two frying pans. Be sure to buy small chickens for frying; larger ones don't have the flavor and don't cook well. *En avant*, Chicken Fryers!

SOUTHERN-FRIED CHICKEN

*I remove the skin from chicken because I don't like the
fatty flavor and because skinned chicken fries crisper. Leave
the skins on if you must, though. Not all Southern cooks use
an egg batter to fry chicken, but the Mobile, Alabama, lady
who taught me this recipe said that the chicken fries better
this way.*

  1 egg
  1 tablespoon water
  ½ teaspoon Worcestershire sauce (optional)
  1 frying chicken, about 1½ to 2½ pounds, cut into pieces
  ⅔ cup flour
  ½ teaspoon freshly ground pepper
  ⅛ teaspoon cayenne (optional)
    salt
    salad oil for frying, preferably peanut oil

In a bowl big enough to hold all the chicken pieces, lightly
beat together the egg, water, and Worcestershire sauce (if used).
Place the chicken pieces in the egg mixture, dipping them to coat
on all sides and leaving them in the mixture until ready to fry.
Shake excess egg off chicken pieces. Put the flour, pepper, and
cayenne (if used) into a paper bag. Put the chicken pieces into the
bag and shake vigorously to coat on all sides. Remove chicken from
bag and shake off excess flour. Pour oil to a depth of about ½ inch
into a large deep frying pan, preferably iron. Heat until about 375°
on frying thermometer or when a cube of bread dropped into hot
oil turns golden brown in 60 seconds or when a little of the egg
mixture dropped into the fat sizzles. Put the dark meat pieces into
the center of the frying pan where they will cook most quickly and
place the light pieces—which take less cooking—around them. Over
high heat, brown pieces for 1–2 minutes. Turn, using tongs (fork
will pierce chicken), and brown for 1–2 minutes on other side. Turn
heat down to low-to-medium and cover frying pan. Cook chicken
for 10 minutes, turn with tongs and cook for 10 more minutes.
Remove cover from frying pan, turn heat to high, and cook for
about 1–2 minutes. Drain chicken on several thicknesses of paper
towels and blot with paper towels before placing on serving platter.

Sprinkle lightly with salt before serving. Keep warm in a low oven while making gravy (see following recipe).

3 SERVINGS

CREAM GRAVY

2 tablespoons fat from frying chicken
2 tablespoons butter
4 tablespoons flour
1 cup milk
1 cup heavy cream
  salt
  freshly ground pepper
  dash Tabasco (optional)
¼ teaspoon paprika

When chicken has been fried, pour off all but 2 tablespoons fat from frying pan. Scrape up all the brown bits clinging to pan. Add the butter, heat, and stir in flour. Cook, stirring constantly, for about 2–3 minutes. Add the milk, cream, and a little salt and pepper. Cook over low heat for about 4–5 minutes, stirring all the time, to cook out raw flour taste—the mixture should be light gold. Season with Tabasco if desired and sprinkle with paprika before serving.

Note:
I would not dare decide whether the gravy is to be served over the chicken or on the side. In any case, it goes well with hot biscuits or corn bread.

MAKES ABOUT 2 CUPS

BATTER-FRIED CHICKEN

Southern

*I prefer a beer batter for batter-fried foods because it is
lighter, thanks to the beer, than a milk batter.*

  1   12-ounce can light beer
1½   cups flour
  2   teaspoons salt
  ½   teaspoon freshly ground pepper
  2   teaspoons paprika (optional)
  2   broiler-fryers, each about 2 to 2½ pounds, cut
         into pieces
         lard, salad oil, or vegetable shortening for frying

Pour the beer into a large bowl. Sift the flour, salt, pepper,
and paprika (if used) into the beer, stirring with a wire whip or
beating with a rotary beater until light, frothy, and smooth. Let
stand at room temperature for from 15 minutes to 2 hours, whisking
occasionally to keep batter mixed. Put enough fat in a large deep
frying pan or shallow saucepan to come up to the height of 1 inch.
Heat to 375° on the frying thermometer or until a cube of bread
dropped into the fat turns golden in 60 seconds. Dip the chicken
pieces into batter, coating on all sides but allowing excess batter to
drain back into the bowl. Drop chicken pieces in hot fat, a few at a
time; they must not touch each other. Cook for about 15 minutes on
one side, turn and cook for 15 more minutes or until chicken tests
fork-tender. Drain chicken on several thicknesses of paper towels
and blot dry with more paper towels. Keep warm on a platter in a
low oven (200°) until all chicken is ready to serve. Garnish platter
with watercress.

6 SERVINGS

OVEN-FRIED CHICKEN

All-American

⅔ cup flour
1 teaspoon salt
½ teaspoon freshly ground pepper
1 teaspoon paprika
1 broiler-fryer, about 2½ pounds, cut into pieces
¼ cup salad oil
¼ cup butter
2 eggs
3 tablespoons milk
⅔ cup grated Parmesan cheese
⅓ cup fine dry breadcrumbs

Put the flour, salt, pepper, and paprika in a bag. Add chicken pieces, a few at a time, and shake vigorously to coat with flour on all sides. Shake off excess flour. Put the oil and butter into an oblong baking pan (13×9½×2 inches) and place in a preheated hot oven (425°). Beat the eggs with the milk. Dip flour-coated chicken in egg mixture, shaking off excess. Combine Parmesan cheese and breadcrumbs and dip egg-coated chicken pieces in mixture. With pot holders, take pan from oven. Place chicken, skin side down, in a single layer in the hot fat. Return pan to oven and cook for about 20 minutes. Turn with tongs and cook for 20 more minutes or until chicken tests fork-tender. Serve on heated platter. If desired, serve with Cream Gravy (see page 70).

Note:
For a simpler dish, omit the egg and cheese-crumb mixture and place floured chicken pieces directly into hot fat.

3–4 SERVINGS

BAKED CHICKEN

From Michigan via New England

      1 broiler-fryer, about 2½ pounds, cut into pieces
        salt
        freshly ground pepper
  ⅓–½ cup flour
      8 tablespoons butter
    ¼ cup boiling water
        dash Tabasco (optional)

   GRAVY
      3 tablespoons flour
      1 cup chicken bouillon
    ½ cup heavy cream

Place the chicken pieces in one layer in an oblong baking dish (13×9×2 inches). Sprinkle lightly with salt and pepper. Sprinkle with flour, beginning with ⅓ cup, and turn pieces to coat lightly with flour. Dot with 4 tablespoons of the butter. Cook in a preheated hot oven (400°) for 10 minutes. Combine the remaining 4 tablespoons butter with the boiling water and Tabasco (if desired). Baste chicken with mixture every 5 minutes for 20 minutes. Chicken should be fork-tender and golden. Turn off oven. Remove chicken to heated platter and keep hot in the oven while making gravy. Pour off all but 3 tablespoons fat from baking pan. Scrape up all the brown bits at the bottom and add the 3 tablespoons flour. Cook, stirring continuously, for 2–3 minutes. Add the chicken bouillon and cream. Cook, stirring all the time, for about 4 minutes to remove raw flour taste. Pour gravy over chicken and serve.

Note:

The gravy may also be made with 1½ cups milk, instead of the bouillon and cream.

3–4 SERVINGS

CHICKEN TETRAZZINI

From New York

This dish of chicken, spaghetti, and sauce is named after the famed coloratura Luisa Tetrazzini, who reigned supreme during the early part of the century. She had an incredibly beautiful voice and was also very portly indeed since she loved to eat. The dish is one that, in an emergency, can be made from kitchen shelf ingredients for unexpected guests. This is one of the fancier versions.

  6 tablespoons butter
  ½ pound mushrooms, thinly sliced
  1 small sweet green pepper, cut into strips
  3 tablespoons flour
  2 teaspoons salt
  ½ teaspoon freshly ground pepper
    dash cayenne
2½ cups half-and-half or equal parts of milk and heavy cream
  3 cups diced cooked chicken, preferably white meat
2–4 tablespoons sherry
  2 egg yolks beaten with 2 tablespoons cream or milk
  ½ pound thin spaghetti
  ½ cup grated Parmesan cheese

Heat 4 tablespoons of the butter in a heavy saucepan. Add mushrooms and green pepper and cook, stirring constantly, for about 3–4 minutes, or until soft but not brown. Blend in the flour, salt, pepper, and cayenne. Cook for 2 more minutes. Stir in half-and-half or milk and cream. Cook over low heat, stirring constantly, until thickened. Add the chicken and sherry. Remove from heat and stir in the beaten egg yolks. Cook the spaghetti in plenty of boiling salted water until almost but not quite tender; drain. Turn into a generously buttered 2½- to 3-quart shallow baking dish. Spoon chicken mixture over spaghetti. Sprinkle with Parmesan and dot with remaining 2 tablespoons butter. Bake in a preheated moderate oven (350°) for about 30–40 minutes or until browned and bubbly. If not sufficiently browned, run the baking dish quickly under the broiler.

6 SERVINGS

CHICKEN CROQUETTES I

All-American

Chicken croquettes should be rescued from oblivion. Served with tomato sauce and a salad they make an excellent lunch. But they must be well seasoned.

  4 tablespoons butter
  2 tablespoons minced onion
  3 tablespoons flour
  1 cup well-seasoned strong chicken bouillon
  1 egg yolk
  ½ teaspoon dry mustard
  1 tablespoon minced parsley
  2 cups cooked chicken, minced
    salt
    freshly ground pepper

FOR BREADING
  ½ cup flour in a bowl
  1 egg, lightly stirred to mix, but not beaten, in a bowl
  ½ cup fine dry breadcrumbs in a bowl
    shortening or oil for frying
    lemon wedges

Heat the butter in a heavy frying pan and add the onion. Cook, stirring constantly, for about 2 minutes or until onion is soft; do not brown. Stir in the 3 tablespoons flour and cook, stirring all the time, for 1–2 minutes; do not brown. Stir in the chicken bouillon. Cook over low heat, stirring briskly, until smooth and thickened. Remove from heat and beat in the egg yolk. Add the mustard, parsley, and chicken. Blend thoroughly. Season with salt if needed (chicken may be salty) and pepper. Turn into a bowl and refrigerate covered for about 30 minutes to 1 hour, or until firm enough to shape.

With lightly floured hands, shape into croquettes measuring about 1×1×2½ inches. To bread, dip each croquette into the bowl of flour and shake off excess flour. Dip into the egg, making sure that all sides are covered. Dip into the breadcrumbs, shaking off excess. As croquettes are ready, place them side by side on a rack. Let stand at room temperature for 1 hour to dry out. Do not refrigerate. Croquettes must be well dried before frying. Heat the shortening or oil in a deep-fryer to a temperature of 375° on the frying thermometer. Cook a few croquettes at a time (they must not touch) for 3–4 minutes on each side or until golden and crisp. Drain on paper towels and place on a plate. Keep warm in oven set at lowest temperature (140°–175°) until all croquettes are fried. Serve hot, with lemon wedges.

Note:

If you do not have leftover chicken, cook a whole small fryer weighing about 2½ to 3 pounds in 1 cup water, covered, over low heat for about 1½ hours. The chicken will yield about 2 to 2½ cups chicken meat and about 1½ cups strong chicken bouillon. Skim the bouillon free of fat, strain, and reduce to 1 cup.

Four slices American bread, toasted but not browned, will yield about ½ cup of crumbs.

MAKES 8 CROQUETTES

CHICKEN CROQUETTES II

All-American

5 tablespoons butter
2 tablespoons minced onion
4 tablespoons flour

1 cup well-seasoned strong chicken boullion
½ teaspoon ground mustard
¼ pound mushrooms, minced
2 cups cooked chicken or turkey, minced
salt
freshly ground pepper

FOR BREADING
½ cup flour, in a bowl
1 egg, lightly stirred but not beaten, in a bowl
½ cup fine dry breadcrumbs plus 3 tablespoons grated
Parmesan cheese, in a bowl
shortening or oil for frying
lemon wedges

Place minced mushrooms in a heavy frying pan. Cook over high heat, stirring constantly, until no liquid remains in pan. Stir in 1 tablespoon of the butter and remove from heat. Cool before adding to croquette mixture and refrigerating. Proceed as in the preceding recipe for Chicken Croquettes I, using the ingredients listed here. In this version of chicken croquettes, Parmesan cheese is added to the breadcrumbs used for breading.

MAKES 8 CROQUETTES

CHICKEN HASH

The recipe also works for cooked turkey.

4 cups chopped cooked chicken meat, white meat only, not too finely chopped
1½ cups heavy cream
1 cup Rich White Sauce (see following recipe)
salt
freshly ground pepper, preferably white pepper
cayenne to taste
⅔ cup freshly grated Swiss cheese

Pick over the meat, removing any small bones, cartilage, and fat. In a large frying pan, heat the meat in the cream. Cook over medium heat, stirring frequently, until the cream has thickened and is reduced by one-third to one-half. Stir in the white sauce and remove from heat. Season with salt, pepper, and cayenne. Turn into a generously buttered 9- or 10-inch shallow baking dish. Sprinkle with the Swiss cheese. Brown under the broiler or in a preheated hot oven (425°) until heated through and bubbly on top.

4–6 SERVINGS

RICH WHITE SAUCE

    2 tablespoons butter
    2 tablespoons flour
    ½ cup hot milk
    ½ cup heavy cream

Heat the butter in the top of a double boiler. Add the flour and cook, stirring all the time, for about 2–3 minutes. Gradually stir in the hot milk, stirring until there is a smooth paste. Cook over simmering water for about 30 minutes, to cook away the raw flour taste. Stir frequently. Stir in the cream and heat through before using; the uncooked cream gives the sauce a fresh taste.

MAKES ABOUT 1 CUP

WHITE DEVILED CHICKEN

From Virginia

A deviled dish is a well-seasoned hot dish of English origin.

    3 cups ½-inch cooked chicken pieces, white meat only
 1⅓ cups heavy cream

   1 tablespoon Worcestershire sauce
   1 teaspoon dry mustard
   ¼ teaspoon Tabasco or to taste
     salt
     freshly ground pepper
     hot buttered toast

Place the chicken in a generously buttered 1½-quart baking dish; the dish should not be too deep. Whip the cream until stiff. Stir in the Worcestershire sauce, dry mustard, Tabasco, and a little salt and pepper. Spoon mixture over chicken. Cook in a preheated hot oven (400°) for 10 minutes. Serve immediately on hot plates, with hot buttered toast.

4 SERVINGS

CHICKEN À LA KING

This dish became popular around the turn of the century and it deserves to be kept in circulation. It lends itself to being made in double and triple amounts and is a good buffet dish, as I know from experience.

   SAUCE
   4 tablespoons butter
   4 tablespoons flour
   2 cups chicken broth
   2 cups light cream or milk
   1 cup heavy cream

   3 tablespoons butter
   1 tablespoon minced onion
   ¼ pound mushrooms, thinly sliced
   1 sweet green pepper, cut into thin strips
   ½ cup chopped pimiento
   3 cups diced cooked chicken (¾-inch dice), preferably
     white meat only

   salt
   freshly ground pepper
 2 egg yolks, beaten
 ½ cup sherry
 ½ cup chopped blanched toasted almonds
   toast, boiled rice, or patty shells

To make the sauce, heat the 4 tablespoons butter in a heavy saucepan. Stir in the flour and cook, stirring constantly, 1–2 minutes. Add the chicken broth and light cream or milk, and cook, stirring all the time, until thick and smooth. Remove from heat and stir in the heavy cream. Reserve.

Heat the 3 tablespoons butter in a frying pan and add onion, mushrooms, and green pepper. Cook over high heat, stirring constantly, for 3–4 minutes; mushrooms must retain their shape. Add the pimiento and chicken and mix well. Season with salt and pepper. Spoon a little sauce into the beaten egg yolks. Turn heat to low and stir egg mixture into chicken. Cook for 1 minute; do not boil. Remove from heat and stir in sherry and almonds. Serve immediately on hot toast, or boiled rice, or hot pastry shells, baked according to package directions. Serve the remaining sauce on the side.

6 SERVINGS

CHICKEN SALAD

All-American

Most chicken-salad recipes advocate more celery than chicken. But what are we eating, chicken salad or celery salad? Marinating the chicken before adding the dressing avoids the dry flavor of so many chicken salads. A chicken that weighs about 3 pounds will yield about 4 cups cooked cubed chicken meat.

½ cup plain French dressing
2–3 drops Tabasco (optional)
4 cups cooked cubed chicken meat
2 cups thinly sliced celery, white part only
½ cup walnuts, broken, not chopped, into pieces
⅔ cup mayonnaise, or to taste
1 cup seedless grapes, stemmed, washed, and dried
shredded salad greens
2 hard-cooked eggs, sliced

Combine the French dressing with the Tabasco (if used) and mix well. Put chicken into a bowl (do not use aluminum) and stir in the dressing. Mix well. Refrigerate covered for 2–4 hours, stirring once. Add the celery, walnuts, and mayonnaise and mix well. Pile in a mound on a serving plate. Stud salad with grapes. Surround the base of the salad with shredded salad greens and top these with egg slices. Serve immediately.

4–6 SERVINGS

CHICKEN SALAD IN AVOCADO SHELLS

From California

There is no mayonnaise in this chicken salad.

2 cups finely chopped cold cooked chicken, white meat only
½ cup finely chopped celery
⅓ cup chopped pitted black olives
2 tablespoons lemon juice
salt
freshly ground pepper
Tabasco to taste
2 large ripe avocados
2 hard-cooked eggs, chopped
lettuce leaves

Combine the chicken, celery, and olives. Stir in the lemon juice and season with salt, pepper, and Tabasco. Cut the avocados in halves, remove pits, and scoop out pulp. Cut pulp into ¼-inch dice and stir carefully into chicken mixture. Fill the avocado shells with the salad and sprinkle each serving with some chopped hard-cooked egg. Serve on plates lined with lettuce leaves.

4 SERVINGS

Beef

———◄◆►———

ANN SERANNE'S PERFECT
RARE RIB ROAST OF BEEF

This different, very successful, and painless way of roasting a rib roast comes from a great cook, food expert, and cookbook writer. This method should only be attempted in a well-insulated oven. The roast must be well trimmed and ready to cook. Count on 2 servings for each rib.

1 2-rib to 4-rib roast of beef, trimmed and short ribs
   removed, weighing about 4½ to 12 pounds
   flour
   salt
   freshly ground pepper

Remove roast from refrigerator 2½ to 4 hours before cooking. Preheat oven to very hot (500°). Preheating will take about 20 minutes and is essential. Place roast, fat side up, in a shallow roasting pan. Sprinkle lightly with flour and rub flour lightly into fat with fingers. Lightly rub in a little salt and pepper. Put roast in preheated oven. Roast according to the following chart. Time exactly and do not open oven door at any time; this is essential. Allow finished roast to remain in oven until oven has cooled to lukewarm, about 2 hours. Roast will be brown and crunchy on the outside and have an internal heat that will be suitable for serving as long as 2–4 hours after taking out of oven, provided it is kept in a warm place. A large roast will keep the internal heat longer than a small one. Make the gravy when you finally take the roast out of the oven.

4 TO 8 SERVINGS (2 PER RIB)

ROASTING CHART

Ribs	Weight without short ribs (pounds)	Roast at 500° (minutes)
2	4½ to 5	25 to 30
3	8 to 9	40 to 45
4	11 to 12	55 to 60

This works out to be about 15 minutes per rib, or about 5 minutes roasting time per pound of trimmed meat.

THIN PAN GRAVY

Pour off any fat from roasting pan. Stir in ½ cup beef bouillon and ½ cup dry red wine, scraping up all the brown bits at the bottom of pan. Bring to boiling point and, if necessary, season with salt and pepper. Cook, stirring all the time, for 1–2 minutes.

BEEF WELLINGTON

All-American

Once a restaurant dish of French parentage, now a perennial favorite of the cook who wants to impress with what is called "Continental Cuisine." This recipe omits the traditional foie gras, mousse de foie gras, or liver pâté, the first two being too expensive and the last unworthy; besides, I don't like the combination of beef and liver. The pastry and the mushroom duxelles (chopped, cooked-down mushrooms) can be prepared a day ahead. The meat may be cooked in the morning (it changes flavor if cooked the previous day) and the whole dish assembled before baking.

PASTRY

3 cups flour
½ teaspoon salt
1½ cups butter, cut into pieces
8 tablespoons sour cream

Put the flour and salt in a bowl. Cut in the butter until mixture resembles coarse meal. Stir in the sour cream. Stir quickly with a fork only until mixture holds together. With the hands shape in a ball. Wrap in waxed paper and refrigerate.

DUXELLES

6 tablespoons butter
2 shallots, or 1 small onion, minced
1 pound mushrooms, chopped fine
salt
freshly ground pepper

Heat the 6 tablespoons butter in a large heavy frying pan. Add the shallots or onion and cook, stirring constantly, until soft and golden. Add the mushrooms and about 1 teaspoon salt. Cook over very low heat, stirring frequently, for about 50 minutes or until mushrooms are very dark and very dry; it is important that they should be very dry or the finished dish will be soggy. Check seasoning and if necessary add more salt and add pepper. Cool thoroughly.

MEAT

1 fillet of beef, weighing approximately 4–5 pounds, well trimmed, at room temperature
salt
freshly ground pepper
2 tablespoons butter
¼ cup brandy

Rub the meat with salt, pepper, and 2 tablespoons butter. Place on a rack in a roasting pan. Roast in a preheated hot oven (450°) for 25 minutes. Remove pan from oven and flame meat with the brandy. Cool completely.

TO ASSEMBLE

1 egg white, slightly beaten
2 egg yolks, slightly beaten with 2 tablespoons cold water

Measure the width and length of fillet. Roll out the pastry between 2 sheets of waxed paper or on a floured board into a rectangle long and wide enough to cover the meat completely. Trim; reserve scraps. Spread about one-third of the mushroom duxelles approximately the width of the fillet, lengthwise down the center of the pastry, leaving about 1½-inch margins at the ends. Lay the meat lengthwise on the duxelles. Spread remaining duxelles on top and sides. Moisten pastry margins with a little beaten egg white. Bring pastry edges together on top of meat and pinch firmly to seal. Fold pastry ends in and pinch to seal. Place seamside down on an ungreased baking sheet; do this transfer carefully in order not to break pastry. Prick lightly twice with a fork to make steam holes. Cut small leaves, half-moons, or rosettes from the reserved pastry scraps. Using beaten egg white as glue, attach these to the meat roll in a decorative pattern. Brush top and cutouts lightly with beaten egg yolk, taking care not to brush over the steam holes. Cook in a preheated hot oven (400°) for about 30 minutes or until pastry is golden. If pastry browns too quickly, reduce heat to moderate (350°). Remove from oven and allow to stand at room temperature for 10 minutes before transferring carefully to a warm serving platter. Meat will be heated through and partly crisp. Use a serrated knife to cut through pastry and meat without tearing. Cut into ¾-inch to 1-inch slices. Garnish with watercress.

Note:

If the meat is not completely cooled before being wrapped in the pastry, it will overcook.

6–8 SERVINGS

EDDIE HERTZBERG'S POT ROAST

From New York

Pot roast is a hunk of not-so-tender beef browned in hot fat, then cooked slowly in a tightly covered pot with a small amount of liquid. Obviously, there are dozens of variations upon this theme. This one—using beef brisket instead of round or rump or chuck—is from a gifted cook.

    1 5- to 6-pound first-cut beef brisket
    ¼ cup butter, salad oil, or chicken fat
    1 Spanish onion (about ½ pound), thinly sliced
    2 garlic cloves, mashed
    1 1-pound can Italian-style tomatoes (about 1¾ cups)
    2 bay leaves
    1 teaspoon ground thyme
       salt
       freshly ground pepper

Cut off all but a thin layer of fat from the meat. Heat the butter, oil, or chicken fat in a heavy frying pan. Over high heat, brown the meat on all sides to a rich dark color. Transfer meat to a large saucepan, ovenproof casserole, or Dutch oven with a tight cover. Add the onion and garlic to the pan juices, and cook, stirring constantly, until browned; do not scorch. With a slotted spoon, transfer onion and garlic to meat and pour off and discard any remaining fat from frying pan. Add the tomatoes to frying pan and mash with a fork. Cook over low heat for about 3–4 minutes, stirring constantly and scraping up the brown bits on the bottom of the frying pan. Pour tomatoes over meat. Add bay leaves, thyme, salt, and pepper. Cover tightly. Simmer over low heat on top of stove, or in a slow oven (300°), for 3–4 hours or until meat is tender but not mushy. Test with a skewer during the last 1½ hours cooking time to avoid overcooking. Set oven to very low (175°–200°). Transfer meat to heated serving platter and keep warm in oven. Skim fat off pan juices, first using a spoon and then blotting the fat with a triple layer of paper towels. Remove bay leaves. If desired, the gravy may be strained or thickened with 1–2 tablespoons flour made into a paste with 1–2 tablespoons cold water, stirred slowly into pan juices and cooked over low heat, with constant stirring for 3 minutes. But it is more flavorful as is. Slice meat and arrange in overlapping slices on serving platter. Spoon some gravy over slices to keep moist and serve remaining gravy on the side. Serve with potato pancakes or noodles or kasha. The leftover cold sliced meat heats up very well in gravy.

8–10 SERVINGS

VARIATIONS:

Eddie Hertzberg's son Bobby suggested two ways of simplifying matters:

(1) Put all ingredients into a "brown-in-bag" according to package directions. Place in a roasting pan and cook in a preheated slow oven (325°) for 2–3 hours or until tender. The pot roast won't be browned, but flavor and texture are excellent.

(2) Put all ingredients into an open roasting pan and cook in a preheated slow oven (325°) for about 2–3 hours or until tender. Baste constantly (about every 7–10 minutes), adding boiling water as the sauce cooks away.

PEKING ROAST

From Texas

*A San Antonio friend made this for me; she could not ac-
count for the name. The coffee flavor must be subtle. Use
ordinary-strength coffee, preferably not instant.*

3   pounds beef bottom round, in one piece
3   garlic cloves, slivered
1   cup cider vinegar
3   tablespoons bacon fat or lard or salad oil
2   cups coffee
2   cups water
    salt
    freshly ground pepper
4   tablespoons flour
1⅔ cups light cream or milk

Cut slits in the meat and insert garlic slivers. Place meat in a
bowl (do not use aluminum) and pour vinegar over it. Turn in the
vinegar several times to make sure vinegar penetrates the garlic
slits. Cover and refrigerate from 24 to 48 hours. Turn several times.
Drain meat and dry thoroughly between paper towels. Heat the fat
in a large heavy frying pan. Over high heat, brown meat on all
sides. Transfer meat to an ovenproof casserole. Pour the coffee and
water over it, bring to boiling point, and remove from heat. Place in
preheated low oven (325°). Cook covered for about 2½–3 hours or
until meat is tender. Turn meat several times, and 30 minutes before meat is ready, season lightly with salt and pepper. Drain
meat and reserve liquid. Reduce oven heat to very lowest, about
140°–170°. Slice the meat and arrange in overlapping slices on a
heated serving dish. Cover the dish with aluminum foil and keep
warm in the oven. Combine the flour and cream or milk to make a
smooth paste. Measure ⅓ cup of the reserved liquid into a small
saucepan. Bring to boiling point and stir into flour mixture. Cook
over low heat, stirring constantly, for about 4–5 minutes or until
thickened and raw flour taste is cooked out. Remove aluminum foil
from meat and pour gravy over it. Serve hot, with buttered noodles
or rice.

Note:

If a stronger coffee flavor is desired, increase the pan liquid in the gravy to ½ cup and reduce the cream to 1½ cups.

6 SERVINGS

BOILED CORNED-BEEF DINNER

From New England

Brisket and boned rump are the best cuts for this. Some corned beef is saltier and spicier than others; this depends on the curing process. If yours seems too salty, soak the meat in cold water for 30 to 60 minutes, depending on saltiness. Drain.

4–5 pounds corned beef
  3 quarts cold water
  3 quarts boiling water
  2 medium onions, peeled and each stuck with 3 cloves
  7 medium carrots
  1 celery stalk, white and green parts
  2 bay leaves
  3 big parsley stalks with leaves, tied together with thread
 12 peppercorns, slightly crushed
  6 medium onions, peeled
  6 small turnips, or 3 large turnips cut into halves
  1 head cabbage, weighing approximately 2–3 pounds
    boiled potatoes, cooked separately
    Parsley Sauce (page 190)
    mustards and pickles

Wash the meat and place in a large kettle. Add the cold water. Bring to boiling point, lower heat, and simmer, covered, for 1 hour. Pour off liquid (changing the water will make for a fresher dish) and add the 3 quarts boiling water, the onions stuck with cloves, 1 carrot, the celery, bay leaves, parsley, and peppercorns. Bring back to boiling and skim. Lower heat and simmer, covered, for 2 to as much as 4 hours, skimming as needed. Cooking time depends on the quality of the meat, which is unpredictable. The meat must be tender but still firm; do not overcook and test frequently with a skewer. When meat is more than three-quarters done (about the last ½ hour of cooking), with a slotted spoon remove the onions stuck with cloves, the carrot, celery, bay leaves, parsley, and as many peppercorns as possible. Add the 6 onions, the remaining 6 carrots, and the turnips. Cut the cabbage into 6 wedges and add for the last 15 minutes of cooking. Prepare Parsley Sauce while the vegetables cook. Drain meat, slice, and place in overlapping slices on a large heated serving dish. Surround with vegetables. Serve with boiled potatoes and Parsley Sauce on the side and, if possible, a variety of mustards and pickles.

Notes:
It is common practice to cook the potatoes along with the meat, but I find that they are apt to disintegrate and are better cooked separately.

It is essential that neither meat nor vegetables be mushy. A way of insuring this is to drain off 4–6 cups of the cooking liquid and cook the vegetables in it, separately. The cooking liquid used for 1 vegetable can be used over again for the others. The potatoes may also be cooked in this liquid.

6 SERVINGS

CORNED-BEEF OR ROAST-BEEF HASH

All-American

In a good beef hash, there is twice as much meat as potatoes. It is important that meat and potatoes be hashed separately—that is, cut with a knife into ¼-inch dice. They must not be ground or processed in a food processor.

5–6 tablespoons beef drippings, or 3 tablespoons butter
    and 2 tablespoons oil
  1 medium onion, minced
  2 cups finely diced boiled potatoes
  4 cups finely diced cooked corned beef or roast beef
    salt
    freshly ground pepper
 ½ cup heavy cream (optional)
    poached eggs
    chili sauce

Heat drippings or butter and oil in a large heavy saucepan.
Add the onion and cook, stirring constantly, until soft and golden.
Add the potatoes. Over medium heat, stirring lightly once or twice
with a fork, cook until potatoes are beginning to crisp at the edges.
Add the meat and again stir with a fork, to mix well. Season with
salt and pepper and smooth top of mixture to make an even layer.
If desired, add the heavy cream and again press hash down in the
frying pan. Cook over very low heat for about 20–25 minutes or
until hash is crusty on the bottom. Do not stir hash but check by
lifting edge carefully with a spatula. Fold in pan like an omelet,
slide onto a heated serving dish. Top with poached eggs and serve
chili sauce on the side.

4 SERVINGS

CHICKEN-FRIED STEAKS

From Texas

*People in the Southwest do not generally care for the un-
dercooked beef favored by Easterners. This typical ranch
dish is good for people like myself who don't like rare meat.*

  2 pounds beef round steak, approximately ½-inch thick
 ⅓ cup flour
1½ teaspoons salt
 ½ teaspoon freshly ground pepper
 ½ cup shortening (approximately)

Trim all fat off the meat. Cut it into 6 slices. Combine the flour, salt, and pepper. Sprinkle over sliced meat, pressing it into both sides of the meat. Heat the shortening in a heavy frying pan. Add the meat and cook over medium heat for about 3–4 minutes, then turn and cook on the other side for the same length of time.

4–6 SERVINGS

SAVORY PEPPER STEAK

Western

    2 pounds beef round, about ½-inch thick
    ¼ cup flour
      salt
      freshly ground pepper
    ¼ cup bacon fat, salad oil, or shortening
    ½ cup chopped onion
    1 garlic clove, minced
    1 cup canned or fresh tomatoes, chopped
  1½ cups water
    1 tablespoon Worcestershire sauce
    2 large sweet green peppers, seeded and cut into strips
      hot cooked rice

Trim the fat off the meat and cut meat into 3-inch strips. Combine the flour, salt, and pepper and toss the meat in the mixture. Shake off excess flour. Heat the bacon fat, oil, or shortening in a large heavy saucepan. Over high heat, cook meat for 3–4 minutes or until browned. Lower heat and add the onion, garlic, tomatoes, water, Worcestershire sauce, and green peppers. Simmer covered for about 45–60 minutes or until meat is tender. Serve with hot boiled rice.

Note:
For crisper pepper strips, add them to the meat only 10 minutes before meat is ready.

4–6 SERVINGS

OLD-FASHIONED
BROWN BEEF STEW

From the Midwest

This stew may be stretched with more potatoes, carrots, and onions. Coating the meat generously with flour and browning it thoroughly enriches the flavor, as does the use of lard or bacon grease.

   3 pounds round or chuck, cut into 1½-inch pieces
     flour
4–6 tablespoons lard or bacon grease
   2 cups water
   1 medium onion, cut into quarters
     salt
     freshly ground pepper
   ⅛ teaspoon ground allspice
   4 medium-sized or large potatoes, peeled and cut into
     1½-inch pieces
   4 large carrots, cut into 1-inch slices
6–8 small (pickling) onions (unpeeled)

Remove all fat or gristle from the meat. Roll the pieces in flour until they are thickly coated. Heat 4 tablespoons of the fat in a large heavy frying pan. Over high heat, brown the meat a few pieces at a time until dark and crusty. Transfer the browned meat to a casserole. If necessary, add the 1 or 2 tablespoons more fat to the frying pan for browning. Add the water and the quartered onion to the meat and bring to boiling point. Reduce heat to very low and cover the pan. Simmer for 1 to 1½ hours, stirring occasionally. Check the moisture; the pan gravy should be the consistency of thick cream; if necessary, add more water, a few tablespoons at a time. Stir in the salt, pepper, and allspice. Simmer covered for 30 minutes. Add the potatoes and carrots. Simmer, covered, until vegetables are tender, checking the moisture; more water may be needed for the proper gravy. While the stew is simmering, cook the small onions in boiling water until they are almost tender. Drain and run cold water over them, then peel and add to the stew and cook for 15 more minutes. Serve with coleslaw or sliced tomatoes and corn bread.

Note:

As in all stews, the amount of liquid needed depends on the amount of flour used in coating the meat and the way the potatoes absorb liquid, as well as on whether you want a thick or a thin stew.

6–8 SERVINGS

BOB HOLLERON'S SAN ANTONIO CHILI CON CARNE

(*Author's Note: According to all who've eaten it, this is the best chili ever. Bob is a distinguished amateur cook and I give the introduction to the recipe in his own words because they make things clear. Like other chili buffs, he considers putting beans into chili a vulgarity.*)

"*Essentially, chili con carne, a Tex-Mex dish, is nothing more than a well-designed and well-thought-out stew. As with other classic stews, certain ground rules are important.*

"*1. The meat, chuck, round, or sirloin, must be carefully trimmed. This means that if you want to come up with 6 pounds trimmed meat you must buy 6–7 pounds untrimmed. Every bit of fat which would make the chili greasy must go. This takes time, but it must be done. Depending on the meat, the fat and gristle usually amount to 1–2 pounds.*

"*2. The meat must be thoroughly dried. This means, very well browned. This takes quite a bit of time since the meat at first gives out quite a lot of water. This water evaporates as the meat browns.*

"*3. The meat is best browned in a good vegetable oil. The traditional fat to brown chili is lard, which is all right if you like the flavor. You can also use rendered beef fat. When a large quantity of chili is made, as in this recipe (chili can be warmed up successfully again and again), it is best to brown the meat in batches, using a heavy iron frying pan. The pan must be heavy.*

"4. A word about chili meat. Ground beef will not do. In Texas, they sell coarser ground so-called chili meat, which I guess people like because it saves cutting up the meat. Real honest chili is cut by hand into tiny dice."

6 pounds trimmed weight, lean beef (chuck, round, or sirloin)
   approximately ½ to ¾ cup salad oil
1 large onion, cut into tiny dice
1 large garlic clove, crushed
1 8-ounce can tomato sauce
   approximately 2 cups hot water
6 tablespoons Gebhard's Chili Powder (available in Latin American groceries) or other good-quality chili powder
4 tablespoons ground cumin
1 tablespoon cracked black pepper
1 tablespoon salt
1 tablespoon paprika
1 generous dash Tabasco or to taste
3 tablespoons masa harina (available in Latin American groceries) or flour (optional)
6 tablespoons warm water (optional)

Cut the beef, which must be absolutely free of all fat and gristle, into ¼- to ½-inch cubes. Heat about ¼ cup salad oil in a large heavy frying pan. Add part of the meat and brown over medium heat until meat is totally dry and there is no liquid in the frying pan. This takes much longer than one thinks—at least 5 to 10 minutes depending on amount of meat. Transfer browned meat to heavy casserole or kettle. Add some more oil to frying pan and continue browning meat and transferring it until all the meat is used up. Add the onion and garlic to frying pan and cook until just soft. Add to meat and mix well. To frying pan, add the tomato sauce, hot water, chili powder, cumin, pepper, salt, paprika, and Tabasco. Bring to boiling point and stir into meat. Cover casserole and simmer over very low heat for about 1½–2 hours. Stir frequently. If chili is in danger of scorching, add a little water. If it is too thin, blend masa harina or flour and water to a paste and stir into chili. Cook, stirring frequently, for 10 more minutes.

Note:

If the meat was properly trimmed, there should be no or very little fat (this depends on the meat) in the chili. If there is some fat, skim it off with paper towels. Or refrigerate chili and remove congealed fat.

Make sure that the spices are fresh, or the chili won't have any flavor. For a hotter chili, use more chili powder and Tabasco; for a milder one, use less. However, as is, the recipe has proved successful.

10–12 SERVINGS

CREOLE GRILLADES WITHOUT GRAVY

From New Orleans

A traditional breakfast dish, served with grits, and also good as a main course, with red or white beans and rice. The traditional beef cut is the round.

1½ pounds beef round, approximately ½-inch thick
salt
freshly ground pepper
sprinkling of cayenne (optional)
2 tablespoons lard or salad oil
1 small onion, thinly sliced
1 garlic clove, minced
1 medium-sized to large tomato, chopped, or ½ cup canned tomato
parsley for garnishing

Trim fat off the meat. Cut into 3- to 4-inch squares. Using a meat mallet or the back of a heavy plate, pound each square to about ¼-inch thickness. Season well on both sides with salt and pepper and a pinch of cayenne (if desired), rubbing seasonings into meat with the hands. Heat a large heavy frying pan and add the lard or oil. When hot, add the onion and garlic and cook, stirring constantly, until browned; do not scorch. Add the tomato and cook for 2 minutes. Add the meat and turn over to coat it on both sides with frying-pan contents. Cover tightly. Cook over low heat for about 10 minutes or until tender and well browned. Serve hot, garnished with parsley.

4–6 SERVINGS

CREOLE GRILLADES
WITH GRAVY

From New Orleans

Originally a breakfast dish, but good for any meal.

1½ pounds beef round, approximately ½-inch thick
     salt
     freshly ground pepper
     sprinkling of cayenne
   2 tablespoons lard or salad oil
   1 small onion, thinly sliced
   1 garlic clove, minced
   1 tablespoon flour
   2 large tomatoes, chopped, or 1 cup canned tomatoes
1–2 tablespoons vinegar, preferably wine vinegar
   1 cup hot water

Trim fat off meat. Cut into 3- to 4-inch squares. Using a meat mallet or the back of a heavy plate, pound each square to about ¼-inch thickness. Season well on both sides with salt, pepper, and cayenne, rubbing seasonings into meat with the hands. Heat a large heavy frying pan and add lard or oil. When hot, add the onion and garlic and cook, stirring constantly, until golden. Stir in the flour and cook until browned. Add tomatoes and cook for 2 minutes. Add meat and turn over to coat on both sides. Brown meat over medium heat. Combine the vinegar and water and pour over meat. Cover tightly and simmer over low heat for about 20–30 minutes, turning over once and stirring the sauce. Turn into a heated serving dish. Serve with grits or rice.

4–6 SERVINGS

NEW ENGLAND
HAMBURGER DISH

As eaten at the table of an Exeter, New Hampshire, Unitarian minister.

    4   tablespoons butter
    1   small onion, minced
    ¼   cup minced parsley
    1   pound lean ground beef
        salt
        freshly ground pepper
    ⅛   teaspoon ground nutmeg
    ½   pound mushrooms, thinly sliced
    1   8-ounce package medium noodles, cooked and drained
    ¼   cup light or heavy cream

Heat 2 tablespoons of the butter in a large deep frying pan. Add the onion and parsley and cook, stirring constantly, until onion is soft and golden. Add the beef. Cook, stirring with a fork, for about 7–10 minutes or until the meat is cooked and browned. Season with salt, pepper, and nutmeg. Keep hot. In another frying pan, heat the remaining 2 tablespoons butter. Add the mushrooms and cook, stirring frequently, for about 5 minutes; mushrooms should be firm still. Combine the meat, mushrooms, and noodles in the meat frying pan. Heat through. Stir in the cream and heat through again. Serve with a green vegetable or a salad.

4 SERVINGS

SYLVIA'S RIBERA, NEW MEXICO, PICADILLO

A good buffet dish, easily doubled or tripled.

2 tablespoons salad oil
1 large onion, thinly sliced
3 garlic cloves, minced
1 pound ground lean beef or equal parts ground beef and
  ground pork
  salt
  freshly ground pepper
¼ teaspoon ground cumin
  pinch cloves
1 bay leaf, crumbled
½ cup dry white or dry red wine
2 large tomatoes, peeled and chopped, or 1 cup canned
  tomatoes, undrained
½ cup dark or golden raisins, plumped in hot water and
  drained
1 sweet green pepper, seeded and cut into strips
1 hard-cooked egg, chopped

Heat the oil in a large deep frying pan or saucepan. Cook the garlic and onion, stirring constantly, until they are soft and golden. Add the meat, salt, pepper, cumin, and cloves. Mix well. Cook over medium heat, stirring constantly, until the meat is browned. Add the bay leaf, wine, tomatoes, and raisins, mix, and cover. Simmer over low heat, stirring frequently, for about 15 minutes. If too liquid, cook without a cover; if too thick, stir in a little hot water, one tablespoon at a time. Stir in the green pepper and cook 2 more minutes; the pepper should be crisp. Sprinkle with chopped hard-cooked egg before serving with boiled rice or as a taco or tamale stuffing.

4–5 SERVINGS

SWEEPINGS CORDON BLEU

A specialty of Olivet College, Michigan, improved with sour cream and seasonings by alumnus R. Hertzberg. It's a good tasty dish to make when you come home at 7:00 and have to have dinner on the table by 7:30.

      4 tablespoons butter
      1 large onion, minced
      1 pound good quality lean ground beef
         salt
         freshly ground pepper
    4–6 tablespoons sour cream or to taste
         cooked rice or noodles or mashed potatoes

Heat the butter in a large frying pan. Cook the onion in it until soft and golden. Add the meat. Stir with a fork to break up the meat lumps. Cook, stirring all the time, until meat is browned but still pinkish inside; otherwise it will be too dry. Season with salt and pepper. Stir in sour cream and heat through. Serve over rice, noodles, or mashed potatoes, with a green salad.

VARIATION:

R. Hertzberg occasionally adds 1 teaspoon to 1 tablespoon of either paprika or curry to the beef, or 1–2 tablespoons drained capers to the finished dish.

4 SERVINGS

CREAMED CHIPPED BEEF

All-American

    ¼ pound dried beef, snipped into pieces
    4 tablespoons butter
    3 tablespoons flour

  2 cups half-and-half or light cream or milk
     freshly ground pepper
     salt
  2 tablespoons minced parsley (optional)
     hot buttered toast, popovers, or baked potatoes

If the beef is only slightly salty (a taste will confirm this), rinse under running cold water. If it is very salty, cover with boiling water, let stand 3 minutes, and drain. Heat the butter in a deep frying pan. Add the beef. Cook over low heat, stirring constantly, for about 3–5 minutes. Stir in the flour and cook, stirring all the time, for 3 minutes. Stir in half-and-half, cream, or milk, and cook until sauce is thickened. Season with pepper and if necessary (taste first) a little salt. Sprinkle with parsley if desired before serving over hot buttered toast.

VARIATIONS:

If avid for a less stark dish, add about 1 cup sautéed sliced mushrooms and/or 2–3 tablespoons sherry, or season with a dash of ground nutmeg or mace.

3–4 SERVINGS

BROWNED DRIED-BEEF GRAVY

From West Virginia

A survival dish from the Depression.

  ¼ pound dried beef
     water
  1 well-rounded tablespoon butter
  1 well-rounded tablespoon bacon fat
2½ tablespoons flour
1½ cups milk
  ½ cup water in which peeled potatoes were boiled
     salt
     freshly ground pepper

Break the beef into small pieces and put in a medium (8-inch) deep frying pan. Cover with water and add the butter and bacon fat. Bring to boiling point. Cook until water has boiled away and beef has been frizzled brown in the fat. Lower heat and stir in the flour, milk, and potato water. Stir and cook until mixture is thickened, smooth, and evenly browned. Serve hot, over mashed potatoes.

2–3 SERVINGS

DESPERATE MOTHER'S QUICK FRANK STEW

The desperate mother lived on a Maine island without stores, where the grocery van visited once a week. She had four hungry children.

2 tablespoons butter
1 medium onion, minced
1 sweet green pepper, seeded and chopped
2 tablespoons flour
2 10½-ounce cans condensed vegetable soup, undiluted
1 cup water
1 pound (or more) frankfurters, sliced diagonally
2 tablespoons minced parsley
1 tablespoon Angostura bitters (optional but good)

Heat the butter in a large deep frying pan. Add the onion and green pepper and cook until vegetables are soft. Stir in flour. Add the undiluted soup and the water. Add the frankfurters and cook for 10 minutes, stirring occasionally. Before serving, stir in the parsley and the bitters (if used). Serve with rice.

6 SERVINGS

Pork

————◄◆►————

STUFFED CROWN ROAST
OF PORK

A crown roast of pork is made by removing the backbone from one or two half loins and tying the ends together to form a circle. The rib ends are frenched and served garnished with paper frills or small fruit such as crab apples or kumquats. This is a luxury roast that must be especially ordered; figure on two ribs per serving to determine the size of the roast. If your butcher will grind the trimmings for you, use them in meatloaf or spaghetti sauce. Make sure the butcher removes the backbone for easier carving and frenches the rib ends.

This recipe calls for a 5-pound crown roast; if the roast is much smaller than that, it won't be long enough to make a circle, and if it is much larger the crown will look ungainly. When you are estimating cooking time you should plan on 30–35 minutes per pound; the stuffing is put in when the roast is about four-fifths done.

To carve, use a sharp knife and slice down between each two ribs and remove one chop at a time.

1 5-pound crown roast of pork
  salt
  freshly ground pepper

STUFFING
2 pounds yams or sweet potatoes
1 pound tart apples
½ cup brown sugar
1 teaspoon ground cinnamon
½ teaspoon ground nutmeg
½ cup chicken bouillon or dry white wine
  watercress for garnish

Let the meat stand at room temperature for 1 to 1½ hours before preheating oven to hot (425°). Cover the rib ends with aluminum foil to keep from charring. Place the roast, rib ends up, in a large shallow roasting pan. Sprinkle with salt and pepper. Place in oven and immediately turn oven down to moderate (350°). As roast is cooking, prepare the stuffing. Cook the yams or sweet potatoes in boiling water to cover until they can be pierced with the point of a knife. Drain and when cool enough to handle peel and cut into ¼-inch dice. Peel and core the apples and cut into ¼-inch dice. Combine potatoes, apples, sugar, cinnamon, nutmeg, and bouillon or wine. Mix well and reserve. After roast has cooked for 2 hours, remove from oven. With a bulb baster skim off as much fat as possible from pan. Fill the center of the crown with the stuffing. Put any remaining stuffing into a greased baking dish. Return roast to oven, along with baking dish of stuffing. Cook for 30–45 more minutes. With two pancake turners or large spoons, transfer the roast to heated platter. If possible, let stand for 10–15 minutes before carving. Remove the foil from the rib ends and either place a paper frill on each rib end or place fruit on alternate ends. Garnish the base of the roast with a wreath of watercress.

6 SERVINGS

ROAST FRESH HAM

All-American

A fresh ham is a leg of pork, which can weigh about 8 to 16 pounds. The usual roast fresh ham is half a leg, either shank or butt end. The butt end is leaner and meatier but harder to carve, unless the butcher removes the small aitchbone. The shank is less meaty but easier to carve; this is the cut usually found in supermarkets. For this recipe it is essential that the ham keeps its skin or rind, which in roasting becomes crunchy, crisp, and delicious crackling.

½ fresh ham, butt or shank, weighing about 5–6 pounds
  salt
  freshly ground pepper
2 teaspoons ground sage or thyme or to taste
  ice water

With a sharp knife, cut into the skin and fat of the ham until you reach the meat. Score the ham lengthwise and crosswise, at about 1-inch intervals. Rub salt, pepper, and sage or thyme into the incisions. Place the ham on a rack in a roasting pan. Insert a meat thermometer in the center of the ham, but do not let it touch the bone. Roast the ham in a preheated slow oven (300°) for about 30 minutes per pound or until the thermometer shows a temperature of 165–170°. During the last hour of roasting, sprinkle the ham 4 times with about 1–2 tablespoons ice water to crisp the skin. Do not baste the meat. Turn off the oven, transfer the ham to a platter, and return it to the oven, leaving the oven door half-open. Let the ham rest for 15 minutes before carving.

GRAVY
4 tablespoons fat
3 tablespoons flour
2 cups hot water or milk
  salt
  freshly ground pepper

Skim the fat off pan juices and pour off all fat but 4 table-spoons. Scrape up all the brown bits at the bottom of the pan. Over medium heat, stir the flour into the fat and cook, stirring all the time, for about 3–4 minutes or until golden brown. Stir in the hot water or milk and cook, stirring constantly, until smooth and thickened. Taste the seasoning and add salt and pepper to taste. Bring to the boiling point, turn into a sauceboat and serve with the ham.

8–10 SERVINGS

VARIATION:
Instead of using 2 cups hot water or milk, use 1½ cups hot water and ½ cup medium sherry.

ROAST LOIN OF PORK

All-American

*For easier carving have the butcher remove the chine bone
which runs the length of the loin. I think the center cut
nicest.*

   1 4- to 5-pound loin of pork, at room temperature
½ cup minced parsley
¼ cup minced onion
   1 tablespoon dried sage
      grated rind of 1 lemon
      salt
      freshly ground pepper
      ice water
½ cup dry white wine (optional)

Trim all excess fat off the meat. Combine the parsley, onion,
sage, and lemon rind and mix well. Spread a little of the mixture
between the chops into which the loin is divided. Rub the whole
loin with salt and pepper. Tie it lengthwise with a piece of soft
kitchen string to keep the stuffing from oozing out. Place the loin,
fat side up, on a rack in a shallow roasting pan. Roast in a preheated slow oven (325°) for about 2 to 2½ hours or for 30 minutes
per pound. If you are using a meat thermometer, insert it in the
center of the meat, away from the bone. When the meat is ready,
the thermometer should read 165° to 170°. During the last hour of
roasting, sprinkle the meat 4 times with about 1–2 tablespoons ice
water; this crisps the surface. When the meat is ready, turn off the
oven. Transfer the meat to a heated platter and return it to the
oven but keep the oven door half open. The meat should rest for
about 10 minutes in a warm place, and the opened oven door will
cool the oven sufficiently to prevent the meat from cooking further.
Skim the fat from the pan juices, add the wine (if used), and
scrape up all the little brown bits at the bottom of the pan. Carve
the meat downward, cutting between the bones, and arrange on a

heated serving platter. Drizzle the pan juices over the meat and serve hot.

6 SERVINGS

PORK CHOPS BAKED WITH ORANGE

From Florida

4-6 lean center-cut loin pork chops (about 2 pounds)
     salt
     freshly ground pepper
     flour
3-4 tablespoons butter
  1 large orange or 2 small ones
  ½ cup fresh orange juice
     watercress

Rub the chops on both sides with salt and pepper. Dredge in flour, shaking off excess flour. Heat the butter in a large frying pan. Over high heat, quickly brown chops on both sides. Transfer browned chops to a large shallow baking dish; make only one layer. Peel yellow and white peels off orange and cut it into thin slices. Top each chop with one or two orange slices. Pour the orange juice over meat and orange slices. Put cover on baking dish or tie on a cover of aluminum foil. Bake in a preheated moderate oven (350°) for about 1 hour or until tender; baking time depends on thickness of chops. Serve in a heated serving dish lined with watercress.

4-6 SERVINGS

PORK GOULASH

American-Hungarian

3 pounds boneless pork
2 tablespoons lard or bacon fat
4 large onions, thinly sliced
2 tablespoons sweet paprika or to taste
2 tablespoons vinegar
   salt
1 tablespoon caraway seed
   approximately 1½ to 2 cups beef bouillon
1 tablespoon flour
2 tablespoons water
½ cup sour cream

Cut the pork into 2-inch cubes and remove every trace of fat or the goulash will be greasy. Heat lard or bacon fat in a heavy saucepan. Add the onions and cook, stirring constantly, for about 3–4 minutes or until soft and golden; do not brown. Stir in the paprika and cook, stirring, for 2 more minutes. Stir in the vinegar. Add the meat, salt, and caraway seed. Mix well. Add enough bouillon to barely cover the meat; quantity depends on saucepan size. Simmer covered over low heat, stirring occasionally, for about 1 hour or until meat is almost but not quite tender. Blend the flour and water to a paste and stir in. Stir in the sour cream. Simmer, covered, for 15 minutes or until meat is tender. The sauce should be the consistency of heavy cream. If too thin, cook without a cover to allow evaporation; if too thick, add a little more bouillon, 1 tablespoon at a time. Serve with boiled potatoes or buttered noodles.

6 SERVINGS

BARBECUED SPARERIBS

From Texas

2 tablespoons butter
1 cup minced onion
1 large garlic clove, minced
½ cup tomato ketchup or chili sauce or half-and-half
   grated rind of 1 lemon
   juice of 1 lemon
2 tablespoons Worcestershire sauce
⅔ cup water
½ teaspoon dry mustard or to taste
½ teaspoon salt
½ teaspoon freshly ground pepper
   dash Tabasco
1–2 tablespoons brown sugar
3 pounds meaty spareribs

Combine all ingredients except the spareribs in a heavy saucepan. Bring to boiling point, lower heat, and simmer without a cover for about 5 minutes or covered for 10 minutes. Trim all excess fat from spareribs. Cool sauce a little before using. Place the spareribs in a baking pan and cover with the sauce. Cook in a preheated moderate oven (350°) for about 2 hours, basting occasionally with pan liquid. Serve hot or cold.

Note:
If desired, spareribs can be cut into serving pieces before cooking.

4–6 SERVINGS

CHINESEY SPARERIBS

American-Chinese

Ribs to be cooked out of doors should be left in one piece. Otherwise, they may be cut into 2-rib chunks before cooking or left in one piece and cut afterward.

⅓ to ½ cup soy sauce
½ cup water
 1 cup fresh orange juice
½ cup light-brown, dark-brown, or granulated sugar
    (brown gives a better color)
 6 garlic cloves, mashed
    grated rind of 1 orange
 1 tablespoon fresh grated ginger, or 1–2 teaspoons
    ground ginger
 3 pounds meaty spareribs, trimmed of excess fat
    salt
    freshly ground pepper

Combine the soy sauce, water, orange juice, sugar, garlic, orange rind, and ginger in a small saucepan. Bring to the boiling point and boil 2–3 minutes. Cool. On both sides of spareribs, rub in salt and pepper. Place ribs into a bowl and pour the marinade over them. Marinate ribs for a few hours or overnight, turning them frequently. Drain; reserve marinade. Place ribs on the rack of a shallow roasting pan. Cook in a preheated hot oven (425°) for about 20–30 minutes. Turn heat to low (300°) and continue cooking about 25 minutes per pound, or until well done. To test for doneness, make a small cut near center of meaty section; there should be no pinkness in the meat.

Note:
Ribs may also be roasted at a temperature of 325° for 35 minutes per pound. But I think the first method gives a better color and flavor.

4 SERVINGS

CHOP SUEY

American-Chinese

*To assuage nostalgia for American-Chinese restaurants.
Neither American nor Chinese, this dish is said to have been
invented in San Francisco in the nineteenth century.
Alas, in this day of so-called authentic Chinese restaurants,
chop suey has all but disappeared. It's our loss because
chop suey is good.*

3	tablespoons salad oil
2	cups shredded Chinese cabbage
2	cups sliced celery
1	cup sliced onion
1–2	cups cooked pork, beef, or chicken, cut into strips
2	cups fresh or canned bean sprouts, washed and drained
½	cup sliced canned water chestnuts, drained
3	tablespoons cornstarch
¼	cup chicken stock or bouillon (can be made with cube or powder)
3	tablespoons soy sauce
	salt
	dash of cayenne

Heat the oil in a heavy saucepan. Add cabbage, celery, and
onion. Cook over medium heat, stirring constantly, for about 3–4
minutes or until vegetables are wilting. Add the meat, bean sprouts,
and water chestnuts and mix well. Lower heat and cook for 5 minutes, stirring frequently. Mix cornstarch and stock or bouillon to a
smooth paste. Return heat to medium and stir in cornstarch paste.
Cook, stirring constantly, until clear and thickened. Remove from
heat and stir in the soy sauce, salt if needed, and pepper. Serve
over hot rice.

4 SERVINGS

BACON AND TOMATO
BREAKFAST DISH

A Pennsylvania Dutch friend made this for me.

4 large or 6 medium-sized tomatoes
salt
freshly ground pepper
flour or fine dry breadcrumbs
½ pound thick-sliced lean bacon
light-brown or dark-brown sugar
1 tablespoon flour
⅓ cup milk or half-and-half

Cut the tomatoes into ½-inch slices. Place them in a colander to drain off excess liquid; leave in colander about 10–15 minutes. While the tomatoes are draining, cut the bacon into 1-inch pieces and place in a heavy frying pan. Cook over low heat, turning occasionally, until the bacon is beginning to brown. With a slotted spoon or a fork, remove the bacon to a plate. Reserve. Sprinkle the tomatoes lightly with salt and pepper and dip them into flour or breadcrumbs on both sides. Place them in the hot bacon fat. Cover the frying pan and cook over low heat for about 10 minutes, turning once. The tomatoes should be golden brown. Place 1 teaspoon of sugar on each tomato slice and cook without a cover until the sugar is melted. With a pancake turner, transfer the tomatoes to a heated platter and keep hot in a low oven. Stir about 1 tablespoon flour into the pan juices. Then stir in the milk or half-and-half to make a gravy. Return the bacon pieces to the frying pan. Heat thoroughly, stirring constantly, and spoon over tomato slices. Serve very hot with Spoon Bread (page 211), or any kind of corn bread, or with Popovers (page 204).

4 SERVINGS

BAKED HAM WITH
MADEIRA SAUCE

From New England

This is a simple way of making a practical ready-to-eat canned ham more interesting. (Be sure it is a ready-to-eat and not a ready-to-cook ham.) The sugar and the Madeira can be doubled or tripled according to the size of the ham. Baking time is 15 minutes per pound of ham, in a slow oven (325°).

1 2-pound canned ham
⅓ cup dark-brown sugar
2 tablespoons Madeira or medium sherry

Remove the ham from the can and remove any fat and any gelatin coating. Place the ham in a roasting pan. Combine sugar and Madeira into a paste and spread over the top of the ham. Cook in a preheated slow oven (325°) for about 30 minutes. Transfer to a serving platter and let stand for 5 minutes before slicing. Serve with Madeira Sauce (see following recipe).

6 SERVINGS

MADEIRA SAUCE FOR
BAKED HAM

¼ cup butter
1 tablespoon minced onion
3 tablespoons flour (for a thicker sauce, use 4 tablespoons flour)
2 cups undiluted hot consommé
⅓ cup golden raisins, plumped in hot water and drained
⅓ cup Madeira or medium sherry
salt
dash of cayenne pepper or to taste

Heat the butter in a saucepan. Add onion and cook over low heat, stirring constantly, until the onion is golden brown. Stir in flour and cook for 3 more minutes or until golden brown; do not scorch flour. Gradually stir in the consommé and cook, stirring all the time, until smooth and thickened. Add the raisins and the Madeira or sherry. Mix well. Taste and if necessary add a little more salt (consommé is salty) and the cayenne. Heat through but do not boil. Serve hot.

MAKES ABOUT 2½ CUPS

BAKED HAM IN COCA-COLA

From the South

Do not use aged country ham or Smithfield ham, but a tenderized ham. The ham, being already on the sweet side, may be served without the sugar-mustard-crumb coating if desired. Ginger ale or cider may be used instead of Coca-Cola.

    1 tenderized ham, weighing about 10 pounds
      Coca-Cola
    ½ cup brown sugar
    2 cups fine dry breadcrumbs
    2 teaspoons dry mustard
    2 tablespoons prepared sharp mustard

Place the ham, fat side down, in a roasting pan. Add enough Coca-Cola to half-cover the ham. Cook in a preheated moderate oven (350°) 15 minutes per pound of ham. Baste ham frequently with the Coca-Cola and if necessary add more Coca-Cola. Remove ham from liquid and cool until easy to handle. Drain pan. Skin ham. Combine the sugar, breadcrumbs, and mustards into a paste. With hands, pat paste into ham. Return ham to baking pan and oven. Cook 30–40 minutes longer, basting occasionally with fresh Coca-Cola. Transfer ham to a platter and let rest at room temperature for 15 minutes before slicing. Serve hot or cold.

10–20 SERVINGS

FRIED HAM WITH MILK GRAVY

Southern

    2 tablespoons dark-brown sugar
    2 tablespoons flour
    ½ teaspoon ground ginger
    1 slice cooked ham (center slice), about 2 inches thick
      butter
1 ½ cups milk
    ¼ cup minced chives or onion

Mix together the sugar, flour, and ginger. Trim all fat off the ham and reserve the fat. Sprinkle the sugar mixture on both sides of ham and rub in with hands. Heat the ham fat in a large deep and heavy frying pan. If fat looks insufficient for browning the ham, add 1–2 tablespoons butter. Add ham. Over medium heat, cook ham for about 3–4 minutes or until golden brown. Turn and brown other side. Add the milk and cover frying pan. Cook over low heat for about 20–30 minutes or until ham is tender. If it seems to be drying out, add a little more milk. The sauce will curdle slightly but that's the way it is. Carve the ham in thin diagonal slices and place on a heated serving platter. Serve the gravy separately. Good with Spoon Bread or grits (page 211).

4–6 SERVINGS

CREAMED HAM FOR PATTY SHELLS

All-American

Unless you wish to express yourself in puff pastry, I suggest buying the excellent frozen puff pastry patty shells found in supermarkets. Though no longer as fashionable as in a more genteel American past, patty shells filled with any creamed mixture make a pleasant first course, or a light

*main course for lunch or supper with a tossed mixed green
salad. This recipe is also good served on hot toast or over
plain hot rice. Besides, it's a fine way of using ham leftovers, improved by sherry and brandy.*

3 tablespoons butter
1 pound cooked ham, preferably smoked ham, coarsely
   chopped or cut into ¼-inch pieces
2 cups half-and-half
2 tablespoons flour
3 tablespoons milk or water
3 tablespoons dry or medium sherry
2 tablespoons brandy
  salt
  freshly ground pepper
8 frozen patty shells, heated according to package
  directions

Heat the butter in a double-boiler top or in a heavy saucepan. Add the ham and stir in the cream. Cook over boiling water or
very low heat until the mixture is boiling. Combine the flour and
water to a smooth paste and stir into ham mixture. Simmer until
thoroughly heated through. Stir in sherry and brandy and simmer
for 3 more minutes; do not let the mixture boil. Taste and if necessary add a little salt, but ham is most likely salty. Add plenty of
freshly ground pepper or to taste. Fill mixture generously into patties, letting some spill over the sides; skimpily filled patties are sad.
Serve warm, on heated plates. Or serve over freshly made toast,
buttered or not.

Note:

Different kinds of ham have different amounts of moisture in
them; smoked hams and Smithfield and similar hams, are drier than
ordinary tenderized or canned hams. If the mixture looks too liquid,
cook it a little longer to allow the liquid to evaporate, or thicken it
with more flour—that is, use 3 or even 4 tablespoons flour combined
with ¼ cup milk, and let it cook long enough to get rid of any raw
flour taste.

FILLING FOR 8 PATTIES; 4 SERVINGS AS A MAIN
DISH, OR 8 AS A FIRST COURSE

COOKED HAM LOAF

All-American

*A Kansas friend's version of an all-time favorite which can
be made with ham leftovers and odds and ends. But a ham
loaf is only as flavorful as the ham that goes into it. Most
ham nowadays, even the smoked kind, is rather bland, so
that seasonings have to be increased and even improvised.
Taste as you go along and season to taste.*

2 pounds cooked ham, preferably smoked ham, with fat
1 medium onion, minced
1 medium or large apple, peeled and minced
1 tablespoon prepared spicy mustard, or to taste
1 tablespoon brown sugar
2 eggs, beaten
1 cup white breadcrumbs made from stale bread
3 slices bacon
¼ teaspoon each ground cloves and ground nutmeg,
     or 1 tablespoon grated lemon rind (optional)

Grind the ham in a meat grinder or food processor, or chop
very, very fine.

Combine all ingredients except the bacon and optional seasonings in a bowl. Mix well with hands. Taste and if necessary add
more mustard, or add the ground cloves and ground nutmeg, or the
grated lemon rind, instead of the spices. Press into a 1½-quart loaf
pan or baking dish. Top with the bacon slices. Cook in a preheated
moderate oven (350°) for about 1 hour or until firm. Serve hot or
cold, with mustard, chutney, pickles, and potato salad.

6 SERVINGS

SALT-PORK GRAVY

From New England

This was one of the settlers' staples, and as they moved west, this basic food went with them. It still is good.

1½　pounds lean salt pork
　4　tablespoons flour
　2　cups milk
　　　salt
　　　freshly ground pepper

If the pork is very salty, put it in a bowl and cover with boiling water. Let stand 3 minutes, drain, and rinse under cold running water. Dry between paper towels. Cut into ½-inch dice and put in a large heavy frying pan. Cook over medium heat, stirring frequently, until crisp. Remove pork dice with a slotted spoon and reserve. Pour off all but about 4 tablespoons fat from frying pan. Stir in the flour. Cook over low heat, stirring constantly, until smooth. Stir in the milk. Cook, stirring all the time, until sauce is thickened and smooth. Add the pork dice and heat through. Taste for seasoning; add a little more salt if necessary and add pepper. Serve over baked or mashed potatoes.

4 SERVINGS

Lamb

————◄◄►►————

ROAST LEG OF LAMB

From Minnesota

This is a Swedish way of roasting lamb, which the Swedish settlers in the Midwest brought with them from the old country. The coffee, not discernible as such, flavors the gravy and also removes the muttony flavor that may be found in the mature spring lamb commonly sold in America. Lamb has never been very popular in the United States, and I think one reason, and possibly the main one, is that American lamb meat is very fat. As is, lamb fat is not appetizing like that of beef or pork, and when cold, it is horrid. But the American lamb producers of the West have never admitted to the excessive fat of their animals; at least I have never seen any of their publicity recipes suggest cutting off excess fat. Unfortunately, most of the lamb recipes circulating through the nation don't say that either. Lamb should not be overcooked to a sorry gray and stringy state, but neither should it be left too pink, as called for in French recipes; these apply to very young baby lamb, seldom found in our country. I think that our mature American lamb, when undercooked, tastes like mutton, but that is a matter of opinion.

For this recipe, use the shank half of the leg of lamb (2½ to 4½ pounds average weight) and make sure it is oven ready. This means that the end of the leg, which is bone and no meat, has been trimmed away by the butcher prior to weighing the meat; otherwise you are paying for useless bone. Unfortunately, in most prepackaged supermarket lamb this useless piece of bone is right there for you to pay for. If you are cooking a whole leg of lamb (5 to 9

*pounds average weight), double the other ingredients. I
suggest you beware of cooking too much lamb; after the
first meal of cold roast lamb, leftover lamb needs to be
jazzed up into a curry, stew, casserole, or pie, and any
way you look at these dishes, they are still leftover lamb,
boring but too expensive to be wasted.*

    1 4- to 4½-pound leg of lamb (shank half)
    1 tablespoon salt
    2 tablespoons pepper
    1 cup hot medium-strength coffee
    ½ cup heavy cream
    2 teaspoons sugar

Remove as much fat as possible from the meat and also
remove the thin membrane known as fell (the butcher may have
removed all or some of this, but there shouldn't be any). If the meat
hangs in loose folds, tie it to keep its shape. Rub the meat with salt
and pepper. Insert a meat thermometer in the center of the meat,
taking care that it does not touch the bone; this is the most reliable
method for achieving a desired degree of doneness. Place the meat
on a rack in a baking pan. Roast in a preheated hot oven (450°) for
20 minutes. Pour off any fat or remove with a spoon or baster. Reduce oven temperature to moderate (350°). Combine the coffee,
cream, and sugar and pour over meat. Roast, basting frequently
with pan juices, until thermometer shows 140° for medium-rare
lamb, or about 12–14 minutes per pound, counted from the time the
oven was reduced to moderate. For medium lamb, roast to 150°, or
14–16 minutes per pound; for well done, to 160°, or 16–18 minutes
per pound. If you want the lamb rare, roast to 130°, or 10–12 minutes per pound. (Personally, I prefer medium.) Turn off oven and
transfer meat to a heated serving platter. Return meat to oven, but
keep oven door half-open. Let the meat rest for 10 minutes while
you make the gravy.

    GRAVY
    pan drippings, plus half-and-half or milk to make 2 cups
    1 tablespoon flour
    salt
    freshly ground pepper
    2 teaspoons red currant jelly

After the meat has been put to rest in the oven, pour off all the pan drippings into a small bowl. Skim off all fat; reserve fat. Measure the pan drippings and add enough half-and-half or milk to make 2 cups. Put roasting pan on low heat and scrape off all the brown bits at the bottom. Add about 2 tablespoons fat to the roasting pan, or, if you prefer, 2 tablespoons butter. Heat the fat and stir in the flour. Cook over low heat, stirring constantly, for about 3 minutes or until flour is golden brown. Gradually stir in the drippings mixture. Cook, stirring all the time, until smooth and thickened. Remove from heat and stir in the currant jelly.

Slice the meat (horizontally for better-looking slices) and arrange in overlapping slices on a heated platter. Drizzle a little of the gravy over the meat to keep it moist and serve the remaining gravy in a sauceboat. Serve hot, with mashed or boiled potatoes and any desired vegetable.

4-6 SERVINGS

ROAST RACK OF LAMB

All-American

A rack of lamb is the rib end of the saddle. One side will serve two people, allowing two chops per person. Ask the butcher to remove any fat from the bones and trim the cut edges of the bones so that they project. Make sure he cracks the bones so that the chops can be carved separately. My butcher says this delicious cut of meat is a disappearing species because it is so expensive.

1 double rack of lamb, weighing approximately 2½–3 pounds
  salt
  freshly ground pepper
2 tablespoons butter
1 garlic clove, minced
1 cup fresh white breadcrumbs

  1 tablespoon minced chives
  ¼ teaspoon dried thyme
     grated rind of ½ lemon
     juice of ½ lemon

Trim as much fat as possible from the lamb. Place meat in a roasting pan, fat side down. Sprinkle with salt and pepper. Roast in a preheated hot oven (500°) for 15 minutes. While lamb is roasting, heat the butter in a small saucepan. Add the garlic and cook, stirring constantly, for 2 minutes. Stir in the breadcrumbs, chives, thyme, and lemon rind. When the 15 minutes are up, reduce heat to 400°. Take pan with lamb from oven and spread with the crumb mixture, patting it into the meat with the back of a knife or a spoon. Return meat to oven and roast for 10 more minutes. Sprinkle with lemon juice and carve into chops. Serve with scalloped potatoes and a green vegetable.

4 SERVINGS

LAMB STEW WITH VEGETABLES

All-American

The sherry makes it more interesting.

  2 pounds any cut boneless lamb, cut into 1½-inch pieces
     salt
     freshly ground pepper
     flour
  3 tablespoons butter or salad oil
  1 large onion, thinly sliced
  ½ teaspoon dried thyme or marjoram
  1½ cups chicken bouillon
  ⅓ cup sherry
  1 cup diced turnips
  2 large carrots, diced
  2 cups fresh peas, or 1 10-ounce package frozen peas,
     thawed
  ¼ cup minced parsley

Cut all fat and gristle off the meat. Sprinkle pieces with salt and pepper and roll in flour. Heat the butter or oil in a large heavy saucepan. Over high heat, and stirring constantly, cook lamb until lightly browned on all sides. Add the onion, thyme, chicken bouillon, and sherry. Bring to boiling point. Lower heat and simmer, covered, for about 30–40 minutes or until meat is almost tender. Add the turnips and carrots and cook for 5 more minutes. Add the peas and cook for 5 more minutes or until vegetables are tender but not mushy. Sprinkle with parsley before serving.

4–6 SERVINGS

ZELMA LONG'S PIQUANT LAMB CHOP MARINADE

From California

This is also good for marinating pork chops.

- ¼ cup soy sauce
- ¼ cup dry sherry
- 1 tablespoon sugar
- 1 teaspoon dry mustard
- ¼ teaspoon ground ginger
- 1 large garlic clove, mashed
- 8 rib or loin lamb chops, trimmed of excess fat

Combine all the ingredients except the chops and mix thoroughly. Dip each chop into marinade on both sides and place chops in a bowl. Pour any remaining marinade over them. Let stand at cool room temperature or in refrigerator for 30–60 minutes. Broil chops in the usual manner.

MAKES ABOUT ½ CUP

Veal

———◆———

CASSEROLE-ROASTED VEAL

Italian-American

This method cooks the veal in its own juice, and the meat does not require the usual larding; on the contrary, the boned veal must be free of all fat and gristle. The flavor trick is not to sear the meat first, but to combine all the ingredients cold. The meat must be cooked in a casserole or saucepan with a really tight cover, and the casserole should be just large enough to hold the meat. Use a boned, rolled shoulder of veal, which is less expensive than the rump or the loin.

1 3-pound boneless roast of veal, rolled and tied, free
    of fat
    salt
    freshly ground pepper
½ teaspoon dried thyme or ground sage (optional)
2 tablespoons butter
2 tablespoons olive oil
¼ cup ice water

Rub the meat on all sides with salt, pepper, and thyme or sage (if desired). In a heavy casserole or saucepan just large enough to hold the meat, combine meat, butter, and olive oil. Heat slowly over low heat. Turn heat to medium and cook, turning the meat several times, until it is reddish on all sides. Sprinkle meat with the ice water. Reduce heat to very low. Simmer *tightly* covered for about 1½ hours, basting about three times with the juices in the casserole. If necessary to prevent sticking, add a little cold water, 1 tablespoon at a time. The veal is done at a meat thermom-

eter reading of 165°; it should not be overdone. At the end of cooking time, there should be about ½ to ⅔ cup of pan juices. Turn off
the oven, transfer meat to a platter, and return it to oven to keep
warm. Set casserole with pan juices on low heat and scrape up all
the brown bits at the bottom. Taste the seasoning and, if necessary,
add a little salt and pepper. Remove the strings from the meat and
cut it into slices. Arrange the slices in an overlapping pattern on a
heated serving dish and drizzle the pan gravy over it. Serve hot,
with mashed potatoes and buttered green beans or spinach.

6 SERVINGS

VEAL LOAF

This version comes from a New Haven, Connecticut, cook.

    2 pounds ground veal
    1 pound ground lean pork
  ⅔ cup fresh white breadcrumbs
  ¼ cup grated onion
    2 garlic cloves, mashed
  ⅔ cup minced parsley
    1 teaspoon ground thyme
    2 eggs, well beaten
      salt
      freshly ground pepper
      approximately ½ pound sliced bacon

Combine the veal, pork, and breadcrumbs in a bowl and mix
well. Add the onion, garlic, parsley, thyme, the beaten eggs, salt,
and pepper. Mix thoroughly. Mold the mixture into a firm oblong
loaf. Line a shallow roasting pan with bacon slices. Place the meatloaf on the bacon and cover completely with more bacon slices.
Cook in a preheated moderate oven (350°) for about 1½ hours, basting with the pan juices after the first half-hour; baste frequently.
Serve hot with mashed potatoes and a green vegetable, or serve as
a cold cut.

Note:

In season, I use ⅓ cup minced fresh parsley and ⅓ cup minced fresh basil leaves. In fact, you may flavor the loaf in any way to your taste.

6–8 SERVINGS

Game

LARRY CORNWALL'S
BREAD-PAN PHEASANT

From Connecticut

The timing on this recipe was for a 4-pound bird cooked in a 9×5-inch pan for 40 minutes. Cooking times may have to be adjusted depending on size and age of birds. When cooking more than one bird, put each into its own pan. The standard 8×5- or 9×5-inch bread pans will do for most birds.

1 pheasant, ready for cooking, weighing approximately
  3½–4 pounds
  salt
  freshly ground pepper
1 medium onion, cut into quarters
1 apple, preferably tart, cored but not peeled,
  cut into quarters
3 slices bacon
  chicken bouillon
  dry red wine
  red currant jelly

Rub the pheasant inside and out with salt and pepper. Stuff the cavity with the onion and apple. Fit the bird, breast down, into a bread loaf pan that holds it tightly with no room to spare. Cover the back with the bacon slices. Add equal parts of chicken bouillon and red wine to come halfway up the sides of the pan. Roast uncovered in a preheated moderate oven (375°) for 40 minutes. Transfer to a heated serving dish and serve with red currant jelly on the side. Good by itself, along with a tossed green salad.

2–3 SERVINGS

VENISON SWISS STEAK

This may also be made with beef round.

salt
freshly ground pepper
1½ pounds venison steak, about 1½ inches thick
flour
3 tablespoons bacon fat or shortening
3 large onions, sliced
1 celery stalk, chopped
1 medium carrot, chopped
1 cup canned tomatoes
2 tablespoons Worcestershire sauce
1 teaspoon dried marjoram
dry white or dry red wine (optional)

Rub salt and pepper into both sides of the steak. Dredge in flour. Heat the fat in a heavy saucepan. Over high heat, brown meat on both sides. Add the remaining ingredients. Cover and cook in a preheated moderate oven (350°), or on low heat on top of stove, for about 1½ hours or until tender. Check for moisture and if necessary add a little hot water or dry white or dry red wine, about 2 tablespoons at a time. Remove steak and keep hot. Purée the pan liquids in a blender or press through a sieve. Slice the steak and arrange in overlapping slices on a heated serving dish. Drizzle sauce over meat and serve hot.

4 SERVINGS

VENISON CHILI

From Texas

Texans are great hunters.

¼ cup salad oil, bacon fat, or lard
2–3 pounds ground venison
3–6 tablespoons chili powder, or to taste
3–4 cups beef bouillon
  3 garlic cloves, mashed
  3 bay leaves
  1 teaspoon ground cumin
  1 teaspoon dried marjoram
 ½ teaspoon cayenne pepper (optional)
  2 teaspoons paprika
  1 square (1 ounce) unsweetened baking chocolate,
     chopped
     salt
     freshly ground pepper
  2 tablespoons cornmeal or masa harina
  2 tablespoons water
  2 cups cooked red kidney beans (1 1-pound can,
     drained)

Heat the fat in a heavy 6-quart casserole or kettle. Add the meat and cook, stirring constantly with a fork, until the meat is loose and browned. Pour off any excess fat. Stir in the chili powder. Cook, stirring constantly, for 3 minutes. Add 3 cups of the beef bouillon, the garlic, bay leaves, cumin, marjoram, cayenne (if used), paprika, and chocolate. Mix well. Taste and season as necessary with salt and pepper. Bring to the boiling point and lower heat to very low. Simmer covered, stirring frequently, for about 1 hour. Check the moisture; if usng 3 pounds of meat you may have to add the remaining cup of bouillon or part of it. Combine the cornmeal or masa harina and water to form a smooth paste and stir into the chili. Cook, stirring frequently, for 5 minutes. Add the beans, mix well, and heat through. Serve with boiled rice or tamales.

6–8 SERVINGS

Fish and Seafood

BAKED STUFFED STRIPED BASS

From Connecticut

Sandy Blanchard, a successful and enthusiastic fisherman, catches the fish; his wife, Marjorie, stuffs and cooks it.

STUFFING

- 3 tablespoons butter
- ¼ cup minced onion
- 1 cup mushrooms, chopped
- 1 small tomato, peeled, seeded, and chopped
- 1 tablespoon minced parsley
- 1 teaspoon minced chives

¾ cup fresh white breadcrumbs
    salt
    freshly ground pepper

FISH
1 striped bass (3–4 pounds), cleaned
1 tablespoon lemon juice
½ cup dry white wine
3 tablespoons melted butter

To make the stuffing, heat the butter in a frying pan. Add the onion and cook, stirring constantly, until soft; do not scorch. Add the mushrooms and cook for 3 more minutes. Add the tomato and cook for 5 more minutes. Stir in the parsley, chives, breadcrumbs, salt, and pepper. Cool mixture. Stuff the fish loosely with stuffing mixture. Close the cavity with small skewers or sew it closed with coarse thread. Line a baking dish with heavy aluminum foil. Butter the foil, and place the fish on it. Mix the lemon juice and wine and sprinkle over the fish. Spoon the melted butter over the fish. Cook in a preheated hot oven (400°) for 30 minutes. Baste occasionally with pan juices.

Note:
A 5- to 6-pound bass must be cooked for 40–45 minutes.

4 SERVINGS

SANDY BLANCHARD'S
FOIL-BAKED BLUEFISH

From Connecticut

1 4- to 5-pound bluefish, filleted
4 tablespoons butter
    salt
    freshly ground pepper
1 lemon, thinly sliced and seeds removed
3 sprigs fresh dill or parsley
    lemon wedges

Cut pieces of heavy foil large enough to enclose fillets completely. Place fillets on foil. Dot with butter and with salt and pepper. Top with the lemon slices and dill or parsley sprigs. Wrap the fish in the foil, closing the edges and folding them over to insure a tight seal. Place fish package on a baking sheet. Cook in a preheated hot oven (400°) for 30 minutes. If fillets are unusually thick, cook for 10 more minutes. To unwrap fish, place the closed package in a shallow dish (fish will be juicy). Cut the foil open with kitchen scissors and unfold. With two pancake turners, transfer the fish to a heated serving dish and serve with lemon wedges.

Note:
This foil-wrapped fish may also be cooked over charcoal.

4–6 SERVINGS

FILLET OF FLOUNDER WITH OYSTERS

From Cape Cod

    1-pound fillet of flounder; if frozen, thawed
12 large oysters, shucked and drained
    salt
½ cup milk
    fine dry cracker crumbs
 4 tablespoons melted butter
    Cucumber Sauce (see following recipe)

Dry the fish fillet thoroughly between paper towels. Cut fillet into 12 even pieces. Sprinkle the oysters with a little salt. Stir 1 teaspoon salt into the milk. Wrap a piece of flounder around each oyster, making a small roll, and secure with toothpicks. Dip each roll first in milk and then in crumbs. Place in one layer in a generously buttered shallow baking dish. Sprinkle with the melted butter. Bake in a preheated very hot oven (475°) for 5–7 minutes. Transfer to a heated serving dish and serve with Cucumber Sauce.

3–4 SERVINGS

CUCUMBER SAUCE

1½ cups peeled, seeded cucumber, cut into tiny dice
1 tablespoon vinegar, preferably white vinegar
  salt
  freshly ground pepper
1 teaspoon minced onion
¼ cup minced pimiento

Combine all the ingredients in a bowl. Let stand for at least 15 minutes to mellow the flavors.

MAKES ABOUT 1¾ CUPS

RED SNAPPER
STUFFED WITH SHRIMP

From Louisiana

Since large whole fish can be very expensive, it may be necessary to stuff small fish instead. But red snapper is a very bony fish, so I would recommend stuffing a large one for people who don't like to pick out fish bones. The following stuffing is sufficient for 1 4- to 6-pound fish or 6 small red snappers, total weight about 3½ to 4 pounds. All the fish are cleaned, but with heads left on. If fresh ginger root is not available, omit the ginger. And if you don't have red snapper, use any other firm-fleshed fish of the same size.

STUFFING (about 3 cups)
4 tablespoons butter
4 scallions, with 2 inches of green tops, minced
1 tablespoon minced fresh ginger root (if available)
2 tablespoons minced celery
2 tablespoons minced parsley

4 tablespoons flour
½ teaspoon salt or more (see rice)
¼ teaspoon freshly ground pepper
⅔ cup milk
1 cup cooked rice (if rice was salted when cooked,
     use only ½ teaspoon salt)
1 to 1½ cups cooked shelled shrimp, chopped
     (about ½- to ¾-pound raw unshelled shrimp)

Heat the butter in a frying pan. Add the scallions, ginger (if available), celery, and parsley. Cook, stirring constantly, for about 3–4 minutes or until vegetables are tender. Stir in the flour and cook for 2 more minutes. Stir in salt and pepper. Add milk and cook, stirring constantly, until thickened and smooth; sauce should be medium-thick. Add the rice and shrimp and mix well. Cook for 3 more minutes. Cool before using.

FISH

1 large red snapper (4–6 pounds), or 6 small red snappers
     juice of ½ to 1 lemon
3 tablespoons butter
     lemon wedges

Generously grease a baking pan large enough to hold all fish in one layer. Line it with foil and grease the foil; this will help in getting the cooked fish out in one piece. Sprinkle fish cavities with a little lemon juice. Stuff fish with stuffing. Fasten with small skewers or sew up with large needle and white thread. Place in one layer in pan. Dot with butter; use ½ tablespoon for each small fish. Bake in a preheated hot oven (400°) about 20–30 minutes for small fishes and about 30–40 minutes for 1 large fish. Test the fish with a toothpick *before* the minimum time; fish should flake. It must not be overcooked. After 15 minutes' cooking time, baste every 5 minutes with pan juices. Serve hot, with lemon wedges, on heated platter.

6 SERVINGS

BAKED SHAD WITH
DISAPPEARING BONES

From Connecticut

This recipe has been used for many years by natives of the Connecticut River area where shad abound in the late spring. Some people say that shad loses flavor cooked in this way, but I don't agree; I think the disintegrated bones flavor it. In any case, it makes eating this excessively bony but very delicious fish a pleasure.

1 whole shad (3–4 pounds), cleaned, head and tail removed
3 tablespoons melted butter
  salt
  freshly ground pepper
4–5 slices bacon
2 cups water, or 1 cup water and 1 cup clam juice or fish stock if available
  lemon wedges

Preheat oven to very hot (450°). Brush the fish inside and out with melted butter. Sprinkle inside and out with salt and pepper. Line a baking pan the size of the fish with heavy foil. Let about 4 inches of foil hang out over the pan's four edges. Place fish on foil. Top with bacon slices. Add 2 cups water or water and clam juice or fish stock. Fold overhanging foil edges back over fish. Cover tightly with more foil, joining foil edges *underneath* the bottom of the baking pan. Place pan in oven and immediately reduce heat to very low (225°). Cook for 6–7 hours. After the first 3 hours, check fish every hour for moisture; if necessary, add more water, ½ cup at a time. Keep fish covered tightly during the whole cooking time. Six hours is the minimum length of time to allow for a 3- to 4-pound fish. A larger shad (4–6 pounds) will take 7 hours. To serve fish, cut foil open. With two pancake turners very carefully transfer fish (fish breaks easily) to a heated serving platter. Serve with lemon wedges.

4 SERVINGS

BAKED SHAD STUFFED WITH SHAD ROE

From New York

You need a 5- to 6-pound whole shad to get about 2 pounds of fillets, plus trimmings for stock. Ask the fish man to cut the fish to make two fillets of even size and to give you the head, tail, and bones for stock—you are paying for it.

STOCK

head, tail, and bones from a 5- to 6-pound shad
1 small onion, sliced
1 3-inch piece celery, sliced
½ teaspoon salt
¼ teaspoon freshly ground pepper
2 cups water

Combine all the ingredients in a large saucepan. Bring to boiling point. Simmer covered over low heat for 30 minutes. Strain into a bowl. Wash out saucepan and return strained stock to it. Cook over high heat until stock is reduced to about 1 cup. Cool before using.

FISH

approximately 2 pounds shad fillets
1 pair shad roes
1½ tablespoons butter
1½ tablespoons flour
¾ cup fish stock
1 egg yolk
½ teaspoon water
1 slice white bread with crusts trimmed off, crumbled
2 teaspoons lemon juice

Spread fillets open and wipe dry with paper towels. Crumble the roes and reserve. Heat the butter in a frying pan, add the flour, and cook, stirring constantly, for 1–2 minutes; do not brown. Stir in the fish stock and, stirring vigorously, cook until thickened. Remove from heat. Blend the egg yolk and water and stir into fish stock. Return to low heat and add the crumbled roes. Add the crumbled bread and lemon juice and blend. The mixture will seem dry, but this is necessary since the fish releases juices during baking; the bread will keep the stuffing from oozing out in baking. Remove from heat and cool. Place one of the fillets skin side down, spread the stuffing on it, and top with the other fillet, skin side up, as if making a sandwich. With a large sewing needle and white cotton thread, sew the fillets together. Place the fish in a generously buttered baking dish that can go to the table. (The cooked shad can be transferred to a hot platter, but it is fragile and the less it is handled, the better.) Bake in a preheated hot oven (400°) for 20 minutes, basting continuously. After 15 minutes' cooking time, the fish will have released some of its juices. Bake for 5 more minutes or until a toothpick will easily go through the center of the fish. Do not overcook; the roe will have been precooked by the hot sauce before it is stuffed into the fish. Serve hot.

5–6 SERVINGS

TROUT WITH
CREAM-AND-ALMOND SAUCE

From Minnesota

4 fresh trout, weighing about 1 pound each, ready for
  cooking
  salt
  freshly ground pepper
  flour
½ cup butter
½ cup slivered blanched almonds
¾ cup heavy cream
¼ cup minced chives or parsley

Wash and dry the trout. Sprinkle the cavity of each with a little salt and pepper. Coat on all sides with flour. Heat the butter in a large frying pan. Add trout in one layer and cook over medium heat for about 4–5 minutes. Turn with pancake turner and cook for 3–4 minutes or until golden brown. Fish should flake when pierced with a toothpick. Carefully transfer the fish to a heated serving platter and keep warm in a low oven. Cook the almonds in the same frying pan, stirring constantly, until crisp and golden; do not brown. Add the cream and cook, stirring all the time, for 3–4 minutes longer or until sauce is thoroughly heated and thickened. Pour the sauce over the fish and sprinkle with minced chives. Serve hot.

4 SERVINGS

LEMON BAKED FISH

From California

1½ to 2 pounds fish fillets, washed and dried (if
    frozen, thaw and dry)
  2 large lemons
  ¼ to ⅓ cup olive oil or salad oil
    salt
    freshly ground pepper
  ¼ teaspoon paprika
    lemon wedges

Place the fish in one or two layers in a generously buttered shallow baking dish. Grate the yellow peel of 1 lemon and sprinkle over the fish. With a sharp knife, peel off the white peel of the first lemon and both yellow and white peels of the second lemon. Slice both lemons thin and remove seeds. Place lemon slices over fish. Combine the oil, salt, pepper, and paprika and sprinkle over the fish. Cook in a preheated moderate oven (350°F) for about 15 minutes or until fish flakes at the touch of a fork. If fish looks too dry, sprinkle with a little more oil, 1–2 tablespoons at a time. Serve with lemon wedges.

4–6 SERVINGS

MARGARET'S PINE-BARK STEW

From South Carolina

This classic and always pungent rural river and seacoast dish uses such traditionally available fish as bass, trout, blue bream, or any salt-water fish. Like all dishes of its kind, it also reflects the different cooks. The origin of the name is moot: some say it comes from the pine bark that kindled the fires over which the stew was cooked; others, from its color, which resembles that of pine bark. Still others claim that since there were no seasonings available during Revolutionary War days, the tender, deep-down roots of pine trees were used to flavor the stew.

½ pound lean bacon, chopped (some use fatback)
½ pound onions, chopped
1 cup chopped canned or fresh tomatoes
4 tablespoons Worcestershire sauce
⅓ cup tomato ketchup
¼ teaspoon hot red pepper or to taste, or 1 tablespoon curry powder
hot water
salt
freshly ground pepper
4–5 small whole fish such as blue bream, bass, or trout, dressed, each weighing approximately 1 to 1½ pounds

In a large heavy frying pan, fry bacon until crisp. With a slotted spoon, remove bacon bits from pan and reserve. Pour off all fat except about 4 tablespoons. Add the onions. Cook, stirring constantly, until soft and browned; do not scorch. Add the tomatoes, Worcestershire sauce, ketchup, and red pepper, and mix well. If mixture is too thick, add a little water, 2 tablespoons at a time. Season with salt and pepper. Add the fish, preferably in a single layer. Cover the frying pan and cook over medium-low heat for about 10 minutes or until fish flakes easily. As fish cooks, spoon sauce over it several times. Sprinkle with reserved bacon bits before serving.

Note:
Another version layers the fish in the sauce alternately with thinly sliced raw potatoes—Irish potatoes, as they are called in the South.

6 SERVINGS

FINNAN HADDIE DELMONICO

From New York City

A famous old Delmonico restaurant recipe. Finnan haddie —the name is Scots for smoked haddock—is found in better fish stores.

1 pound finnan haddie fillet, cut into strips
1 cup heavy cream
2 tablespoons butter
4 hard-cooked eggs, thinly sliced
  cayenne pepper or Tabasco to taste
¼ cup minced parsley
  boiled rice or buttered toast

Place the fish in a heatproof casserole and cover with cold water. Over low heat, let come to boiling point but do not boil up. Keep barely simmering over low heat for about 20 minutes. Drain thoroughly. While fish is simmering, pour the cream into a heavy frying pan and add the butter. Cook over low heat for about 10 minutes or until reduced by about one-quarter. Flake the fish and add to the cream along with the sliced eggs. Season with cayenne or Tabasco and sprinkle with parsley. Serve with rice or buttered toast.

Note:

This is a more-or-less dish, which should be neither stiff nor soupy.

4 SERVINGS

CODFISH BALLS

From New England

Excellent nostalgia, to my mind.

1½ cups shredded salt codfish (1 12-ounce package)
1½ cups hot water
   2 cups hot mashed potatoes
   2 tablespoons butter
   2 tablespoons minced onion
   ½ teaspoon ground mace or nutmeg or allspice
   ½ cup flour
      oil or shortening for deep frying
      tomato sauce
      coleslaw

Soak the codfish in the hot water for 3 minutes. Drain and, with hands, squeeze as dry as possible. (Codfish will expand when wet, but after squeezing it packs back into about 1½ cups.) In a bowl, mix together the codfish, potatoes, butter, onion, and spice. Blend thoroughly. With hands, shape into 1½-inch balls. Roll balls in the flour. Heat oil or shortening to the temperature of 375° on frying thermometer or until a bread cube browns in 60 seconds. Fry 1–2 minutes or until balls are golden brown on all sides. Drain on paper towels and serve with tomato sauce and coleslaw.

Notes:

The mixture may also be shaped into patties and cooked in butter until browned.

For crisper codfish balls, dip into flour, beaten egg yolk, and fine dry breadcrumbs before frying.

MAKES 24–30 1½-INCH BALLS
6 SERVINGS

THE SIMPLEST CRABMEAT

From Maryland

Mrs. McGowen, my wartime Maryland cook (who always wore a hat), made this for Sunday breakfast. The butter was brought to us weekly by Mr. Orlando Rideout, a gentleman farmer on the Eastern Shore, because he liked my family. The dish was served with Spoon Bread (page 211) and broiled tomatoes. Grits would be good too.

½ cup (1 stick) sweet butter (it really should be sweet—unsalted—butter)
1 pound cooked backfin lump crabmeat
salt
dash of cayenne

Heat the butter in a frying pan, but do not let it brown. Turn heat to low and add the crabmeat. Stir frequently but extremely gently, so as not to break up the lumps until heated through. The butter must be absorbed by the crabmeat. Do not boil. Sprinkle with a little salt and a dash of cayenne. Serve very hot.

3 SERVINGS

CRAB CAKES

From Maryland

Inspect crabmeat before buying it. Though they sell it as cleaned, dishonest fish dealers leave an ungodly amount of shell and cartilage, for which you pay heavily, as crabmeat is very expensive. If you must, use frozen crabmeat, thawed and picked over, but it isn't as good in this dish as fresh crabmeat.

- 1 pound fresh crabmeat
- 4 tablespoons butter
- 2 tablespoons minced onion
- 1 egg, beaten
- ½ teaspoon ground mustard
- ½ teaspoon salt
- ⅛ teaspoon freshly ground pepper
- pinch cayenne pepper
- ½ teaspoon Worcestershire sauce
- ½ cup fine dry breadcrumbs

Put the crabmeat in a bowl. Pick it over to remove any remaining shell bits and cartilage but leave as much meat as possible in lumps. Heat 1 tablespoon of the butter in a frying pan. Cook the onion until soft, but do not brown. Add to crabmeat, together with the beaten egg, mustard, salt, and pepper, cayenne, and Worcestershire sauce. Mix carefully to blend ingredients. Shape into small cakes about 3½ inches in diameter. Coat on both sides with breadcrumbs. Heat the remaining butter in the frying pan until browned. Add the crab cakes and cook for about 3–4 minutes on each side. Turn the cakes carefully with a pancake turner both in the breadcrumbs and when frying, because the cakes are fragile and tend to fall apart easily.

MAKES 8 SMALL CAKES

DEVILED CRABS

From New Orleans

This dish should be well seasoned. You will have 4 hard-cooked egg whites left over from the ingredients—I suggest eating them.

2 tablespoons butter
2 tablespoons flour
1 cup light or heavy cream
4 hard-cooked egg yolks
2 teaspoons minced parsley
2 teaspoons Worcestershire sauce
1 pound cooked crabmeat, picked over and flaked
  salt
  cayenne pepper
4 tablespoons fine dry breadcrumbs mixed with 2
  tablespoons melted butter
  lemon wedges

Heat the butter and stir in the flour. Cook, stirring constantly, for about 2 minutes. Stir in the cream and cook, stirring all the time, until smooth and thickened. Remove from heat and cool. Crumble the egg yolks into the sauce and add the parsley, Worcestershire sauce, and crabmeat. Stir carefully to blend. Season with salt and cayenne and mix well. Turn into buttered crab shells or scallop shells (this amount will fill about 8 shells) or into individual baking dishes. Sprinkle with the buttered crumbs. Bake in a preheated moderate oven (350°) for about 20 minutes or until golden brown. Serve hot, with lemon wedges.

4–6 SERVINGS

SCALLOPED OYSTERS

From New England

Once upon a time, oysters were so plentiful and cheap that people had to invent new ways of using them. In any cooked oyster dish, never allow more than two layers of oysters; if there are three layers, the middle one will not be properly cooked.

  1 pint shucked oysters, with liquid
  1 cup freshly rolled coarse cracker crumbs
  ½ cup coarse fresh white breadcrumbs
  ½ cup melted butter
    salt
    freshly ground pepper
  2 tablespoons butter
  ⅛ teaspoon ground mace or nutmeg (optional)
  ⅓ cup heavy cream

Drain oysters, reserving liquid. Combine cracker crumbs and breadcrumbs and season with a little salt and pepper. Stir in the melted butter and mix well. Generously butter a 1-quart shallow baking dish. Line bottom with one third of crumb mixture. Top with half the oysters. Sprinkle oysters with 2 tablespoons reserved oyster liquid and half of the heavy cream. If desired, sprinkle with a little mace or nutmeg. Top with another third of the crumbs, the remaining oysters, oyster liquid, cream, and spice. Cover with the last third of crumbs. Dot with butter. Cook in a preheated hot oven (400°) for about 20 to 25 minutes. Serve hot.

3–4 SERVINGS

SAUTÉED SCALLOPS

From New York

One of the quickest, easiest, and nicest ways with scallops.

- 1 pint bay scallops, whole, or sea scallops, halved or quartered
- ¼ cup flour
- ½ teaspoon salt
  freshly ground pepper
- 6 tablespoons butter
- ½ cup dry white wine
- 2 tablespoons minced chives or parsley

Dry the scallops on paper towels and spread on dry paper towels. Combine the flour, salt, and pepper and sprinkle over the scallops. Turn to coat on all sides, and shake off excess flour. Heat the butter in a large frying pan. Add scallops. Over medium heat, and stirring frequently, cook scallops for about 5 minutes. With a slotted spoon, transfer to a heated serving dish. Add the wine to the frying pan. Bring to boiling point, scraping up the brown bits in the bottom of pan. Pour over scallops and sprinkle with chives or parsley. Serve hot.

3–4 SERVINGS

SIMPLE WAY OF COOKING SHRIMP

From Connecticut

This easy method, which does not overcook the shrimp, comes from the owners of The Mansion Clam House fish store and restaurant in Saugatuck.

Put raw, unshelled, medium shrimp into a large saucepan or kettle. Run enough hot water from the faucet over the shrimp to cover them completely. For each 2 pounds of shrimp, add 1 table-spoon salt and 2 bay leaves. Over high heat, bring to boiling point, stirring frequently. Boil for 1 minute. Drain into a colander and quickly run cold water over the shrimp. Drain again. Shell and use as desired.

SHRIMP CASSEROLE

From Charleston, S.C.

TO COOK SHRIMP

- 2 quarts water
- 1 small onion, studded with 2 cloves
- 1 stalk celery, white and green parts
- 3 dry red seeded chili peppers
- 1 tablespoon salt
- 1 teaspoon peppercorns
- 2 garlic cloves
- 1 bay leaf
- 1 lemon, sliced
- 2 pounds small raw shrimp

Combine all ingredients except the shrimp in a large sauce-pan and bring to boiling point. Boil covered over medium heat for about 15–20 minutes. Add shrimp. When water returns to boiling point shrimp will be cooked. Drain immediately. Shell and devein shrimp and reserve.

- 8 slices firm white bread with crusts trimmed off, shredded into crumbs
- 1 cup dry white wine
- ½ cup good-quality medium-dry sherry
- 4 tablespoons butter, cut into pieces and at room temperature
- 1 teaspoon salt
- ¼–⅔ teaspoon ground nutmeg
  freshly ground pepper to taste
- 2 pounds reserved shrimp

Place the breadcrumbs in a deep bowl and pour the white wine and sherry over them. Mix well and let stand until thoroughly soaked. With a fork, mash the butter into the crumbs to make a smooth paste. Beat in the salt, nutmeg, and pepper. Add shrimp and mix well to coat with crumb mixture. Turn into a generously buttered 1½-quart casserole. Bake in a preheated moderate oven (350°) for about 30 minutes or until top is crusty and golden. Serve with broiled tomatoes and hot corn bread.

4–6 SERVINGS

SHRIMP NEWBURG

Newburg dishes are refined versions of chowders and stews, containing egg yolks and cream for thickening, and sherry and even brandy for flavoring. Unlike their à la King cousins, Newburgs are never thickened with flour. All these creamed dishes became popular around the turn of the century, along with the chafing dish, for which they are very well suited since they require low, steady heat. They are also easily made in electric skillets with a low, steady temperature. When they are made over direct heat, the heat must be very low. They should be kept warm in a double boiler. Be sure to use a good dry or medium-dry sherry, never a sweet one. Favorites of the Edwardians, Newburgs still make excellent buffet dishes, and along with the chafing dish itself, they deserve a comeback. Wild rice is the most desirable accompaniment.

4 tablespoons butter
1 pound medium shrimp, cooked and shelled
3 tablespoons sherry
1 tablespoon brandy
  salt
  cayenne
1 cup light cream
½ cup heavy cream
2 egg yolks, beaten

Over low heat, heat the butter in a large heavy frying pan. Add the shrimp. Cook, stirring carefully with a fork, for 3 minutes. Stir in the sherry and brandy. Season lightly with salt and cayenne. Cook for 3 more minutes. Combine the light and heavy cream in a bowl and beat together with the beaten egg yolks. Remove the frying pan from the heat and slowly stir in the cream mixture. Return pan to low heat and heat thoroughly, but do not boil or mixture will separate. Serve at once, very hot, on heated plates with wild rice, on buttered toast, or in warm patty shells.

4 SERVINGS

VARIATION:

You may substitute 1 pound cooked lobster meat for the shrimp to make Lobster Newburg.

SHRIMP WIGGLE

From both the Northeast and the Midwest

Once a favorite of college students and for ladies' lunches, Shrimp Wiggle has disappeared from our tables. A pity, because it is one of those good, practical, inoffensive dishes that cooks fall back on when they don't know what to serve. I don't know the origin of the name; could it be from the wiggly shape of the shrimps?

         4 tablespoons butter
         2 tablespoons flour
     1⅓ cups milk
         1 cup cooked and shelled small shrimp
         1 cup cooked drained peas
            salt
            freshly ground pepper
            paprika
         2 tablespoons sherry (optional)
            buttered toast

Heat the butter. Stir in the flour and cook, stirring constantly, for 2 minutes. Gradually stir in the milk. Cook, stirring all the time, until smooth and thickened. Add the shrimp, peas, salt, pepper, and a little paprika. Over low heat, heat through thoroughly. Stir in the sherry (if used) before serving on hot buttered toast.

4 SERVINGS

POTATO-SHRIMP SALAD

From South Carolina

There should be as nearly as possible equal amounts of shrimp and potatoes.

¾ cup mayonnaise
1⅓ to 1½ cups lemon juice
1 tablespoon prepared mustard
1 teaspoon salt
½ teaspoon freshly ground pepper
1½ pounds boiled potatoes, diced (about 2½–3 cups)
1½ pounds shelled cooked shrimp, chopped (about 2½ cups), or 2 pounds unshelled raw shrimp, cooked, shelled, and chopped to make about 2½ cups
½ cup finely chopped celery
   salad greens
3 tablespoons chopped fresh dill weed

Combine the mayonnaise, lemon juice, mustard, salt, and pepper and mix well. Put the potatoes, shrimp, and celery into a bowl and toss with the mayonnaise mixture. Taste the seasoning and if necessary add a little more salt and pepper. Line a salad bowl with salad greens. Pile salad on the greens in a mound and sprinkle with chopped dill. Serve cold but preferably not chilled.

Note:
You may want to add 1 or 2 chopped hard-cooked eggs.

4–6 SERVINGS

Vegetables and Salads

BOSTON BAKED BEANS

*In the old days, the beans were often baked in a commu-
nity oven, usually in the cellar of a tavern. The baker called
for the beans on Saturday morning and returned them in
time for Saturday supper. Beans are best baked in a narrow-
throated earthenware bean pot with bulging sides; this
seems to keep in the flavor. Lacking this, a deep casserole,
preferably an earthenware one, will do; earthenware seems
to cook long slow dishes better. As in all folk recipes there
are variations. Some baked-bean recipes use more salt pork,
others use dry mustard, others omit the sugar or even omit
the salt pork. I like my beans molassesy and not too fat.
Though I think home-baked beans are better, one or two
commercial varieties, the ones without tomatoes, come on*

*as very reasonable facsimiles, especially when heated up
with a few extra spoonfuls of molasses.*

  2 pounds small white pea beans
    cold water to cover
  2 quarts cold water
    boiling water
  ½ pound well-streaked salt pork
  2 teaspoons salt
  1 cup dark molasses
  ¼ cup dark-brown sugar

Wash the beans, picking out dud ones. Cover with cold
water and soak overnight. In the morning, drain, put into a kettle,
and add 2 quarts water. Bring slowly to the boiling point. Cover
and simmer—*do not* boil—over low heat until the skins are about to
burst when you take a few on the tip of a spoon and blow on them.
(Not overcooking the beans allows them to stay whole and not become mushy during baking.) Drain, reserving cooking liquid. Pour
boiling water to cover over the salt pork and let stand 3 minutes.
Drain and cut 1-inch gashes into the pork without cutting into the
rind, spacing the cuts about 1 inch apart. Put drained beans into a
bean pot or casserole, add the pork and push it down until all but
the rind is covered. Measure 1 cup of the bean liquid into a saucepan and stir in the salt, molasses, and brown sugar. Bring to boiling
point and pour over the beans. Add enough of the remaining bean
liquid to cover the beans; reserve any remaining liquid. Cover bean
pot. Put into a very slow oven (250°). Bake for a minimum of 6 to 8
hours. Check for dryness about once an hour and if necessary add
remaining bean liquid or a little boiling water, ¼ cup at a time.
Beans should be moist but not soupy. Uncover the pot for the last
hour to crisp the pork rind. Serve hot, warm, or cold.

10–12 SERVINGS

GREEN BEANS WITH BACON

Midwestern

1½ pounds green beans, trimmed
  4 slices bacon, chopped
  1 medium onion, thinly sliced
  1 cup water
     salt
     freshly ground pepper
 ½ teaspoon sugar

Cut beans into 1½- to 2-inch pieces. Put the bacon and onions into a large heavy saucepan. Cook over medium heat, stirring constantly, until onions are soft but not mushy. Add the beans, water, salt, pepper, and sugar. Bring to boiling point and reduce heat to low. Simmer covered, stirring frequently, for about 20 minutes or until beans are tender. Check moisture and, if necessary to prevent scorching, add a little hot water, 2 tablespoons at a time.

4–6 SERVINGS

NONA'S MOTHER'S GEORGIA GREEN BEANS

Use either pole beans or bush beans; pole beans are Southern favorites. This recipe is typical of the Southern way with vegetables—they are overcooked and delicious. And nobody ever called them rabbit food, whereas the crisp, crunchy, and (one is led to hope) vitamin-filled vegetables beloved by Easterners and Californians only too often deserve that name.

 ½ pound salt pork with a lean streak
1½ cups water
1½ pounds green beans, trimmed
     salt

Wash excess salt off salt pork. Place it in a saucepan large enough to hold the beans, and add the water. Simmer covered for 30 minutes. Add the beans and bring to boiling point. Lower heat and simmer covered for about 40 minutes. Beans will be a pale green. Turn beans with a spatula two or three times to insure even cooking. When done, there should be very little pan liquid.

Notes:

Be careful not to overcook the beans or they will be mushy. It is important that beans be firm enough to hold their shape when dished up. Depending on age and size of beans, the cooking time may have to be adjusted.

Old-fashioned streaky salt pork is not easy to find. Few supermarkets carry it and it is generally necessary to go to an old-fashioned butcher. Nona's mother says that when she has no streaky salt pork, she puts the beans in the water and lays very thin bacon slices across the top of the beans instead of boiling the bacon first.

4–6 SERVINGS

PURÉED BROCCOLI

From New York

Puréed vegetables are found in all good restaurants because they will stay fresh and flavorful, whereas braised or sautéed vegetables will not. Leftover vegetables may also be puréed, but freshly cooked are better.

- 2 bunches broccoli
    boiling salted water
- 2 large potatoes, peeled and cut into pieces
- 2 tablespoons butter
    salt
    freshly ground pepper
- ⅛ teaspoon ground nutmeg
- 2–4 tablespoons heavy cream

Cut off all tough parts from broccoli and break into flowerets. Cook until tender in boiling salt water to cover. Drain and purée in a food processor or food mill. Cook the potatoes in boiling salted water until tender. Drain and mash with a potato ricer or push through food mill. Combine the two vegetables in a saucepan or the top of a double boiler and mix well. Stir in the butter, salt, pepper, and nutmeg and 2 tablespoons of the heavy cream. Heat through, stirring constantly. If too thin, continue to cook, stirring all the time, to let liquid evaporate; if too thick, add the remaining cream. Serve hot. Or keep hot over boiling water until serving time.

6 SERVINGS

CREAMED CABBAGE

Midwestern

If you have leftover cooked peas, add them to the hot cabbage and heat through.

1 medium-sized cabbage, weighing about 2 pounds
  boiling salted water
2 tablespoons butter
1 cup heavy cream or half-and-half
  salt
  freshly ground pepper
  ground nutmeg to taste

Trim the cabbage, discarding any blemished leaves and cutting out the hard core. Cut the cabbage into four parts and shred thin. Wash and drain cabbage. Plunge into a large saucepan full of boiling salted water. Cook without a cover for about 3 minutes. Drain and squeeze out as much moisture as possible. Heat the butter in a saucepan. Add the cabbage and mix well. Add the cream or half-and-half, pepper, and nutmeg and mix thoroughly. Simmer covered over low heat for about 5 minutes, stirring frequently. The cabbage should be very hot and still crisp.

4–6 SERVINGS

CRISP SHREDDED CARROTS

The finished dish may be seasoned with a pinch of allspice, ginger, nutmeg, thyme, or chives.

3 cups shredded carrots
  hot water
2 tablespoons butter
  salt
  freshly ground pepper
  additional seasoning to taste
2 tablespoons minced parsley (omit if chives are used)

Place the carrots in a heavy saucepan. Add enough hot water to come about ¼-inch above carrots. Cover saucepan and cook carrots over medium heat for 2 minutes. Remove cover and cook for 2 more minutes. Drain off any remaining water and stir in butter. Season with salt, plenty of pepper, and allspice, ginger, nutmeg, thyme, or chives (as above). Turn into heated serving dish. Sprinkle with parsley (if not seasoned with chives).

4–5 SERVINGS

CREAMED CELERY
WITH PECANS

From Georgia

     1 large bunch celery (about 1½ pounds)
  1½ cups boiling water (approximately)
     1 tablespoon lemon juice
     1 teaspoon salt
     3 tablespoons butter
     3 tablespoons flour
   ½ cup heavy cream
       freshly ground white pepper
   ⅔ cup pecan halves

Trim the celery and cut stalks into 2-inch diagonal pieces. Put celery into a saucepan that will hold it in two layers, and add water, lemon juice, and salt. Water should reach two-thirds of the way up the celery; accurate amounts depend on size of saucepan. Simmer covered over low heat for about 10–15 minutes or until celery is tender but still crisp. Drain, reserving liquid. Place celery in a buttered shallow 1½- or 2-quart baking dish. Measure 1 cup reserved celery liquid. In a saucepan, heat the butter and stir in the flour. Cook, stirring constantly, for about 2 minutes. Stir in the 1 cup celery liquid and the cream. Cook, stirring constantly, until sauce is thickened and smooth. Check seasoning and if necessary add more salt. Add pepper. Pour the sauce over the celery. Top with pecan halves. Cook in a preheated moderate oven (350°) for about 20–25 minutes or until browned and bubbly.

4–6 SERVINGS

CELERY VICTOR

From California

Victor Hirtzler, once chef of the St. Francis Hotel in San Francisco, created this dish, which became very fashionable. It is very good and deserves to be enjoyed at our modern tables.

    3 large bunches celery
       chicken bouillon
       bouquet garni: 3 sprigs parsley, 1 bay leaf, and
       1 teaspoon dried thyme tied together in a little cheese-
       cloth bag. If fresh thyme is available, use 1 sprig
    1 medium onion, sliced
    1 carrot, cut into pieces
  1½ cups olive oil
    ½ cup white wine vinegar
       salt
       freshly ground pepper
    6 anchovy fillets, drained
    6 strips pimiento

Remove tough outer stalks from celery, cut off green tops and roots, and trim all 3 bunches to a length of approximately 6 or 7 inches. Split each bunch into halves lengthwise. (The tender green leaves of the celery hearts may be left or trimmed away, as preferred.) Place celery in a single layer in a large saucepan or fireproof baking dish. Add chicken bouillon to barely cover celery. Add the bouquet garni, onion, and carrot. Bring quickly to boiling point and reduce heat to low. Simmer, covered for about 10 minutes or until celery is tender but still firm; accurate cooking time depends on the size and variety of celery. Drain and strain out carrot and onion pieces. Reserve broth for other uses. Cool celery and when cooled, gently press out excess liquid with clean hands. It must be well drained. Place celery in one layer in a serving dish. Combine the oil, vinegar, salt as needed (the bouillon may have been salty), and pepper and mix well. Pour over celery and chill in the marinade for at least 2 hours. At serving time, serve it in the dish, garnishing each half-bunch with 1 anchovy fillet and 1 pimiento strip, crossed. Serve with roast meats or as an appetizer.

6 SERVINGS

THE BEST WAY TO COOK CORN ON THE COB

Have ready a kettle with 3–6 quarts boiling water. Shuck corn just before cooking it. Place shucked corn in a deep saucepan. Pour in boiling water to cover corn. Do *not* add sugar or salt. When the water returns to boiling point, remove pan from heat. Cover and let corn stand in water from 5 to 10 minutes, though it can stand as long as 20 minutes without great damage. Drain corn and serve immediately.

FRESH CORN MEDLEY

All-American

A more-or-less dish.

4 slices lean bacon, chopped
1 medium or large onion, minced
1 garlic clove, minced
1 sweet green pepper, seeded and cut into strips
3 medium-to-large tomatoes, peeled and chopped
2–3 cups fresh corn kernels, cut off the cob (about 4 to 6 ears)
   salt
   freshly ground pepper
¼ teaspoon sugar
½ teaspoon dried thyme

Fry the bacon until crisp in a casserole large enough to hold all the ingredients. Remove the bacon bits with a slotted spoon and reserve. Pour off all but 3 tablespoons bacon fat. Add the onion, garlic, and green pepper. Cook, stirring constantly, for about 4–5 minutes or until soft; do not scorch. Add the tomatoes, corn, salt, pepper, sugar, and thyme and mix well. Cook covered over medium heat for about 8–10 minutes or until corn is tender. If necessary, add a little water, 2 tablespoons at a time, to prevent scorching. Sprinkle with the reserved bacon bits and serve hot, from the casserole.

4 SERVINGS

CORN PUDDING

Eastern Seaboard and Midwest

3 cups fresh corn kernels (approximately 6 large ears)
1 tablespoon cornstarch
1 teaspoon sugar
1 teaspoon salt
⅛ teaspoon mace (optional)
4 tablespoons melted butter
¾ cup light cream, half-and-half, or milk
3 large eggs, separated

Turn the corn into a bowl. Stir in the cornstarch, sugar, salt, mace (if used), and melted butter. Beat together the cream, half-and-half, or milk, and the egg yolks, and stir the mixture into the corn. Beat the egg whites until stiff and fold into the corn mixture. Turn into a buttered 1½-quart baking dish. Cook in a preheated moderate oven (350°) for about 30 minutes or until a knife inserted in the middle of the pudding shows clean. Serve immediately.

Note:
The mace is my idea for flavoring a rather bland dish. The pudding can be flavored with any herb, or with a dash of Tabasco.

4–6 SERVINGS

CORN AND SHRIMP PUDDING

A Carolina version of a Southern favorite

Short of having an old-fashioned spiky corn grater, this is how home cooks grate their corn, as a North Carolina friend showed me. For mature corn, with a sharp knife, go around and around the cob (as if peeling an apple), taking off a thin layer of corn from top to bottom. When finally down to the cob itself, scrape the cob with the sharp or dull end of the knife blade. With younger corn, the following method works best. With a sharp knife, slit each row of kernels down the middle. Then scrape downward with the blade turned slightly toward you.

5   large ears of corn, grated to make about 3½ to 4 cups, or 2 10-ounce packages frozen kernel corn, thawed and drained
3   eggs, separated
2   tablespoons melted butter
½   cup milk
1   teaspoon salt
1   teaspoon sugar
1   pound cooked shelled shrimp (about 2 pounds raw unshelled medium shrimp)

If frozen corn is used, process for a second or two in blender or food processor to bruise kernels. Turn the grated corn into a bowl. Beat the egg whites and egg yolks separately. Stir beaten yolks into corn. While stirring, add the butter, milk, salt, sugar, and shrimp. Gently fold in the beaten egg whites. Turn mixture into a generously buttered 2-quart baking dish. Cook in a preheated moderate oven (350°) for about 30–40 minutes or until golden brown. Serve with any kind of corn bread.

Note:
Frozen kernel corn will do, but it does not have quite the flavor of scraped corn.

6 SERVINGS

KALE WITH SOUR CREAM

From a Georgia lady tired of conventional kale

    3 pounds kale
      boiling salted water
    2 tablespoons butter
      salt
      freshly ground pepper
    ⅛ teaspoon ground nutmeg
    1 cup sour cream

Wash the kale in cold water. Trim off heavy stems and
blemished leaves. Put in a saucepan and cover with boiling salted
water. Simmer covered for 10–15 minutes or until tender but not
mushy. Drain well and chop fine. Return to saucepan and stir in the
butter, salt, pepper, and nutmeg. Heat thoroughly. Reduce heat to
very low and stir in the sour cream gradually. Heat through but do
not boil.

4–6 SERVINGS

LEEKS AU GRATIN

From California's Napa Valley

    12 medium-to-large leeks
    1¼ cups beef or chicken bouillon
     1 cup dry white wine
     4 tablespoons butter
     ¼ cup flour
       salt
       freshly ground pepper
     1 cup grated Swiss or Parmesan cheese

Trim the leeks, removing all but 2 inches of the green leaves.

Holding each leek leafy side down, cut with a sharp knife through the white part up to 2 inches from the root, cutting through the whole length of the leek. (This will make washing away the sand between the leaves easier.) Wash thoroughly to remove all sand. Combine the bouillon and wine in a large shallow saucepan and bring to the boiling point. Lower heat and carefully place leeks in the stock. Simmer covered over low heat for about 5–7 minutes or until leeks are barely tender. Drain and reserve stock (there should be about 2 cups; if not, make up the difference with wine or bouillon). Place the leeks in a buttered shallow baking dish in one or two layers. Heat the butter in a saucepan and stir in the flour. Cook for 2 minutes. Gradually stir in the leek stock, and cook, stirring constantly, until thickened and smooth. Stir in salt and pepper and ¾ cup of the cheese. Cook until cheese is melted. Spoon the sauce over the leeks and sprinkle with the remaining cheese. Place under broiler or in a hot oven and cook until top is browned and bubbly.

4–6 SERVINGS

MUSHROOMS IN CREAM

From New Orleans

Fresh mushrooms must be washed because they are grown in compost. But wash them quickly and dry thoroughly to prevent sogginess. Serve this as a first course or for brunch.

    1 pound mushrooms
    3 tablespoons butter
       salt
       freshly ground pepper
    ¼ teaspoon ground mace
    2 tablespoons flour
    ⅓ cup dry sherry
    ⅔ cup heavy cream
    1 egg yolk
       buttered toast fingers

Wash and trim mushrooms; if very large, cut into halves or quarters. Place in a saucepan with 2 tablespoons of the butter. Simmer covered for about 10 minutes. Season with salt, pepper, and mace. Stir in the flour and mix well. Stir in the sherry. Cook, stirring constantly, for about 2–3 minutes. Beat together the cream and egg yolk. Remove saucepan from heat and stir in the cream mixture. Return to heat and heat through, but do not boil. Stir in one remaining tablespoon of butter. Serve very hot, over buttered toast fingers.

4 SERVINGS

CRUSTLESS MUSHROOM PIE

From Napa Valley, California

This can be used as a luncheon or supper main dish or served as an appetizer.

    1 pound mushrooms, preferably tiny ones
    3 tablespoons butter
    1 small onion, minced
    1 garlic clove, minced
      grated rind of 1 lemon
    1 tablespoon lemon juice
      salt
      freshly ground pepper
    ¼ teaspoon cayenne pepper or to taste
    3 eggs, beaten
  1 ¼ cups sour cream
    ⅛ teaspoon paprika

Wash and trim mushrooms. If large, cut in halves or quarters. Heat the butter in a deep frying pan. Over medium heat, cook onion and garlic until onion is soft; do not brown. Add mushrooms, lemon rind, and lemon juice and mix well. Cook, stirring constantly, for about 5–8 minutes; the mushrooms should be still firm and white. Remove from heat and season with salt, pepper, and cayenne. Cool. Beat together the beaten eggs, sour cream, and paprika. Put the mushrooms in a generously buttered deep 8- or 9-inch pie pan. Spoon sour-cream mixture evenly over mushrooms. Bake in a preheated moderate oven (350°) for about 30–40 minutes or until firm and golden on top. Remove from oven and let stand at room temperature for 5 minutes before cutting into wedges.

4–5 SERVINGS

CRISP FRIED OKRA

From the South

    1 pound fresh young okra
      flour
    1 egg, beaten with 1 tablespoon salad oil or water
    1 cup yellow or white cornmeal or fine dry breadcrumbs
    4 tablespoons lard, bacon fat, or salad oil
      salt
      freshly ground pepper

Trim off the tips and stems of the okra pods. Cut the pods diagonally into ¼-inch slices. Dip the slices first in flour, coating them on all sides, then in the beaten egg, and finally in the cornmeal or breadcrumbs. The okra should be evenly coated; shake off excess meal or crumbs. Put the okra slices on paper towels. Heat the fat in a large heavy frying pan. Add the okra slices. Over medium heat, sauté the okra for about 2 minutes or until golden brown. Turn and sauté 1–2 minutes longer, or until evenly browned on all sides. Drain on paper towels and place on a heated serving dish. Sprinkle with salt and pepper and serve hot.

4 SERVINGS

CREOLE STEWED OKRA

From Louisiana

1 pound fresh okra, preferably small, or 2 packages
  frozen okra, thawed and sliced
2 tablespoons bacon fat, lard, or butter
1 small onion, minced
1 garlic clove, minced
1 medium-sized sweet green pepper, seeded and cut
  into 2-inch strips
1 cup tomato sauce, or 1 cup chopped fresh tomatoes
  salt
  freshly ground pepper
½ teaspoon ground thyme (optional)
  Tabasco to taste
3 tablespoons minced parsley

If fresh okra is very small and tender, leave it whole. If not,
trim off tops and bottoms and slice the pods. In a heavy saucepan,
put okra, the fat, onion, garlic, and green pepper. Cook over low
heat, stirring constantly, for about 5 minutes. Add tomato sauce or
chopped tomatoes, salt, pepper, thyme, and Tabasco and mix well.
Simmer covered, stirring frequently, for about 10 minutes or until
okra is tender.

4 SERVINGS

DORIS'S ONION PIE

From Lancaster in Pennsylvania Dutch country

*Good as a main dish, excellent on a buffet, and popular
with men, women, and children.*

CRUST

3 cups flour
1 tablespoon salt
1 cup lard
½ cup ice water

Sift the flour and salt into a bowl. Cut in the lard with two
knives or a pastry cutter until mixture resembles coarse meal. Add
water, 1 or 2 tablespoons at a time and just enough to make dough
hold together when stirred with a fork. Roll out dough in two
rounds to fit a deep 10-inch pie pan. Line pan bottom with one
crust and refrigerate both until ready to use.

FILLING

6 large yellow onions, thinly sliced
  boiling water
  milk
4 tablespoons butter
  salt
  freshly ground pepper
2 tablespoons flour
2 hard-cooked eggs, sliced

Place the onions in a saucepan and add boiling water to
cover. Cook over medium heat 3–4 minutes or until tender but not
mushy. Drain thoroughly and place in the pastry-lined pie pan.
Add enough milk to barely cover the onions. Dot with the butter.
Sprinkle with salt and pepper and flour. Top with the egg slices.
Cover with top crust in the usual manner. Bake in a preheated
moderate oven (350°) for about 35–40 minutes. Serve hot or warm.

8 SERVINGS

FRENCH-FRIED ONION RINGS

All-American

2 large Spanish or Bermuda onions
    approximately 1⅔ cups milk
1⅓ cups flour
    salt
    freshly ground pepper
2 eggs, well beaten
2 tablespoons melted butter or salad oil
5 cups vegetable oil for frying

Peel the onions and cut into ¼-inch-thick slices. Separate the slices into rings and place in a large pie pan in one or two layers. Pour about 1 cup milk over the onion rings. Let stand in refrigerator or at cool room temperature for 1 hour, turning frequently. Prepare batter: In a shallow bowl, mix together the flour, salt, and pepper. Stir in the remaining ⅔ cup milk, the beaten eggs, and the melted butter or salad oil. Beat until smooth with a rotary beater or wire whip. Heat the vegetable oil in a heavy 2-quart saucepan to a temperature of 365°–375° on frying thermometer (see following note). When oil is hot, with metal tongs or a fork remove a few onion rings from milk and drain and dry on paper towels. Dip rings into the batter, making sure they are coated on both sides. Shake off excess batter. Place in hot oil. Turn once or twice. When browned and crisp (in about 2–3 minutes), remove from oil and drain on paper towels. Pat dry with more paper towels. Place on a serving dish and keep hot in a low oven until all rings are fried. Then salt the rings and serve immediately.

Note:
   If you do not have a frying thermometer, judge the heat of the oil this way: Cut a few 1-inch-square cubes of bread. When you think oil is hot enough, drop in a couple of cubes and count slowly to 60, or use a timer for 60 seconds. If the cubes brown in this time, the oil will be around 365°. Do not wait for it to smoke before making this test; smoking means that it is beginning to break down and that food will overbrown on outside and be raw inside.

If there are any bits of batter floating in the hot oil between frying batches of rings, remove them with a slotted spoon or they will burn and flavor the oil.

3–4 SERVINGS

FRIED PARSNIPS

From Michigan

A humble vegetable cooked in an unsuspectedly pleasant way by my husband's mother. The recipe can easily be doubled or tripled.

1 pound parsnips
  boiling water
2 tablespoons butter
  salt
  freshly ground pepper

Trim and peel the parsnips and cut them into match sticks. Put in a saucepan and cover with boiling water. Cook without a cover for 2–3 minutes or until just barely tender. Drain. Heat the butter in a frying pan. Add parsnips. Cook over medium heat, stirring with a fork, for about 3 minutes or until golden. Sprinkle with salt and pepper and serve hot.

2–3 SERVINGS

CREAMED PEAS AND
NEW POTATOES

From New England

This really should be made only with fresh peas and new potatoes.

2 quarts unshelled new peas
2 quarts tiny potatoes (1- to 1½-inch diameter)
½ pound salt pork, blanched and diced small
1 small onion, minced
⅔ cup heavy cream
   salt
   freshly ground white pepper

Shell the peas, reserving 3 pods. Scrub the potatoes but do not peel. Cook potatoes in boiling salted water to cover for 7 to 10 minutes or more, until they are just tender but not mushy. Drain. Cooking time depends on size and age. Put potatoes in a fireproof casserole and keep warm. Heat the salt pork and fry until the pieces are golden. Add the onion and cook, stirring constantly, until onion is soft. Add the pork, onion, and fat to the potatoes and keep warm. Cook the peas and reserved pods in about ½ cup boiling water for 3 minutes. Remove pods and add peas and their liquid to casserole. Mix the contents with a fork and place over low heat. Cook until heated through. Add the cream and heat, but do not boil. Season with a little salt and pepper. Serve on heated plates.

4 SERVINGS

PENNSYLVANIA DUTCH
POTATO FILLING

This savory dish is little known outside Pennsylvania Dutch country. It is not a stuffing, but a potato side dish. The dish is not one of the prettiest, but the flavor makes up for it, as does its popularity with men and children.

      4 tablespoons butter
      1 medium onion, minced
        bread cubes, made from 3 slices stale white bread
        without crusts
    4-5 cups hot mashed potatoes
      2 tablespoons minced celery
      2 tablespoons minced parsley
        salt
        freshly ground pepper
      ½ cup hot milk
      ½ cup hot chicken bouillon
      1 egg, beaten

Heat 3 tablespoons of butter in a large heavy frying pan. Add the onion and cook, stirring constantly, until soft but still white. Add the bread cubes. Stirring with a fork, cook until onion and bread cubes are golden. Add the hot mashed potatoes and mix well. Beat in the celery, parsley, salt, and pepper. Combine the hot milk and hot bouillon and gradually stir into mixture. Beat until light with a wooden spoon, or, better, with an electric beater. Beat in the beaten egg. Turn mixture into a buttered 2-quart baking dish. Dot with remaining butter. Bake in a preheated moderate oven (350°) for 20–30 minutes or until golden.

Note:
This may also be made with either 1 cup milk or 1 cup chicken bouillon, but the mixture is best.

6 SERVINGS

SCALLOPED POTATOES

All-American

Since potatoes, depending on their age and kind, absorb liquids differently, a little more cream or milk may have to be added during cooking. Scalding the cream—or milk— helps to prevent the sauce from being curdled by the enzymes in the raw potatoes.

4 cups thinly sliced potatoes (about ⅛- to ¼-inch thick)
⅔ cup minced onions
  salt
  freshly ground pepper
2 tablespoons flour
3–4 tablespoons butter
1½ cups light cream or milk, scalded

Layer the potatoes and onions in a generously buttered 2-quart baking dish. Sprinkle each layer with a little salt and pepper, flour, and 1–2 tablespoons of the butter. Dot top with the remaining butter. Pour the scalded cream over the potatoes. Cover baking dish with a lid or with aluminum foil. Cook in a preheated moderate oven (350°) for about 40 minutes. Uncover and cook for 20 more minutes or until potatoes are tender and golden on top and almost all the liquid has been absorbed.

VARIATION:

Substitute 1 or 2 cups peeled sliced celeriac for 1 or 2 cups of the potatoes.

4 SERVINGS

SWEET-POTATO PONE

From South Carolina

I find this a welcome change from the usual baked sweet potatoes. Serve as a side dish with meats or poultry.

1¼ cups boiling water
  4 tablespoons butter
2½ pounds sweet potatoes, peeled and grated to make about 4 cups
  salt
  freshly ground pepper

2   teaspoons ground allspice
½   teaspoon ground mace
    grated rind of ½ lemon
2   tablespoons sugar

Boil the water in a large saucepan. Add 2 tablespoons of the butter and stir until melted. Add the sweet potatoes, salt, pepper, allspice, mace, lemon rind, and sugar. Mix thoroughly. Turn into a generously buttered 2-quart baking dish. Dot with the remaining butter. Cook in a preheated moderate oven (350°) for about 1 hour or until firm.

6 SERVINGS

SPINACH AT ITS BEST

An eternal verity: fresh spinach always tastes better than frozen spinach. This is the perfect way to cook it.

Choose fresh spinach that is bright, crisp, and green. Cut off the tough stems and blemished leaves, and wash the spinach in several changes of water. Put it into a large pot with the water that clings to the leaves. Cover and cook over high heat for 3–4 minutes (depending on the amount) or until the spinach is barely cooked. Drain, and with a spoon squeeze it as dry as possible. (The spinach does not have to be as dry as when you put it into a soufflé; see following recipe.) Return to pot, season with salt and a generous amount of freshly ground pepper, and add butter—the more the better. Heat through quickly and serve immediately, very hot.

SPINACH SOUFFLÉ

From the Midwest

If more soufflé is wanted, it is better to make two soufflés rather than to double the quantities of the ingredients and make them in one dish.

1½ pounds fresh spinach, or 2 10-ounce packages
       frozen spinach, thawed
   3 tablespoons butter
   3 tablespoons flour
   1 cup half-and-half or light cream or milk
       salt
       freshly ground pepper
  ⅛ teaspoon ground nutmeg
  ¼ pound (1 cup) grated Swiss cheese
   4 eggs, separated

Remove all the tough stems and damaged leaves from fresh
spinach and cut the large leaves into 2 or 4 pieces. Wash in several
changes of water. Put the spinach into a saucepan with the water
that clings to the leaves. Cover, and cook over high heat for about 3
minutes or until barely tender. Drain and squeeze dry; this is best
done with the hands. (Or cook thawed frozen spinach according to
package directions, drain, and squeeze dry.) Reserve spinach. Heat
the butter in a saucepan large enough to take all the ingredients.
Stir in the flour and cook, stirring constantly, for 2 minutes. Stir in
the half-and-half or cream or milk and cook over low heat, stirring
constantly, until thick and smooth. Add the cheese and stir until
melted. Add the spinach and mix well. Remove from heat and cool
to lukewarm. Beat the egg yolks until thick and beat them into the
spinach mixture. Beat the egg whites until stiff but not dry and fold
into spinach mixture. Turn into a generously buttered 1½- to 2-
quart baking dish. Bake in a preheated slow oven (325°) for about
30 minutes or until set. Serve immediately.

4 SERVINGS

BAKED ACORN SQUASH WITH BOURBON

From Tennessee

3 medium acorn squashes
6 teaspoons butter
6 teaspoons light-brown or dark-brown sugar
6 teaspoons bourbon
  salt
  freshly ground pepper
  ground mace

Cut squashes into halves and remove seeds. Place the halves side by side in a buttered baking dish. Into each half, put 1 teaspoon butter, 1 teaspoon brown sugar, and 1 teaspoon bourbon. Sprinkle lightly with salt, pepper, and a pinch of mace. Cover dish tightly with aluminum foil; if necessary, tie the foil on with string. Bake in a preheated moderate oven (375°) for about 45 minutes or until tender. (Test tenderness with a toothpick or a cake tester.) Uncover and serve hot, with extra butter if desired.

6 SERVINGS

BAKED MASHED SQUASH

A Boston version of an All-American dish

Can be easily doubled or tripled.

2 pounds butternut squash or other winter squash
⅔ cup heavy cream
  salt
  freshly ground pepper
  pinch of ground allspice or nutmeg or ginger
  or mace (optional)

Cut the squash into halves lengthwise. Remove seeds and stringy parts. Place cut side down in a shallow baking dish. Add about ½-inch water. Bake in a preheated moderate oven (375°) for about 30 minutes or until tender; baking time depends on the kind of squash. Cool slightly and scrape out the pulp. Mash pulp with a fork. Place in a saucepan and beat in the cream. Season with salt and plenty of pepper and a little allspice or other spice if desired. (I don't use spices because I like the pristine flavor of squash.) Heat thoroughly and serve hot.

3–4 SERVINGS

SQUASH SOUFFLÉ

From New York State

This soufflé can be made from any firm yellow squash, but not from the zucchini-like yellow summer squash. It is possible to use only 4 egg whites, but 6 egg whites make a lighter soufflé.

    3 tablespoons butter
    3 tablespoons flour
 1⅓ cups light cream or half-and-half
 1½ cups cooked puréed yellow squash, on the dry side
    4 egg yolks
      salt
      freshly ground pepper
      Tabasco to taste
    6 egg whites
  ½ teaspoon cream of tartar

Heat the butter and stir in the flour. Cook, stirring constantly, for 2 minutes. Stir in the cream or half-and-half and cook, stirring all the time, until smooth and thickened. Beat in the squash and mix well. Remove from heat and stir in the egg yolks, one at a time, beating well after each addition. Season with salt, pepper, and Tabasco; this soufflé should be well seasoned. Beat the egg whites until frothy and add the cream of tartar. Beat until stiff and glossy. Fold gently into squash mixture. Generously butter a 1½-quart baking dish. Turn mixture into dish. Set in a pan containing 2 inches of water. Cook in a preheated moderate oven (350°) until firm and puffy. Serve immediately on heated plates.

5–6 SERVINGS

CALABACITA

From New Mexico

You will need a deep 12-inch frying pan for this.

3 tablespoons bacon fat or shortening
1 medium onion, chopped
1 garlic clove, minced
2 pounds zucchini, trimmed and cut into ½-inch pieces
1 cup corn kernels, fresh, canned, or frozen
1 sweet green or red pepper, cut into strips
salt
freshly ground pepper

Heat the fat in a large deep frying pan. Add all the vegetables. Cook over medium-to-high heat, stirring constantly, for about 5 minutes or until almost all the liquid given up by the vegetables has cooked away; the vegetables should be just tender and crisp. Season with salt and pepper and serve hot.

6 SERVINGS

TOMATOES À LA CRÈME

From a Connecticut hostess

I had this served to me as a first course, and I in turn have served it with broiled fish and with roast or broiled chicken.

6 large ripe but firm tomatoes
3 tablespoons butter
  salt
½ cup heavy cream
  freshly ground pepper

Do not peel the tomatoes. Cut off a thin slice at the stem end. Cut the tomatoes into halves crosswise. Heat the butter in a large frying pan, preferably one that can go to the table, or in a flame-proof shallow baking dish. When the butter is bubbling, add the tomatoes, cut side down. Puncture the rounded side with the point of a kitchen knife 2 or 3 times. Cook over medium heat for about 3–4 minutes. Turn the tomatoes over with a pancake turner. Sprinkle lightly with salt. Cook for 3 more minutes. Turn again with a pancake turner, to let the juices run out. Stir the cream into the pan juices and blend it in. Sprinkle with a little more salt if necessary and sprinkle with the pepper. When the sauce is very hot and bubbly, serve immediately from the pan or baking dish, or turn into a heated serving dish.

4 SERVINGS

AUNT HARRIET'S
FRIED GREEN TOMATOES

From Connecticut

This formidable lady, lover of good food, added the garlic touch which improves the dish.

4 large firm green tomatoes, sliced ⅜-inch thick
  cornmeal
1 garlic clove, cut in half
3 tablespoons butter
  salt
  freshly ground pepper
  light-brown or dark-brown sugar
½ cup heavy cream
  hot buttered toast

Dip the tomatoes into cornmeal and coat on all sides, shaking off excess cornmeal. Rub the frying pan thoroughly with the cut ends of the garlic; throw away garlic. Heat the butter over medium heat. Add tomato slices in one layer. Season each slice with salt and pepper and about ¼ teaspoon brown sugar. Cook about 3 minutes and turn carefully with pancake turner. Season other side too. Turn heat to low (300°). Simmer covered for about 5–8 minutes or until crisp. Place a slice of hot buttered toast on each of 4 heated plates. Top with tomato slices and keep warm. Stir the cream into the frying pan and bring to boiling point. Remove from heat and spoon over tomatoes. Serve hot.

4 SERVINGS

TURNIP OR PARSNIP STEW

From New England

Use as a lunch or supper main dish.

    4 cups diced turnips or parsnips
    2 cups peeled, diced potatoes
    ⅔ cup diced salt pork
    4 cups hot milk
    2 tablespoons flour
    2 tablespoons water
      salt
      freshly ground pepper
      dash Tabasco (optional)

Combine turnips, or parsnips, and potatoes in a saucepan and add water to cover. Simmer covered over low heat for about 10 minutes or until tender. In a small frying pan, brown the salt pork. Add to vegetables, along with the milk. Combine the flour and water and stir to a smooth paste. Stir into vegetable mixture. Cook, stirring constantly, until thickened. Season with salt and pepper and stir in Tabasco if used. Serve hot.

4–6 SERVINGS

VEGETABLE STEW

From California

1 medium eggplant, peeled and cut into 2-inch cubes
  salt
½ cup olive oil
2 large onions, thinly sliced
2 garlic cloves, minced
2 large sweet red or green peppers, cut into strips
4 large tomatoes, peeled and chopped
4 small zucchini or yellow summer squashes, sliced,
  or 2 of each
1 cup fresh sliced okra
2 cups fresh corn kernels
  freshly ground pepper
3 tablespoons minced fresh basil leaves or 1
  tablespoon dried basil
⅓ cup minced parsley

Sprinkle the eggplant with about 2 tablespoons salt and place in a colander. Weigh down with a plate topped by a full bowl of water or several cans of food. Stand in sink and let stand for about 30 minutes, to drain off excess moisture. In a heavy casserole, heat the olive oil over low heat. The oil must be warm but must not smoke. Add the onions, garlic, peppers, and eggplant. Over low heat, cook but *do not fry or brown* vegetables for about 30 minutes or until very soft. Add tomatoes, squash, okra, and corn. Taste for saltiness (eggplant may be salty) and season with salt and pepper. Simmer covered over low heat for 15 minutes. Add the basil and parsley and simmer without a cover for 15–25 minutes to let excess moisture evaporate. The stew should not be too soupy but neither should it be dry. Serve with ham or cold cuts, or as a main dish with corn bread.

6 SERVINGS

Salads

COLESLAW WITH
SOUR-CREAM DRESSING

All-American

Using both red and green cabbage makes for a nicer-looking dish. For crisp cabbage, shred cabbage and set in a bowl of ice water. Refrigerate for 1–2 hours. Drain and dry between paper towels.

    2 cups finely shredded green cabbage
    2 cups finely shredded red cabbage
    ¼ cup finely diced celery
    ⅓ cup finely chopped onion
      Sour-Cream Dressing (see following recipe)
    2 tablespoons minced pimiento
    2 tablespoons minced parsley

Put the cabbage, celery, and onion into a salad bowl. Add Sour-Cream Dressing and pimiento. Mix lightly and sprinkle with parsley.

4–6 SERVINGS

SOUR-CREAM DRESSING

    ¼ cup sour cream
      salt
      freshly ground pepper

1 teaspoon ground horseradish, or ⅛ teaspoon Tabasco
1 tablespoon cider vinegar
1 teaspoon lemon juice

Combine ingredients and mix well. Refrigerate covered until used.

MAKES ABOUT ⅓ CUP

WILTED LETTUCE

Midwestern

This salad is best served immediately after mixing.

6 slices bacon, preferably lean, cut into ¼-inch dice
⅓ cup white or cider vinegar
2 bunches leaf lettuce, washed, dried, and shredded,
or 4 cups shredded lettuce
¼ cup minced scallions
¼ to ½ teaspoon salt
¼ teaspoon freshly ground pepper
2 teaspoons sugar
2 hard-cooked eggs, chopped

In a large frying pan, cook the bacon until crisp. If bacon is fat, pour off all but 4–6 tablespoons of fat. Add the vinegar to bacon and fat. Heat through over very low heat. Remove from heat and add the lettuce, scallions, salt, pepper, and sugar. Toss 1–2 minutes to wilt the lettuce. Add the chopped eggs and toss again.

4 SERVINGS

SOUR-CREAM POTATO SALAD

German-American from Illinois

2 pounds new or waxy potatoes
⅓ cup French dressing (made with equal parts salad oil and mild vinegar)
1 cup finely diced celery (white part only)
¼ cup chopped sweet pickles
¼ cup drained chopped pimiento
2 hard-cooked eggs, coarsely chopped
1 tablespoon prepared mustard
1 teaspoon salt
¼ teaspoon freshly ground pepper
1 cup sour cream
⅓ cup minced parsley
2 hard-cooked eggs, sliced
paprika

Cook the potatoes until tender but still firm; they must not be mushy. Peel and, while still hot, cut into ½-inch slices. Put into a large bowl. (There should be about 4–5 cups.) Add the French dressing to the hot potatoes and toss carefully with a fork so as not to break the slices. Cool thoroughly. Add all the other ingredients except the parsley, sliced hard-cooked eggs, and paprika. Again toss carefully to blend. Chill for 1 hour, but do not overchill. At serving time, turn into a serving dish and sprinkle with the parsley, top with the hard-cooked egg slices, and sprinkle with a little paprika.

6 SERVINGS

SPINACH, BACON, AND MUSHROOM SALAD

All-American

As with all salads, adjust amount and flavors of dressing to individual tastes. It is essential that the salad be made with fresh, young, small spinach leaves only; use the big leaves for cooked spinach.

6 tablespoons olive oil or salad oil
3 tablespoons wine vinegar
1 garlic clove, mashed
2 teaspoons Dijon mustard or other prepared mustard
   salt
   freshly ground pepper
¼ pound mushrooms, thinly sliced
6–8 slices bacon
1½ to 2 pounds fresh spinach (amount depends on size of leaves)
¼ cup minced chives or parsley

Make the dressing by combining the oil, vinegar, garlic, mustard, salt, and pepper. Mix well. Put the mushrooms into a salad bowl and pour the dressing over them. Toss to mix. Cook the bacon until crisp; drain and crumble. Reserve. Trim the spinach, selecting only the young, small, and tender leaves for the salad. Wash in several changes of water. Drain and dry between paper towels. At serving time, add crumbled bacon and spinach to mushrooms, toss, and sprinkle with chives or parsley. Serve immediately.

4–6 SERVINGS

TOMATO ASPIC

All-American

Tomato aspic does not deserve to be forgotten since it is nice with chicken or seafood salads. To my mind, it is also one of the very, very few gelatin affairs (so prettily called congealed salads in Southern cookbooks) worth eating. It is tastier made with canned or fresh tomatoes than with tomato juice. As a matter of fact, it is rather like eating a well-spiced nonalcoholic Bloody Mary.

1 2-pound 3-ounce can Italian-style tomatoes (4 cups), or 4 pounds fresh tomatoes, peeled, seeded, and coarsely chopped to make 4 cups pulp
2 teaspoons dried basil
2 teaspoons celery salt
¼ teaspoon salt
¼ teaspoon freshly ground pepper
⅛ teaspoon Tabasco
⅛ teaspoon Worcestershire sauce
2 tablespoons (2 envelopes) unflavored gelatin
½ cup water
juice of 1 lemon

Combine the tomatoes, basil, celery salt, salt, pepper, Tabasco, and Worcestershire sauce. Purée in a blender or food processor or push through a food mill; the last method will remove seeds better, but you can always strain blended or processed tomatoes. Measure 1½ cups of purée into a bowl. Sprinkle the gelatin over the water and stir to mix. Add gelatin mixture and lemon juice to 1½ cups purée and stir to mix. Put the remaining purée in a saucepan and bring to boiling point. Simmer without a cover over low heat for 3 minutes. Stir into the cold purée, blending thoroughly. Cool to room temperature, stirring occasionally. Rinse a 1½-quart mold, preferably a ring mold, with cold water. Pour in purée. Chill until set. At serving time, run a knife around edges of mold and set mold in warm water for 1–2 seconds. Invert over a serving dish. Serve as is, or filled with any mayonnaise salad.

Note:

This amount of aspic will also go into a 1-quart mold, but so close to the edge that it easily slops over when being handled.

6–8 SERVINGS

WALDORF SALAD

From New York

We forget how good this is. It must be freshly made.

  2 cups diced celery, white part only (about ½-inch dice)
  2 cups diced, unpeeled apples, preferably red (about ½-inch dice)
  1 cup chopped walnuts or pecans
1¼ cups mayonnaise or Boiled Salad Dressing (p. 194) or to taste
    salt
    freshly ground pepper
    salad greens

Combine the celery, apples, walnuts, and dressing and mix well. Taste (the dressing may be sufficiently seasoned) and if necessary season with salt and pepper. Serve piled on a bed of salad greens.

6 SERVINGS

GOLDEN GLOW SALAD

Midwestern

An old-time gelatin salad for which some people have nostalgia.

    1 cup pineapple juice less 2 tablespoons
    1 cup boiling water less 2 tablespoons
    1 package lemon-flavored gelatin
    2 cups grated carrots
    1 cup drained crushed canned pineapple
  ½ cup chopped pecans
      lettuce
      mayonnaise

Combine the pineapple juice and boiling water and bring to boiling point. Pour over the gelatin and stir until gelatin is completely dissolved. Chill. When mixture is about to set, stir in the carrots, pineapple, and pecans and mix well. Turn into a rinsed 1½-quart mold and chill until firm. Unmold on a bed of lettuce and serve with mayonnaise.

6–8 SERVINGS

Sauces and Dressings

A Note on Sauces

※

American cooking prides itself on its plainness, and there was a time when the presence of a sauce on a dish was taken as proof that the dish needed to be gussied up. This section, therefore, is necessarily short, but other sauces and gravies to accompany particular dishes appear in the book following the dishes in which they are used. These, like the ones included here, are listed in the index under sauces.

WHITE SAUCE

All-American

This sauce is used by itself or as the base for mustard, horseradish, cheese, egg, and parsley sauces. The liquid may be milk or half milk and half light cream or broth only or broth combined with milk or cream. This is the French Béchamel Sauce, a most practical sauce that allows many variations.

- 2 tablespoons butter
- 2 tablespoons flour
- 1 cup hot milk or broth or a combination of both
  - salt
  - freshly ground pepper
  - ground nutmeg (optional)

Over low heat, melt the butter in a heavy saucepan. Stir in the flour, preferably with a wooden spoon. Cook, stirring constantly, for 2–3 minutes or until well blended; do not brown. Remove the saucepan from the heat and stir in the hot liquid. Keep stirring until smooth. Return to low heat and cook, stirring all the while, for 3–4 minutes, or until thickened and smooth. Season with salt, pepper, and nutmeg (if desired) to taste. Use the sauce as is, or to make the three following recipes. If the sauce is not to be used straightaway, cut a piece of waxed paper large enough to fit inside the saucepan. Butter one side of the paper and lay it, buttered side down, on the sauce. This prevents a skin from forming on the surface of the sauce.

MAKES ABOUT 1 CUP MEDIUM SAUCE

WARM HORSERADISH SAUCE

All-American

1–2 tablespoons drained bottled horseradish, squeezed
   dry, or to taste, or 1–2 tablespoons fresh grated horseradish, moistened with 1 tablespoon fresh lemon juice
  1 cup hot White Sauce (see preceding recipe)

Stir the horseradish into the hot sauce and mix well. Serve
with boiled beef, corned beef, or chicken.

MAKES ABOUT 1 CUP

WARM MUSTARD SAUCE

All-American

1–2 tablespoons Dijon mustard or other prepared mustard
   or to taste
  1 cup hot White Sauce (page 188)

Stir the mustard into the hot sauce and mix well. Simmer for
2–3 minutes. Serve with boiled or broiled fish or shrimp.

MAKES ABOUT 1 CUP

CHEESE SAUCE

All-American

½ cup grated sharp Cheddar or grated Swiss cheese
1 cup hot White Sauce (page 188)
    dash Tabasco (optional)

Stir the cheese into the hot sauce and mix well. Add a dash of Tabasco. Simmer over very low heat, stirring constantly, until cheese is melted. Quickly remove from heat or cheese may become stringy. Serve with hot vegetables.

MAKES ABOUT 1 CUP

PARSLEY SAUCE

From New England

For corned beef, boiled fish, and vegetables.

4 tablespoons butter
4 tablespoons flour
1 cup chicken, beef, or fish bouillon, or liquid from
    cooking corned beef
1 cup light cream or half-and-half
    salt
    freshly ground pepper
1 cup minced parsley leaves
    juice of ½ lemon

Heat the butter in a saucepan and stir in the flour. Cook, stirring constantly, for about 1 minute. Stir in the bouillon or corned beef liquid and cook, stirring constantly, until thickened. Stir in the cream or half-and-half. Add salt if needed (the bouillon may be salty) and pepper. Cook over low heat, stirring constantly, for about 5 minutes or until thickened and smooth. Stir in the parsley and cook for 2 more minutes. Remove from heat and stir in the lemon juice. Serve hot.

MAKES 2 CUPS

TOMATO SAUCE

Italian-American

3 pounds fresh ripe plum tomatoes, cut into halves and
  seeded, or 4 cups Italian-style canned tomatoes (1
  2-pound 3-ounce can) drained, plus 1 cup of the juice
1 medium onion, cut in half
1 medium carrot, minced
1 celery stalk, minced
  salt
  freshly ground pepper
¼ cup minced parsley
⅓ cup bacon fat or olive oil or salad oil

In a heavy saucepan, place the tomatoes, tomato juice, one half of the onion, the carrot, celery, salt, and pepper to taste, and the parsley. Bring quickly to boiling point. Cook over high heat, stirring constantly, for about 3–4 minutes or until tomatoes are soft. Purée in a blender, food processor, or food mill. Strain. Mince the remaining half onion, and cook in bacon fat or oil until soft. Add strained tomatoes and check seasoning. Cook over medium heat, stirring frequently, for 5–10 minutes, no longer. The quick cooking preserves the fresh flavor of the tomatoes.

MAKES ABOUT 4 CUPS

HELEN BROWN'S
HOTTISH BARBECUE SAUCE

From California

The late Helen Brown was one of the most talented—and personally charming—cooks America has ever brought forth. Her recipes, developed in the '40s, '50s, and early '60s, are as good as ever. All her books are most worthwhile to own, especially Helen Brown's West Coast Cook Book *(Boston: Little, Brown, 1952, 1956), from which the following recipe is taken verbatim. The books are out-of-print, but I urge readers to try to get secondhand copies; the* West Coast Cook Book *is to this day the best, and a superior best, of any written on the subject. Barbecue sauces come in endless, personal variations—ah well, to each his or her own, or should it be her or his own?*

4 cloves garlic
1 tablespoon salt
1 cup olive or salad oil
½ cup vinegar
1 small onion
1 small green pepper
1 tablespoon chili powder
1 cup tomato juice
1 teaspoon oregano

Squash 4 cloves of garlic with a tablespoon of salt. Add a cup of olive oil or salad oil, ½ cup vinegar, a small onion, minced, a small green pepper, minced, a tablespoon (that's a lot) of chili powder, a cup of tomato juice, and a teaspoon of oregano. Simmer this for 10 minutes, and strain before using. There's nothing to prevent your adding Worcestershire, Tabasco, mustard, cayenne, smoked salt or even sugar to this recipe if that's what you want—but I won't have any part of it.

MAKES ABOUT 2 ¾ CUPS

CREAMY COLD
HORSERADISH SAUCE

All-American

*You may substitute ½ cup well-drained bottled horseradish
for the fresh ingredient and omit the vinegar or lemon
juice. Fresh horseradish should be grated just before using.
For boiled meats, ham, and sausages.*

¾ cup grated fresh horseradish root
 1 tablespoon vinegar or lemon juice
 1 teaspoon sugar (optional)
    salt
    freshly ground pepper, preferably white pepper
 1 cup heavy cream

Put the grated horseradish into a small bowl. Stir in the vinegar or lemon juice, sugar (if used), salt, and pepper. In another bowl, whip the cream until stiff. Stir horseradish into cream and mix well. Chill quickly before serving. Serve soon after making, since the ingredients tend to separate upon standing.

MAKES ABOUT 1½ CUPS

SHRIMP COCKTAIL SAUCE

All-American

½ cup tomato ketchup
¾ cup chili sauce
 1 small garlic clove, mashed
 1 tablespoon grated onion
 1 tablespoon horseradish (drain if bottled)
 2 teaspoons minced celery
 1 tablespoon lemon juice
 1 teaspoon Worcestershire sauce

Combine all ingredients and mix well. Cover and refrigerate for 2 hours, stirring occasionally. Serve with cooked shrimp.

MAKES 1½ CUPS

BOILED SALAD DRESSING

All-American

Boiled dressings flourished in the age before vinaigrette became popular and before there was ready access to olive oil or salad oil. Today they are mainly used on coleslaw, yet they are also good instead of mayonnaise on chicken or shrimp salad. Many boiled dressings date from an age with blander and sweeter tastes than ours, when vinegars seem to have been less powerful. I have found that white, cider, and malt vinegars (wine vinegars are not good for boiled dressings) all vary greatly in acidity and need adjusting slightly according to taste and food; coleslaw needs a stronger vinegar flavor than chicken salad.

    2 tablespoons flour
 1½ tablespoons sugar
    1 teaspoon salt
    1 teaspoon ground mustard
  ½ cup water
    2 tablespoons butter
    2 egg yolks
    2 tablespoons white, cider, or malt vinegar
  ¼ cup heavy cream or sour cream

Sift the flour, sugar, salt, and mustard into the top of a double boiler. Stir in the water and blend until smooth. Cook over boiling water, stirring constantly, until thick and smooth. Beat in the butter. Beat the egg yolks and vinegar together and stir into water mixture, beating constantly, cook until thickened. Remove from heat and cool to lukewarm, stirring occasionally. Then stir in the cream and mix well.

MAKES ABOUT 1½ CUPS

PEACH CHUTNEY

From New York

*My neighbors and friends Letty Warner and Nona Clarke
make this every year. The procedure is somewhat more
elaborate than for other chutneys since the ingredients
are simmered separately part of the time. The reason is
that if they are simmered together from the beginning
the fruit completely loses its character before the syrup
thickens sufficiently. This rule, by the way, applies to any
chutney made with soft fruit, such as mango or plum.*

     15 pounds peaches (about 40 medium-sized peaches)
      2 pounds white sugar
      2 quarts cider vinegar
      3 pounds light-brown or dark-brown sugar
      1 pound golden raisins
      6 garlic cloves
         yellow rind of 1 lemon, chopped
    6–8 ounces fresh green ginger, peeled and chopped
         coarsely
      1 pound onions, chopped
      1 tablespoon salt
    3–4 tablespoons ground coriander
    3–4 tablespoons mustard seed
    1–3 teaspoons chili powder
    1–2 teaspoons ground cinnamon
      1 teaspoon ground cloves

Use heavy stainless steel, iron, or porcelain-coated saucepans
rather than aluminum ware. Do not peel peaches. Wash them and
with a terry-cloth towel rub off most of the fuzz. Pit peaches and
slice thin or cut into ¼-inch chunks. Put peaches into a large kettle
and add the white sugar. Simmer without a cover over low heat
until the peaches give up at least 1 quart liquid. Stir frequently.
Remove from heat. Pour off the syrup into a heavy saucepan and
reserve the peaches. Over low heat, simmer the syrup until it has
the consistency of heavy pancake batter. Stir very frequently to
prevent scorching. Remove from heat and reserve. In another heavy

saucepan, combine 1½ quarts of the vinegar, the brown sugar, and ¾ pound of the raisins. Over low heat and without a cover, simmer for about 1 hour or until thickened. Remove from heat and reserve. In a blender or food processor, blend the remaining ½ quart vinegar with the remaining ¼ pound raisins, the garlic, lemon rind, and one-half the ginger. (This may have to be done in several batches.) In a large heavy kettle, combine peaches, peach syrup, vinegar, brown sugar, and raisin mixture, and blended vinegar mixture and mix thoroughly. Stir in the remaining ginger, the onions, salt, coriander, mustard seed, chili powder, cinnamon, and cloves. Blend to mix well. Simmer without a cover over low heat, stirring frequently to prevent scorching, for 1–1½ hours or to desired thickness. Ladle boiling chutney into sterilized pint jars to ⅛-inch from top. Wipe rims and seal. The chutney can also be kept in unsterilized containers in the refrigerator for at least 1 month.

VARIATION:

This same recipe serves for ripe mangoes or plums.

MAKES ABOUT 12 PINT JARS

KAY'S CRANBERRY KETCHUP

From Cape Cod

    4 cups fresh cranberries, chopped fine
    1 teaspoon ground cinnamon
    1 teaspoon ground cloves
    1 teaspoon ground allspice
    2 cups sugar
    ½ teaspoon salt
    1 cup vinegar
      dash of cayenne
    1 teaspoon pepper

Combine all the ingredients. Bring to the boiling point. Lower the heat and cook, stirring constantly, for about 5 minutes, or until the mixture is thick. If necessary, add a little water to prevent scorching. Store in sterilized containers or in refrigerator. Good with rich meats.

MAKES ABOUT 4 CUPS

MAPLE SYRUP AND NUT SAUCE

From Vermont

For ice cream and puddings.

2 cups maple syrup
½ cup chopped walnuts or butternuts

Pour the maple syrup into a small heavy saucepan. Cook over low heat, stirring frequently, until reduced to about half. Remove from heat and stir in the nuts. Serve warm.

MAKES ABOUT 1½ CUPS

WHIPPED-CREAM SAUCE

From New York

To serve over fresh berries or stewed pears.

1 cup heavy cream
2 tablespoons sifted confectioners' sugar
½ cup sour cream
1 teaspoon vanilla extract

Whip the heavy cream until it forms soft peaks. Stir in the sugar, sour cream, and the vanilla. Chill 10 minutes before serving.

MAKES ABOUT 1½ CUPS

Hot Breads, Pancakes, and Doughnuts

Thoughts on Biscuits

* * *

The nostalgia provoked by homemade biscuits is easily assuaged by making them rather than buying them in a refrigerated can. Biscuits are not difficult to make, and one gets better with practice. They are worthwhile since they add a bit of glamour to an ordinary meal, as do muffins and popovers. There are different rules for their making, with more or with less baking powder, milk, and so on. The formulas that follow these thoughts are the ones I found to work best after ample experimentation.

As in all baking, bleached white flour (ordinary all-purpose flour) makes a slightly lighter product than unbleached white flour.

I like light biscuits, and I use all-purpose flour. However, all flours vary a little from brand to brand and regionally as well. I find that 2 teaspoons of baking powder are needed for *each* cup of flour when making fluffy risen biscuits. When baking powder or baking soda (used in buttermilk biscuits) is not *thoroughly* mixed in with the flour, little brown spots appear on the baked biscuits.

Lard makes flakier biscuits than other fats but alone makes too lardy-tasting biscuits. I combine lard and butter. The two following recipes can also be made with such other fats as hydrogenated shortening or margarine, used exclusively, though the flavor and texture will be somewhat different.

Buttermilk biscuits, which I prefer because I think that baking with buttermilk results in a tenderer product, contain baking soda. They rise higher and are fluffier if allowed to stand for 5–10 minutes after being cut out and before being baked.

Biscuits should be cut out with a sharp-edged cutter, brought down into the dough in a straight-down motion. This makes for a biscuit that rises more evenly. A duller-edged cutter requires a twist motion in cutting the biscuit that can result in lopsided biscuits.

For crisp sides, bake biscuits on a baking sheet about 1½ inches apart. For soft-sided biscuits, place almost touching in baking pan. For truly hot biscuits, bake in a pie pan that can be brought to the table and serve the biscuits from the pan.

For a shiny-topped biscuit, brush unbaked biscuits with melted butter or milk before baking.

To reheat biscuits, wrap in foil and heat in a preheated moderate oven (350°) for 10 minutes.

BAKING-POWDER
SWEET-MILK BISCUITS

All-American

2 cups all-purpose flour (sifted before measuring)
¾ teaspoon salt
4 teaspoons baking powder

3 tablespoons lard
3 tablespoons butter
⅔ to ¾ cup milk

Sift together the flour, salt, and baking powder into a bowl. Cut in the lard and butter with fingertips, two knives, or a pastry blender until mixture is the texture of coarse meal. Add ⅔ cup of milk. Stir briskly with fork only until dough just holds together in a ball. Add remaining milk only if necessary to get dough to stick together. Turn dough onto a floured board and knead gently 7 or 8 times or until the dough holds together. Again lightly flour the board. Roll out dough gently to the thickness of ⅓ inch, using no more pressure than the weight of the rolling pin or bottle you may be using. If necessary, lightly flour rolling pin. Fold dough over and lightly roll out again, this time to the thickness of ½ inch. With a sharp-edged cutter about 2½ inches in diameter, cut out biscuits, using a straight-down motion. Gather up scraps, roll and cut again. Place on ungreased baking sheet about 1½ inches apart. Bake in a preheated hot oven (450°) for 10–15 minutes or until golden brown.

ABOUT 10–12 BISCUITS

BUTTERMILK BISCUITS

All-American

2 cups all-purpose flour (sifted before measuring)
1 teaspoon salt
3 teaspoons baking powder
¼ teaspoon baking soda
3 tablespoons lard
3 tablespoons butter
⅔ to ¾ cup buttermilk

Proceed as for Baking-Powder Sweet-Milk Biscuits (see preceding recipe), but let cut biscuits stand at room temperature for 10 minutes before baking.

ABOUT 10–12 BISCUITS

MR. HAMPTON ALLEN'S
BEATEN BISCUITS

From North Carolina

Beaten biscuits are one of the foods upon which nostalgia feasts. Nostalgia inspired several Southern friends to make biscuits for this book, biscuits that came up to their memories. They fussed with the formula, trying different combinations of shortening, varied measurements by the ½ teaspoonful and beat from 30 minutes to 1 hour with rolling pin and cleaver or mallet or even processed the dough in a food processor. The biscuits were not what they had been in North Carolina, Alabama, and other points south; we thought our New York flour might have differed, or possibly the lard, the best shortening for biscuits (rather than combined with butter or vegetable shortening). Then Mr. Hampton Allen, from Anson County, North Carolina, came up with the recipe that follows and that did make the biscuits that nostalgia (and the taste of many testers) thought just right. Mr. Allen is a retired feed-mill owner and businessman interested in keeping the old arts alive, as he does in making beaten biscuits, almost a lost cause in the new South. He makes them in an old beaten-biscuit machine that works somewhat like a pasta machine, with two big rollers pounding and flattening the dough. A welcome relief from the old-time beating, though the biscuits have to be in the machine for at least 30 minutes. Mr. Allen's machine has been in continuous use for at least seventy years. Again, these biscuits may not come up to individual nostalgias, but such is life. On the practical side, if you're going to all the trouble of making these biscuits, it is worth making a lot since they keep well in an airtight container.

- 6 cups flour (sifted before measuring)
- 4 tablespoons sugar
- 2 teaspoons salt
- 1 teaspoon baking powder
- 1 cup lard
- ⅔ cup milk
- ⅓ cup water

Sift together the flour, sugar, salt, and baking powder in a large bowl. With the fingers, a pastry cutter, or two knives cut in the lard until the mixture resembles cornmeal. Gradually and alternately add milk and water, but only enough to make a very stiff dough. Knead dough with hands for 3–4 minutes or until it will hold together—otherwise it will fly into bits when beaten. Place dough on a firm flat surface. Beat with a rolling pin, the flat side of a cleaver, or a mallet. It is not necessary to hit with force; beat only hard enough to flatten the dough gradually to about ½ inch thickness. As you beat, fold the dough over on itself frequently, beating and folding for anywhere from 25 to 40 minutes, though the longer the beating the better. Dough will become shiny and rubbery. It may begin to pop as you beat. This is caused by air blisters and when this happens and the surface of the dough looks like satin it has been sufficiently beaten. However, no more than 40 minutes beating is necessary even if the dough does not blister or look satiny; this is because some modern flours don't produce this traditional effect. With a rolling pin, roll out dough to a thickness of about ¼ inch. Fold over and roll out to the thickness of about ⅓ inch. (This step will make the baked biscuits easy to break open in the traditional manner.) Cut with any round cutter 1½-inch in diameter. (Better still, if you have inherited one, is a beaten-biscuit cutter with built-in tines for piercing the biscuits.) Prick the center of each biscuit three times with the tines of a fork, making sure to push all the way through the dough. Place biscuits on lightly greased baking sheets. Bake in a preheated slow-to-moderate oven (325° to 350°) for about 30 minutes or until biscuits are beginning to turn a pale gold. Turn off heat, open oven door, and leave biscuits in oven for 5 minutes. Close oven door and cool biscuits in oven; taking these steps after baking seems to mellow the biscuits. Store in airtight containers until ready to serve with slivers of Southern ham.

ABOUT 5 DOZEN BISCUITS

MUFFINS

All-American

Contrary to some current opinion, muffins are easy to make and a blessing for giving a simple meal more interest.

      2 cups flour
      1 tablespoon baking powder
      1 tablespoon sugar
      ½ teaspoon salt
      1 egg, lightly beaten
      1 cup milk
      ¼ cup melted butter

Grease the bottoms but not the sides of muffin pans. Sift together the flour, baking powder, sugar, and salt into a bowl. Combine beaten egg, milk, and butter and stir lightly to mix. Make a well in the middle of the flour mixture and pour in liquids all at once. Stir lightly and quickly with a fork just to mix; the batter should be lumpy. (Overmixing makes for too close-grained, too solid muffins.) Fill each cup of muffin pans no more than two-thirds full. Bake in a preheated hot oven (425°) for about 20 minutes or until golden brown. Serve hot, with plenty of butter.

ABOUT 1 DOZEN

CORN MUFFINS WITH BACON

All-American

      4 slices bacon
      1 cup yellow cornmeal, preferably stone-ground
      1 cup flour
      ¼ cup sugar
      3 teaspoons baking powder

½ teaspoon salt
1 cup milk
1 egg
¼ cup reserved bacon fat

Cook bacon until crisp. Drain on paper towels. Reserve ¼ cup of bacon fat. Crumble bacon and reserve. Into a bowl, sift together the cornmeal, flour, sugar, baking powder, and salt. Mix together the milk, egg, and reserved bacon fat. Make a well in the center of the cornmeal mixture. Pour in liquid all at once. Add crumbled bacon. Stir lightly and quickly just to mix; batter should be lumpy. Grease bottom but not sides of muffin pans. Fill each cup about two-thirds full of batter. Bake in a preheated hot oven (400°) for about 20 minutes or until lightly browned. Serve hot, with plenty of butter.

12 MUFFINS

POPOVERS

Since many cooks seem to be afraid of making this easy, delicious, and truly American specialty, this is by way of a helping hand. The trick is not in the mixing, but in the baking. Popovers must be baked in smallish containers that are reasonably heavy and deeper than wide. The old-fashioned cast-iron pans are best, but since I, like most people, don't have them, I bake popovers in heavy aluminum muffin pans or in individual glass custard cups. The pans must be heavily greased or buttered on all sides. The batter should be the consistency of heavy cream. Fill pans or cups no more than two-thirds full. While popovers are baking do not peek for 30 minutes or they will collapse. Popovers pop because the large amount of liquid in the batter causes steam to form in the hot oven, expanding the batter into a nearly hollow shell. This shell must be baked until rigid, or it will collapse when the steam condenses upon cooling.

There are two methods of baking popovers, both

*satisfactory although the hot-oven method (which I think
is the easier of the two) turns out a popover with a firmer
inside. If you are using glass or earthenware cups with the
hot-oven method, you must preheat them before greasing.
This is done by placing the cups on a baking sheet in the
oven to heat thoroughly. Remove with pot holders and
grease generously with butter or shortening.*

   1 cup milk
   1 tablespoon melted butter
   1 cup sifted flour
  ½ teaspoon salt
   2 eggs

Hot-oven method:

Preheat oven to very hot (425°). Grease popover pans generously and set aside. (If using glass or earthenware cups preheat
in hot oven before greasing. Remove and grease just before filling.)
With a rotary beater, wire whip, or fork, beat together just until
smooth the milk, butter, flour, and salt. Beat in the eggs one at a
time, but do not overbeat. Fill the greased baking cups less than
two-thirds full. Bake without peeking for 30 minutes. Then reduce
heat to moderate (350°) and continue baking for 5–10 minutes or
until popovers are firm, puffy, and well browned. Serve immediately with plenty of butter.

Cold-oven method:

Mix batter as directed. Fill greased baking cups less than
two-thirds full. Place in a cold oven and set heat at hot (425°).
Bake without peeking for about 30 to 35 minutes or until firm,
puffy, and well browned. If the popovers are browning too quickly,
reduce the heat to moderate (375°) for the last 10 or 15 minutes.

8 MEDIUM-SIZED POPOVERS

SEATTLE DUTCH BABIES

From Washington

*These popover-like baked pancakes were a specialty of the
old-time Manca Restaurant. A good way of serving them is
to sandwich them with jam and, if you must, butter.*

 3 eggs
½ cup flour
½ cup milk
 2 tablespoons melted butter
¼ teaspoon salt
   grated rind of ½ lemon (optional)
   confectioners' sugar
   lemon wedges

In a bowl, beat the eggs. Beat in the flour, 2 tablespoons at a
time, beating just until smooth. Beat in the milk, butter, salt, and
lemon rind (if used). Generously butter two 9-inch pie pans. Divide batter between them. Bake in a preheated hot oven (400°) for
10 minutes. Lower heat to 350° and bake 5 more minutes. Sprinkle
with confectioners' sugar and serve with lemon wedges.

1–2 SERVINGS

DUMPLINGS

*There are many different dumpling recipes, but whichever
you use, dumplings should be light. Unfortunately, much
of the time they are soggy and leaden. To avoid this,
I have found that each dumpling must rest upon a solid
piece of food—meat, potato, vegetable, or fruit—so that it
does not submerge in the gravy. The part of the dumpling
that touches the food and gravy will be wet, but the rest
shoudn't be. If there is too much liquid in the dish that
you're going to top with dumplings, take out part of the*

*gravy or broth and keep it warm in a saucepan, serving it
separately or adding it later.*

*I still think that the old-fashioned method of cook-
ing dumplings in a tightly closed saucepan or kettle is the
best. On no account must you lift the lid and peek until
the cooking time is up. Dumplings cook by steam and when
the air comes in, the steam goes out and the dumplings
get heavy.*

*Since I like airy dumplings, I put more baking
powder into mine than standard recipes call for. And I
add dill or other herbs, especially for chicken dishes.*

2 cups flour (for lighter dumplings, use cake flour)
5 teaspoons baking powder
1 teaspoon salt
1 egg
1 egg yolk
½ cup milk, or more
2 tablespoons fresh dill weed, minced

Sift together the flour, baking powder, and salt and sift twice
more. Beat together the egg, egg yolk, milk, and dill, beating well
after each addition. Pour egg mixture over flour and stir only until
mixed. If too thick (flours absorb liquids differently) add enough
more milk, 1 tablespoon at a time, to make a fairly stiff dough.
Have the meat and broth for the dumplings at a barely simmering
point. Arrange the meat so that the dumplings have a place to rest
on. Drop the dumpling mixture tablespoon by tablespoon into meat
and broth, dipping the tablespoon between times into cold water,
and cover pan at once. Cook for about 15–18 minutes without lifting lid and make absolutely sure that the broth in saucepan is simmering, not bubbling. This is done by keeping heat low.

Note:
If the liquid of the dish needs thickening, do this after cooking the dumplings. Remove them and keep them warm; then return
them to stew or casserole if you are serving from the dish. Or turn
stew into a serving dish and top with dumplings.

ABOUT 2 DOZEN DUMPLINGS

CORN BREAD

All-American

This amount makes 6 cups crumbled, as needed for Corn-Bread Stuffing (page 60).

>   6 tablespoons butter, melted
>   1 cup yellow cornmeal
>   1 cup flour
>   1 tablespoon sugar
>   4 teaspoons baking powder
>   ½ teaspoon salt
>   1 cup milk
>   1 egg, beaten

Into a square 8-inch baking pan, pour 2 tablespoons of the butter. Turn the pan around to coat bottom and all sides. Place pan in a preheated hot oven (400°). Into a bowl, sift together the cornmeal, flour, sugar, baking powder, and salt. Add milk, beaten egg, and remaining 4 tablespoons butter. Stir only until barely mixed. With thick pot holders, remove sizzling pan from oven. Pour in the cornmeal mixture. Return pan to oven and increase heat to 425°. Bake for 20 minutes or until corn bread tests done. Serve hot with butter, or crumble and use for stuffing.

8 SERVINGS

PLAIN BUTTERMILK CORN BREAD

From Texas

>   1½ cups yellow cornmeal, preferably stone-ground
>   ¼ cup flour
>   1 teaspoon baking soda
>   1 teaspoon salt

2 cups buttermilk
1 egg, beaten
   dash Tabasco (optional)
1 cup finely cut cracklings or crumbled crisp bacon
   (optional)

Combine and sift together the cornmeal, flour, baking soda, and salt into a bowl. Beat in the buttermilk and beaten egg, beating until there are no lumps in the batter. If desired, add Tabasco and fold in cracklings or bacon bits. Generously grease a 9-inch iron skillet or a 9-inch square pan. Put on direct heat until very hot. Remove from heat and pour in batter. Bake in a preheated hot oven (425°) for about 25–30 minutes or until corn bread is golden brown on top. Depending on the pan, cut corn bread either in wedges or in squares. Serve hot, with butter.

Note:
This corn bread lends itself very well to Corn-Bread Stuffing (page 60).

6 SERVINGS

JALAPEÑO CORN BREAD

From Texas

2 eggs
1 cup sour cream
⅓ cup salad oil
1 cup cream-style canned corn
1 cup yellow cornmeal
3 teaspoons baking powder
1 teaspoon salt
¼ cup shredded Longhorn or Cheddar cheese
¼ cup diced canned drained green jalapeño peppers
   (remove ultrahot seeds)

Beat the eggs in a bowl. Stir in the sour cream, oil, and corn. Sift into the bowl the cornmeal, baking powder, and salt and beat until smooth. Stir in the cheese and jalapeño peppers. Turn into a greased 13×9½×2-inch baking dish. Bake in a preheated moderate oven (375°) for about 30 minutes or until bread tests done. Cut into squares and serve hot, with or without butter.

Note:

Every child in Texas knows that after touching any hot peppers and chilis (jalapeño, etc.) you must never touch your face or eyes or they will burn badly. Wash your hands with hot water and soap before touching anything else.

10–12 SERVINGS

MAGGIE'S SKILLET CORN BREAD

From North Carolina

As children Pauline, Pauline's daughter, and a longtime friend would eat no other bread. The bread must be made with the white stone-ground cornmeal that Southerners prefer; ordinary cornmeal makes it too grainy, since the meal is not scalded or cooked before baking.

      1 cup buttermilk
      ½ teaspoon baking soda
    1¾ cup white stone-ground cornmeal
      ½ teaspoon baking soda
      1 teaspoon salt
      1 egg, beaten
    2–3 tablespoons butter or bacon fat

Put the buttermilk and soda into a bowl and mix well. Sift into it the cornmeal, baking soda, and salt and beat until smooth. Beat in beaten egg. Heat 2–3 tablespoons butter or bacon fat in a heavy 10-inch frying pan and swish it around to coat bottom and sides of frying pan. Pour any remaining butter into the batter and blend. Pour batter into the hot frying pan. Bake in a preheated moderate oven (375°) for about 30–40 minutes or until set and shrinking from sides of frying pan. Serve hot in wedges, with butter and molasses or sorghum molasses.

4–6 SERVINGS

SPOON BREAD

Southern, of Indian origin, going back to the Indians' cornmeal porridges

There are any number of spoon-bread recipes, and having made most of them I have come to the following conclusions: It is well to scald the cornmeal before baking, though some recipes don't. Buttermilk makes for smoothness and stone-ground cornmeal, favored in the South, is softer and tastier than commercial steel-ground cornmeal. This recipe makes a delicate, pudding-like spoon bread. Serve all spoon breads with meat, as a substitute for potatoes, and with plenty of butter on the side.

    1 cup stone-ground or other white or yellow cornmeal
    1 cup boiling water
    1 cup buttermilk and 1 cup milk, or 2 cups milk
    1 teaspoon salt
 1½ teaspoons baking powder
    ½ teaspoon baking soda (omit if all milk is used)
    3 eggs, well beaten
    3 tablespoons melted butter

Put the cornmeal into a bowl. Pour in boiling water, stirring as you pour to avoid lumping. Cool, stirring frequently to keep smooth. If you use buttermilk and milk, combine in another bowl and stir in salt, baking powder, and baking soda. (If you are using all milk, omit baking soda.) Stir into cooled cornmeal, beating until smooth. Beat in beaten eggs and mix thoroughly. Blend in melted butter. Generously butter a 1½-quart baking dish. Turn batter into baking dish. Bake in a preheated moderate oven (375°) for about 40–50 minutes or until well set and golden brown. Serve from baking dish.

4–6 SERVINGS

SALLY LUNN

From Virginia

This is one of the many colonial breads of English origin that were especially liked in the Southern colonies. The name's origin is unclear; it is said that a girl called Sally Lunn hawked these breads in London. Among the varied versions, this is a nice Sally Lunn.

    4 cups flour
    ¾ teaspoon salt
    1 cup milk
    1 package dry yeast
    ½ cup (1 stick) butter
    ⅓ cup sugar
    3 eggs

Sift together the flour and salt and reserve. Heat the milk to lukewarm. Sprinkle the yeast over milk and stir to dissolve. In a large bowl, cream the butter and add the sugar, beating well for about 3 minutes with an electric beater at medium speed. Add the eggs, one at a time, beating well after each addition. Alternately beat in the yeast mixture and the flour. (If using an electric beater add the last ½ cup flour by hand.) This beating should take about 5–7 minutes, and the dough will be stiff but sticky. Cover the bowl with plastic wrap and let dough rise in a warm place. (An oven

with a pan of boiling water on the lower rack works well if there is
no oven pilot; if there is an oven pilot, just set in oven.) When
dough is doubled in bulk, punch down and beat for 40–50 strokes
with bare hands. Generously butter a 10-inch tube pan or Turk's-
head pan. Turn dough into pan and spread out with a spatula.
Cover and again put in a warm place until doubled in bulk. Bake in
a preheated moderate oven (350°) for about 50 minutes or until
bread tests done. Remove from oven and let stand for 2–3 minutes.
Then loosen edges with knife carefully; bread is somewhat fragile.
To remove from pan, put a plate over the bread, reverse, and tap
bottom of pan until bread falls onto plate. Cover with another plate
and reverse again to stand bread upright. Cool a little. Bread is
very crusty; cut with a serrated knife, using a sawing motion to
keep bread from coming apart. Serve warm with butter and jam.
When stale, the bread toasts well.

1 10-INCH TUBE-PAN LOAF

QUICK SALLY LUNN

Southern

*Acceptable and nice, but not as good as the traditional
Sally Lunn.*

  2 cups flour
  1 tablespoon baking powder
  ½ teaspoon salt
  3 tablespoons butter
  2 eggs, separated
  ½ cup sugar
  ¾ cup milk

Into a bowl, sift together the flour, baking powder, and salt.
Cut in the butter with two knives, a pastry blender, or fingertips
until mixture resembles coarse cornmeal. In another bowl, beat together the egg yolks and sugar until thick and pale. Add flour and

milk alternately to egg mixture, beating well after each addition.
Beat the egg whites until stiff and fold gently into batter. Generously butter an 8×8-inch baking pan. Turn dough into it and
spread out with a spatula. Bake in a preheated moderate oven
(350°) for 40–45 minutes or until bread tests done.

6 SERVINGS

CINNAMON TOAST

All-American

  2 tablespoons sugar
  1 teaspoon ground cinnamon
  6 slices bread
  2 tablespoons butter, at room temperature for spreading

Combine the sugar and cinnamon and mix well. Toast the
bread. Spread each slice with 1 teaspoon butter and sprinkle with
about 1 teaspoon cinnamon-sugar. Place toast, buttered side up, on
an ungreased baking sheet. Bake in a preheated moderate oven
(350°) for about 4–5 minutes. Cut into fingers and serve hot.

3 SERVINGS

FRENCH TOAST

All-American

  2 eggs, beaten
  ⅔ cup milk or half-and-half
  ¼ teaspoon salt
  8 slices firm or stale bread
  4 tablespoons butter, or more as needed

Combine the beaten eggs, milk or half-and-half, and salt in a shallow bowl. Dip the bread slices into the mixture, turning to coat both sides thoroughly. Heat the 4 tablespoons butter in a heavy frying pan. Add bread slices (2 at a time if frying pan is small) and cook until golden brown. Turn with pancake turner and cook until other side is brown. Keep hot in a slow oven until all the bread is cooked. Add more butter to frying pan as needed. Serve hot with fried ham, sausages, or bacon and syrup, or sprinkle with confectioners' sugar and serve with preserves or jelly or with syrup only.

4 SERVINGS

MILK TOAST

The All-American dish to cry into

1 thick slice hot buttered toast
1 cup hot milk or hot half-and-half
  brown sugar (optional)

Place toast in a heated shallow soup bowl or plate. Pour milk over it and sprinkle with brown sugar to taste. Serve hot.

1 SERVING

ELEGANT MILK TOAST

Line a large tray with a doily. On it, place a heated shallow bowl or soup bowl, with the hot buttered toast. Pour the hot milk into a small pitcher. Into another small pitcher pour ½ cup heated heavy cream. Place both on tray, together with sugar bowls filled with white and brown sugars. Take to the table, where the recipient pours milk and cream to taste over the toast and adds white or brown sugar or both. Don't forget a spoon, a fork, and a pretty napkin.

Note:
This is the way an old lady in Boston served milk toast to me.

PANCAKES

All-American

The dry ingredients can be doubled and tripled in quantity, combined, and refrigerated in a covered container. When ready to use, add liquids needed and mix.

1 cup flour
2 tablespoons sugar
1 tablespoon cornmeal
1 tablespoon baking powder
½ teaspoon salt
1 egg
½ to ¾ cup milk
½ cup butter, melted

Sift into a bowl the flour, sugar, cornmeal, baking powder, and salt. Add egg, milk, and butter and stir to mix and blend only until dampened; batter should be lumpy. Heat a greased griddle until a drop of cold water will dance on it. Drop batter, about 3 tablespoons for each pancake, on griddle. Cook until bubbles rise on surface, turn, and brown on other side. Stack cooked pancakes on a heated plate in a low oven (140°–175°) until all are cooked. Serve as soon as possible with butter and syrup.

Notes:
If mixed batter has been standing for a while, stir in ¼ teaspoon additional baking powder before cooking.

Since different flours and cornmeals absorb liquid differently, I suggest you start with ½ cup milk.

ABOUT 1 DOZEN

CORN PANCAKES

All-American

Best made with very young fresh corn. Since these come apart easily during cooking it is best to make small cakes. They should be put together quickly and not let stand before cooking.

- 3 tablespoons flour
- 1½ teaspoons baking soda
- 1½ teaspoons salt
  - corn grated from 3 medium ears, or 1 10-ounce package frozen kernel corn, thawed
- 4 tablespoons yogurt or buttermilk
- 1 egg, beaten
- 1 tablespoon melted butter
  - maple syrup or other syrup or jam

Sift together the flour, baking soda, and salt. In a blender or food processor blend two-thirds of the corn until mashed. Add remaining corn and blend 1 to 2 seconds longer so that corn is coarsely chopped and left almost whole (this is for texture). Beat together yogurt or buttermilk, beaten egg, and butter. Beat into flour mixture. Add corn and mix well. Drop by the heaping tablespoonful on a medium-hot greased griddle. Turn only when top looks firm, lightly browned, and cooked. Then turn and brown other side lightly. Serve hot, with any syrup or jam.

2–3 SERVINGS

BUTTERMILK FLAPJACKS

All-American

1 egg
1 cup buttermilk
2 tablespoons melted butter or salad oil
1 cup flour
1 tablespoon sugar
1 teaspoon baking powder
½ teaspoon baking soda
½ teaspoon salt

In a bowl, beat the egg thoroughly until fluffy. Beat in buttermilk and melted butter or oil. Combine and sift remaining ingredients directly into buttermilk mixture. Drop batter by one-fourth cupfuls onto a greased heated griddle. Cook until puffed and dry around edges. Turn and cook until golden brown. Serve hot, with maple syrup, molasses, or any fruit topping.

Note:
Griddle is hot enough when a few drops of water dropped onto it dance around.

8 4-INCH FLAPJACKS

WAFFLES

All-American

Waffles made with buttermilk are tenderer and stick less to the waffle iron.

2 cups flour
1 tablespoon baking powder
½ teaspoon baking soda

    1 teaspoon salt
    1½ cups buttermilk
    3 eggs
    ½ cup butter, melted

Into a bowl, sift together the flour, baking powder, baking soda, and salt. Make a hole in the center of the flour mixture. Beat together the buttermilk and eggs and pour into flour. Mix with a spoon until the dry ingredients are dampened. Then beat with a rotary beater or electric beater until smooth. With a spoon, blend in the melted butter. Spread in a lightly greased waffle iron. Cook until the iron stops steaming and serve with maple syrup.

8 DOUBLE WAFFLES

DOUGHNUTS

These are rich baking-powder cake-type doughnuts. Making doughnuts takes a certain amount of practice in rolling the dough to an even thickness and in the frying. The dough should not be thicker than ½ inch—if it is, the hole in the doughnut will fill up as the dough rises in the cooking. Since uncooked doughnuts are soft, it is difficult to pick them up without getting them out of shape before they reach the deep-fryer. It helps to use a spatula, first dipping it into the hot oil and then sliding it under each doughnut prior to transporting it into the hot fat. Make sure the oil has heated to the proper temperature, or you will have soggy, oily doughnuts. Since the doughnuts cook for so little time it is a good idea to have a helper at the oil pot while one is cutting out more doughnuts oneself.

    4 cups flour
    2 teaspoons baking powder
    1 teaspoon baking soda
    ¾ teaspoon salt
    ¼ teaspoon nutmeg
    3 tablespoons soft butter

       3 egg yolks
       1 whole egg
    1¼ cups sugar
       ¾ cup buttermilk
       1 teaspoon grated lemon rind
       1 teaspoon vanilla extract
         cooking oil or shortenings for deep-frying
         sifted confectioners' sugar

Sift together the flour, baking powder, baking soda, salt, and nutmeg. Cut in the butter with a pastry blender or two knives until mixture resembles very coarse meal. Reserve. Beat together the egg yolks, whole egg, sugar, buttermilk, lemon rind, and vanilla extract. Add dry ingredients to egg mixture all at once and beat just until smooth and well blended. The dough should be stiff, but if necessary add a little more buttermilk, 1 tablespoon at a time, to make it easier to handle. Cover and chill in refrigerator for at least 2 hours. Roll out dough on lightly floured surface to the thickness of ½ inch. Cut with a 2½-inch doughnut cutter. Put oil or shortening in a deep saucepan or electric deep-fryer, filling it no more than three-quarters full, and heat to 375° on frying thermometer. Fry doughnuts a few at a time for 2–3 minutes on each side, turning with tongs or two long-handled spoons. Doughnuts must not touch each other while frying. Drain on paper towels. When cooled, dust with confectioners' sugar.

Note:
The cut-out doughnut centers may be fried separately in oil or shortening heated to 375° on the frying thermometer.

ABOUT 4 DOZEN DOUGHNUTS 2½ INCHES IN
DIAMETER AND ½-INCH THICK

RAISED JELLY DOUGHNUTS

All-American

The virtue of this dough is that it can also be used for bread or dinner rolls if you don't want so many doughnuts; one third of the dough will make about 1 dozen doughnuts. Since the dough rises in the refrigerator it will keep, refrigerated, for 3–4 days so that it can be used as needed. If you are using part of the dough for bread or rolls, reduce the sugar from ½ cup to ⅓ cup, or the bread will be too sweet; the smaller amount of sugar does not make that much difference in the doughnuts. Odd though it may seem, jelly does not work at all in jelly doughnuts because under heat it liquefies and oozes out; thick jam or preserve must be used.

    2 cups warm water from tap (about 115–120°)
    2 packages granulated dry yeast
    ½ cup sugar
    ½ cup butter, softened and cut into pieces
    1½ teaspoons salt
    2 eggs (at room temperature)
    7 cups flour (sifted before measuring)
      thick jam or preserve
      shortening or oil for deep-frying
      sifted confectioners' sugar

Pour the water into a large bowl. Sprinkle the yeast over water and stir to dissolve. Beat in the sugar, butter, salt, eggs, and 3 cups of the flour. Beat with an electric beater at medium speed for about 3 minutes, or beat energetically by hand for 5 minutes. Then, beating by hand, add as much of the remaining 4 cups of flour as the dough will absorb and still remain soft. (Some flours absorb more liquid than others.) Dough should be sticky but should pull away from sides of bowl. Grease another bowl, turn dough into it, and turn it around in the bowl so that it will be greased on all sides. Cover with plastic wrap or aluminum foil and refrigerate from at least 2½ hours to 3–4 days. Dough will rise in refrigerator. When dough is removed from refrigerator, punch it down and roll out required amount to a thickness of ¼ inch. Using a 2¾-inch biscuit cutter, cut dough into circles. Put 1 rounded teaspoon of jam or preserve on half the circles; if you cut bigger circles you will need more jam. Dip fingers into a container of *warm* water and moisten edges of all circles. Pick up a circle without jam and place it over one with jam, stretching the top ones a little to cover the mound of jam. Press circle edges together firmly and neatly so that jam won't ooze out during frying. Place doughnuts on a large baking sheet covered with greased aluminum foil; this will make doughnuts easier to handle when ready for frying. Repeat until all doughnuts are ready. Cover doughnuts lightly with plastic wrap or foil. Let rise in a warm place for about 45 minutes; doughnuts will rise further in frying. Fill a deep-fryer or heavy saucepan about two-thirds full of shortening or oil. Heat to a temperature of 375° on frying thermometer, or until a bread cube dropped into the hot fat browns in 60 seconds. With a pancake turner, lift each doughnut and slide carefully into the hot fat. Fry for 2–3 minutes, turn, and fry 2–3 minutes on other side. Remove from fat and drain on several thicknesses of paper towels. Cook only a few doughnuts at one time; they must not touch each other but must have plenty of room to swim around in the hot fat. Sprinkle with confectioners' sugar and serve, preferably immediately and warm.

Note:

A frying thermometer is quite essential if you do serious deep-frying. Measure the temperature of the fat before adding new foods; fat cools while food is being taken out of it to drain. Have a bowl of warm water to hold the frying thermometer in use to help prevent breakage, but *be sure to wipe it dry* before plunging it again into the hot fat.

If you want to make cloverleaf rolls with some of the dough, make little balls and put three of them side by side into each cup of a greased muffin pan; they will bake into cloverleaf rolls.

ABOUT 3 DOZEN

Desserts

DESSERT APPLE CAKE

From the Midwest

- 3 large tart apples
  grated rind of 1 lemon
  juice of 1 large lemon
- ½ cup butter
- ⅔ cup sugar
- 1 egg, beaten
- 1½ cups flour
- 1 teaspoon baking soda
- ¼ teaspoon salt
- ½ teaspoon ground cinnamon
- ¼ teaspoon ground ginger

⅛ teaspoon ground cloves
⅛ teaspoon ground nutmeg
½ cup milk
⅔ cup chopped walnuts or pecans

Peel and core the apples. Cut them into ½-inch pieces; there should be about 4 cups. Put into a bowl and add the lemon rind and lemon juice. Mix with the hands to coat all the apple pieces with lemon juice and some rind. Cream the butter until soft and gradually beat in the sugar, a little at a time. Beat in the beaten egg. Sift together the flour, salt, and spices. Beat into the sugar mixture gradually, alternating with the milk. Stir the apples and any remaining lemon juice into the batter. Add the nuts and stir to distribute the fruit and nuts evenly. Generously butter a 9×9-inch baking dish. Turn in the batter and smooth the top with a spatula. Bake in a preheated moderate oven (350°) for 45–50 minutes or until the cake tests done and shrinks from the sides of the pan. Serve with hard sauce or heavy cream.

Note:
As a child in Upper Michigan, my husband was given a simpler version of this cake for supper, served in a bowl with milk poured over it.

6–8 SERVINGS

APPLE CRUMB

From New England

The recipe is easily doubled and even tripled.

4 cups tart apples (about 1 pound), peeled, cored, and sliced
grated rind of 1 lemon
juice of ½ lemon

¼ cup hot water
½ cup chilled butter cut into pieces
½ cup flour
½ cup sugar
  chilled heavy cream

Place the apples in a generously buttered 1½- or 2-quart baking dish. Sprinkle with the grated lemon rind. Combine the lemon juice and hot water and pour over the apples. With your fingers or two knives or a pastry cutter work together the butter, flour, and sugar until the mixture forms coarse crumbs. Spread over the apples. Bake in a preheated hot oven (425°) for 10 minutes. Reduce heat to moderate (350°) and bake for 30 more minutes. The topping should be crisp. Serve with chilled heavy cream.

Note:
I have made this with dark-brown and with light-brown sugar. The results taste good, but the pudding looks too dark.

4 SERVINGS

TANGY APPLES STEWED
IN APPLE JUICE

From New York

2 pounds tart green cooking apples (5–6 apples)
2 cups apple juice or mild cider
1 cup sugar or to taste (depending on tartness of apples)
½ teaspoon ground cinnamon
¼ teaspoon ground nutmeg
¼ teaspoon ground cloves

Have a bowl of cold water ready. Peel the apples, core, and quarter them. If smaller slices are desired, cut the quarters in half. Drop cut apples into cold water to prevent darkening. In a saucepan, combine the apple juice or cider, sugar, cinnamon, nutmeg, and cloves. Bring to boiling point, lower heat immediately, and simmer for 3–4 minutes. Drain apples and add to apple juice mixture. Simmer over low heat for 5–7 minutes or until apples are tender but still keep their shape. Be careful that the juice does not boil over; if it mounts too much, remove from heat for a minute or so to let it sink. Turn apples and juice into a serving dish. Chill and serve with heavy cream.

6 SERVINGS

DRIED-APRICOT CREAM

From California

2 cups dried apricots (1 11-ounce package)
1 cup water
1 cup orange juice
½ cup sugar, preferably superfine sugar
1 tablespoon lemon juice, brandy, or Kirsch
1½ cups heavy cream
½ cup blanched shredded almonds, lightly toasted

Place the apricots, water, and orange juice in a saucepan. Cook without a cover over low heat for about 5–10 minutes or until apricots are very soft. Stir in the sugar and cook, stirring constantly, until sugar has dissolved. Remove from heat. Press through a sieve or purée in a blender or food processor. Stir in the lemon juice or liquor and cool. Whip the cream until very stiff and fold into the apricot purée. Turn into a glass bowl or other serving dish and chill. Sprinkle with almonds and serve with plain cookies.

6 SERVINGS

OLD-FASHIONED
BLACKBERRY FLUMMERY

From Michigan

     2 quarts blackberries
    ½ cup plus 3 tablespoons water
     1 cup sugar
    ⅛ teaspoon ground cinnamon
     1 tablespoon grated lemon rind
     2 tablespoons cornstarch
       heavy cream or vanilla sauce

Pick over the blackberries and place in a saucepan. Add ½ cup water, the sugar, cinnamon, and lemon rind. Bring to boiling point; lower heat and simmer for about 5 minutes. Partly cover the saucepan. Blend the cornstarch and the 3 tablespoons water to a smooth paste. Gradually stir into blackberry mixture. Cook, stirring constantly, for about 3–5 minutes or until slightly thickened and translucent. Pour into serving dish (preferably glass) and chill. Serve with heavy cream or your favorite vanilla sauce.

4–6 SERVINGS

NEW ENGLAND
BLUEBERRY GRUNT

Alas, I don't know where the name comes from—nobody could tell me. This is also called Blueberry Slump or Blueberry Potpie.

     3 cups blueberries, fresh or frozen, picked over
       (fresh are better)
    ⅔ cup sugar
    ½ teaspoon ground cinnamon
    ¼ teaspoon ground nutmeg

¼ teaspoon ground mace
1 cup water
2 tablespoons lemon juice

DUMPLINGS
1 cup flour
2 teaspoons baking powder
1 teaspoon sugar
¼ teaspoon salt
  approximately ¾ cup milk
  heavy cream

If you use fresh blueberries, pick them over. Place the blueberries, ⅔ cup sugar, spices, water, and lemon juice in a heavy 3- to 4-quart saucepan, preferably a wide one. Cook over moderate heat for 2–3 minutes. Remove from heat. To make dumplings, sift together the flour, baking powder, 1 teaspoon sugar, and salt. Beginning with ½ cup milk, stir in enough milk to make a dumpling dough that will slide from a spoon. Return the blueberries to low heat and bring to simmering point. Drop the dumpling dough in heaping tablespoonfuls over the blueberries. The dumplings should be about 1½ to 2 inches long and should lie side by side, not touching each other. Cover tightly and simmer for about 15–20 minutes. To serve, spoon the dumplings into large serving bowls. Spoon the blueberry sauce over them. Serve with heavy cream, plain or whipped.

4–6 SERVINGS

THE COACH HOUSE
BREAD-AND-BUTTER PUDDING

From New York

The Coach House in New York City is one of the finest restaurants in the country, one in which American cooking has been raised to utter glory. No home ever made Bread-and-Butter Pudding like the Coach House's; it is the

*ultimate of its kind, served there with a purée of fresh rasp-
berries as a sauce.*

12 small thin slices French bread
 5 eggs
 4 egg yolks
 1 cup sugar
⅛ teaspoon salt
 4 cups (1 quart) milk
 1 cup heavy cream
 1 teaspoon vanilla extract
   confectioners' sugar

Trim crusts from the bread, and butter each slice on one
side. Beat together the eggs, egg yolks, sugar, and salt until thoroughly blended. Combine the milk and cream in a saucepan, scald,
but do not boil. Stir gradually into egg mixture and stir in the vanilla extract. Butter a 2-quart baking dish. Line it with the bread,
buttered side up. Strain milk, cream, and egg mixture over bread;
straining this custard through a strainer makes for a more satiny
pudding. Set baking dish into a large roasting pan containing about
1 inch water. Bake pudding in a preheated moderate oven (375°)
for about 45 minutes or until pudding tests done. Sprinkle generously with confectioners' sugar and glaze quickly under hot
broiler. Serve hot or cool.

6–8 SERVINGS

CHOCOLATE PUDDING

All-American

*Make this with Dutch-type cocoa; it has the most intensive
chocolate flavor.*

3 tablespoons Dutch-type cocoa
4 tablespoons cornstarch
6 tablespoons sugar
  pinch salt

2 cups milk or light cream
1 teaspoon vanilla extract
   heavy cream or vanilla sauce

Combine the cocoa, cornstarch, sugar, and salt in the top of double boiler or in a heavy saucepan. Add ½ cup of the milk or light cream and stir to a smooth paste. Scald the remaining milk or light cream. Stir gradually into cocoa mixture. Cook over hot water, stirring constantly, until thick and smooth. Stir in the vanilla extract. Pour into a serving dish or 4 individual serving dishes and chill before serving. Serve with heavy cream or your favorite vanilla sauce.

4 SERVINGS

CHOCOLATE FRESH-RASPBERRY CREAM

From Virginia

4 ounces (1 package) sweet cooking chocolate, grated
2 cups heavy cream, whipped
1 tablespoon rum, or ¼ teaspoon almond extract
3 cups fresh raspberries
¼ cup superfine sugar

Reserve 3 tablespoons of the grated chocolate and refrigerate until needed. Combine the remaining chocolate and the whipped cream and blend gently but thoroughly. Stir in rum or almond extract. Reserve ¼ cup of the raspberries and refrigerate until needed. Sprinkle remaining berries with the sugar and toss. Fold berries into chocolate mixture. Spoon into a glass serving dish and chill for 1 hour. Do not overchill or chill too long or the dessert will soften. At serving time, sprinkle with the reserved chocolate and decorate with the reserved berries.

Note:
This may be made, though less flavorfully, with thawed, well-drained frozen raspberries. Use 2 10-ounce packages.

6 SERVINGS

CHERRIES JUBILEE

All-American

Jim Beard, who knows more about food than anybody else in America, thinks this dish is of English origin, dating back to Victoria's reign. It still is an easy, very good, and showy dessert if you prepare it in a chafing dish at the table or serve it flaming (which I don't like as being too dangerous).

- 1 19-ounce can pitted Bing cherries
- ¼ cup sugar
- 1 tablespoon cornstarch
   vanilla ice cream
- ⅓ cup brandy or Kirsch

Drain the cherries; reserve cherries and liquid. Mix together the sugar and cornstarch, preferably in a chafing dish. Stir in the cherry liquid. Cook over low heat, stirring constantly until thickened. Add cherries and cook until cherries are thoroughly heated. Meanwhile have vanilla ice cream ready in a serving dish. Warm the brandy or Kirsch in a small saucepan or in a ladle over low heat and pour over cherries. Flame and carry to the table, or flame at the table, then pour over the ice cream.

4 SERVINGS

MARDY'S GRANOLA

From a Connecticut mother

A welcome change from the overly sweet commercial product, yet sweet enough for children.

- 1 cup soy bean flour
- 1 cup sunflower seeds

    1 cup raw sesame seeds
    6 cups rolled oats
    1 cup pepita seeds
    1 cup powdered milk
    1 cup wheat germ
    1 cup shredded fresh coconut, or 1 cup packaged coconut, preferably unsweetened
    1 cup sesame or safflower oil
    1 cup honey
    2 cups currants or raisins

Combine the soy bean flour, sunflower seeds, sesame seeds, oats, pepita seeds, powdered milk, wheat germ, and coconut in a large bowl. Mix together the oil and honey and stir into dry ingredients. Spread mixture about ½-inch deep in a shallow baking pan. Cook in a preheated very slow oven (225°) for about 30 minutes or until crisp and golden brown. Continue until whole mixture is toasted. Cool and add currants or raisins. Mix well and store in airtight jars.

ABOUT 2 QUARTS

GREEN GRAPES AND SOUR CREAM

From New York

This should be made at serving time or just before.

    4 cups seedless green grapes, stemmed, washed, dried, and chilled
    ⅔ cup sour cream or unflavored yogurt
    ⅓ cup dark-brown sugar

Turn the grapes into a serving bowl and mix with the sour cream or yogurt. Sprinkle with the sugar and serve.

4 SERVINGS

INDIAN PUDDING

From Massachusetts

Indian Pudding must have been the first dessert of the English settlers and I think in its most primitive form—just cornmeal and milk cooked together with a little sweetening of molasses. There are many variations of the recipe, which traditionally calls for yellow cornmeal. Eggs, raisins, and even flour have been added to Indian Pudding, also spices, varying slightly according to individual tastes. I present my favorite version; for those who like a more liquid pudding, increase the hot milk by 1 cup. Chilled, the pudding becomes solid and can be sliced. Good hot, lukewarm, or chilled.

    5 cups milk
    ⅔ cup dark molasses
    ¼ cup sugar
    ½ cup yellow cornmeal
    ½ teaspoon ground cinnamon
    ½ teaspoon ground nutmeg
    ¼ teaspoon ground allspice
    ¼ teaspoon ground ginger
    1 teaspoon salt
    2 tablespoons butter
      heavy cream or vanilla ice cream or hard sauce

Scald 4 cups of the milk in a heavy saucepan. Stir in the molasses, sugar, cornmeal, cinnamon, nutmeg, allspice, ginger, salt, and butter. Cook over very low heat, stirring frequently, for about 10–15 minutes, or until mixture thickens and is smooth. Turn into a buttered 1½- or 2-quart baking dish. Add the remaining cup of cold milk, but do not stir. Bake in a preheated slow oven (300°) for 3 hours, without stirring. The pudding may also be baked at 275° for 4–5 hours. Serve warm or chilled, with heavy cream, vanilla ice cream, or hard sauce.

6–8 SERVINGS

MAPLE FRANGO

From Vermont

A rich, half-frozen cream, best served with lady fingers or plain cookies. Refrigerate an opened bottle or jar of maple syrup; otherwise, it can turn sour.

¾ cup maple syrup
 3 egg yolks, well beaten in a small heavy saucepan
⅛ teaspoon salt
 1 tablespoon grated orange rind (optional)
 1 cup heavy cream, whipped

Heat the maple syrup to boiling point. Pour slowly over the beaten egg yolks, stirring all the time. Cook over very low heat, stirring constantly, for about 5 minutes or until somewhat thickened. Stir in the salt and the orange rind (if used). Cool thoroughly. Combine with the whipped cream. Pour into a china or ceramic serving bowl or individual bowls (do not use glass). Place in the freezing compartment of the refrigerator and freeze until half-frozen.

4–6 SERVINGS

MRS. KRETCHMAR'S SWEET NOODLE PUDDING

From New York

This is a good dessert after a light meal. I serve it with a sauce made from frozen raspberries puréed in a blender or food processor.

½ pound medium noodles, cooked al dente and drained
 2 tablespoons melted butter

    3 eggs, separated
    1 cup sugar
    2 teaspoons ground cinnamon
    ½ teaspoon vanilla extract
    3 well-flavored apples, peeled, cored, and sliced
    ¼ cup raisins

Place the noodles in a large bowl and stir in the melted butter. Beat the egg yolks and add to noodles. Stir in the sugar, cinnamon, and vanilla. Add the apples and raisins and mix thoroughly. Beat the egg whites until stiff and fold gently into noodle mixture. Turn into a generously buttered 1½- to 2-quart baking dish. Bake in a preheated moderate oven (350°) for about 35–40 minutes or until golden. Serve sliced, with preserves or a fruit sauce. Leftover pudding can be sliced, fried in a little butter, and served like French toast.

   6 SERVINGS

RUTH GIVEN'S
BAKED PEACH PUDDING

From West Virginia

6–7 large ripe but firm peaches, stoned and sliced, to fill
       1½-quart baking dish
    3 tablespoons light-brown or dark-brown sugar
    3 tablespoons butter
    1 egg
    1 cup granulated sugar
    1 cup flour
    1 teaspoon baking powder
       heavy cream or ice cream

Turn the peaches into a generously buttered 1½-quart baking dish. Sprinkle with the brown sugar and dot with the butter. In a bowl, beat the egg. Sift into it the granulated sugar, flour, and baking powder. Stir until mixture is blended; it should be crumbly. Pile on top of peaches. Bake for about 35 minutes in a preheated moderate oven (350°). Serve with heavy cream or ice cream.

4–6 SERVINGS

VARIATION:
This recipe may also be made with 5 large tart apples.

PEARS HÉLÈNE

All-American

An easy restaurant dessert that makes a good impression.

    2 cups water
    1 cup sugar
    1 2-inch piece vanilla bean or 1 teaspoon vanilla extract
    4 large ripe but firm pears
    1 pint vanilla ice cream
    ⅔ cup chopped walnuts, pecans, or pistachios
       Fudge Sauce (see following recipe)

In a wide-bottomed saucepan, combine the water, sugar, and vanilla bean or vanilla extract. Bring to boiling point, lower heat, and simmer without a cover for 3–5 minutes. While the syrup is cooking, peel and core the pears. Cut them into halves, lengthwise. Add pears in single layer (or cook half the pears at a time) and simmer over low heat for about 5 minutes or until tender. Pears must not be mushy. Cool pears in syrup and drain. Chill until serving time. Place ice cream in a glass serving dish. Arrange pear halves on it. Sprinkle with nuts. Spoon Fudge Sauce over pears or pass separately.

4 SERVINGS

FUDGE SAUCE

4 squares (4 ounces) unsweetened chocolate
2 tablespoons butter
½ cup heavy cream
1 cup sifted confectioners' sugar
1 teaspoon vanilla extract

Put the chocolate and butter in the top of a double boiler. Over hot—not boiling—water, melt chocolate and butter, stirring occasionally. Stir in the cream. Beat in the confectioners' sugar and vanilla extract. Cook, stirring all the time, until mixture is smooth. Cool a little before using.

AUNT BLANCHE'S PERSIMMON PUDDING CAKE

From North Carolina

Persimmon Pudding is a well-known North Carolina delicacy. In the South, it is made with the native fruit, which differs from the large, juicy Japanese persimmons from California found in northern markets. The southern persimmon is a small round fruit, about 1 to 2 inches in diameter. When these are not available use the large Japanese persimmons. To pulp persimmons, wash them and strain through a sieve or food mill to get rid of seeds and most of the skin.

1 quart persimmon pulp (about 12 large persimmons
  for 1 quart pulp)
1 cup sugar
3 eggs, beaten
2 cups finely grated sweet potato or yam
1 cup shredded coconut
1 cup seedless raisins
1 cup melted butter

¾ cup milk
2 cups flour
3 teaspoons baking powder
1 teaspoon ground cinnamon
1 teaspoon ground nutmeg
1 teaspoon vanilla extract
⅓ cup water
1 tablespoon sugar

In a large bowl, combine the persimmon pulp, 1 cup sugar, eggs, sweet potato or yam, coconut, and raisins and mix thoroughly. Stir in the butter and milk and again mix well. Sift directly into the mixture the flour, baking powder, cinnamon, and nutmeg and again mix thoroughly. Stir in the vanilla. Turn into a greased and floured 10-inch tube pan. Bake in a preheated slow oven (325°) for 1½ hours. Combine the ⅓ cup water and 1 tablespoon sugar and bring to boiling point. Remove cake from oven and slowly drizzle the boiling syrup over the surface; this keeps the cake pudding-like. Return to oven and bake for another 30 minutes. Cool in pan. Turn out on a cake platter and serve with whipped cream.

8 SERVINGS

BAKED PLUM COMPOTE

From Oregon

The idea is to cook the fruit in its own juice. This makes a delicious dish, even without the spices. Pitted fresh cherries can be cooked in the same way. Ripe black Bing cherries need very little if any sugar, and, rather than with spices, I prefer them cooked with a twist of lemon peel.

2 pounds ripe blue Italian plums
2 cups sugar
½ teaspoon ground cinnamon
¼ teaspoon ground cloves
¼ teaspoon ground nutmeg
water
heavy cream (optional)

Wash and pit the plums. Place them in a [...] bean pot; either must have a tight-fitting lid. Sti[...] namon, cloves, and nutmeg and mix well. Add [...] water (1 inch for every pound of plums). Cover tightly. Cook [...] very slow oven (250°) for about 2 hours or until plums are very soft. Check occasionally for moisture; if necessary, add a little more water, 2 tablespoons at a time, to prevent scorching. Chill and serve with heavy cream or serve plain as a relish with pork or ham.

4–6 SERVINGS

PRUNE WHIP

All-American

A charming light, old-fashioned dessert that can also be made with dried apricots or dates. Real prunes, strained, or mashed in a food processor, work much better than the rather liquid baby-food prunes; the strained prunes should be the consistency of very thick applesauce or of a thick preserve.

1⅓ cups pitted prunes
⅓ cup water
⅓ cup sugar
2 teaspoons lemon juice
5 egg whites
¼ teaspoon cream of tartar
   thin egg custard or heavy cream

Wash and drain prunes. Place in a small saucepan and add the water. Simmer, covered, over low heat for about 5–10 minutes or until very soft. Stir frequently to prevent scorching. Rub prunes through a strainer into another small saucepan, or mash in food processor and then put into small saucepan. Stir in the sugar and cook for about 2 minutes or until sugar has dissolved. Cool and stir in the lemon juice. Beat the egg whites until frothy, add the cream of tartar, and continue beating until whites are stiff and stand in peaks. Gradually add prunes to egg whites, folding each addition quickly into the egg whites. The easiest way to do this is to use a rubber spatula, cutting down from the center top to the bottom and folding over. Do not overfold or the whites will be deflated and not rise properly. Turn mixture into a lightly buttered 1½-quart baking dish. Let it stand in peaks. Bake in a preheated slow oven (275°) for about 30–40 minutes or until golden on top. Cool and serve cold or chilled with a thin custard or with plain heavy cream.

4–6 SERVINGS

RED FRUITS

From New York

1½ quarts large ripe strawberries
2 10-ounce packages frozen raspberries, partially
   thawed and drained
1 cup heavy cream
2 tablespoons sugar
1 tablespoon brandy or Curaçao

Wash the strawberries and dry between paper towels. Hull carefully. Place strawberries in a pyramid on a serving dish. Purée the raspberries in a food processor or blender. Pour over strawberries. Chill for 1 hour. At serving time, whip the cream with the sugar; add the brandy or Curaçao. Serve separately.

Note:
For a sweeter dish, sprinkle strawberries with sugar to taste.

4–6 SERVINGS

SWEET-POTATO PUDDING

From South Carolina

- ¾ cup milk or water
- 2½ pounds sweet potatoes, peeled and grated (about 4 cups)
- 1 cup white or light-brown sugar
- 6 tablespoons butter
  grated rind of 1 lemon
- 2 teaspoons ground cardamom or to taste, or any desired spice to taste
- ½ cup golden raisins, plumped in hot water and drained
- ½ cup blanched slivered almonds
  sweet cream or sour cream

Over low heat, bring milk or water to boiling point in a heavy saucepan. Stir in the sweet potatoes and cook, stirring frequently (mixture scorches easily), for about 15 minutes. Stir in the sugar and 4 tablespoons of the butter. Continue cooking over low heat, stirring constantly and scraping down sides and bottom of saucepan, for 10–15 more minutes, or until mixture thickens. Stir in cardamom or other spice, raisins, and almonds and mix well. Turn into a generously buttered 1½- or 2-quart baking dish. Dot with the remaining butter. Cook in a preheated moderate oven (350°) for about 20 minutes or until golden brown. Cool to lukewarm before serving with sweet cream or a dollop of sour cream for each serving.

5–6 SERVINGS

Cakes, Frostings, Pies, and Cookies

Cakes and Frostings

ONE-EGG CAKE

All-American

This very good cake is an echo of a more frugal past. As for all cakes with few eggs and not much shortening it is better to use cake flour; this makes for a lighter cake.

2 cups cake flour
2 teaspoons baking powder
¼ teaspoon salt
¼ cup butter
1 cup sugar
1 egg, beaten
¾ cup milk
1 teaspoon vanilla extract

Sift together the flour, baking powder, and salt. Cream the butter until soft. Gradually beat in the sugar, 2 tablespoons at a time, beating well after each addition. Beat in the beaten egg. Beat in the flour and the milk alternately, starting and ending with flour. Beat in the vanilla extract. Turn into two buttered and floured 8-inch layer-cake pans or into a buttered and floured square 8-inch pan. Bake in a preheated moderate oven (350°) for about 25–35 minutes or until cake tests done.

Note:
The cake may be sandwiched with jam or any filling. The top may be sprinkled with sifted confectioners' sugar or the top and sides frosted as desired.

2 ROUND 8-INCH LAYERS

TWO-EGG CAKE

All-American

The preceding One-Egg Cake and this cake lend themselves to Boston Cream Pie and Washington Pie (pages 244, 246). They are cakes that children like for birthday parties. This is one of the best basic cakes.

2 cups minus 2 tablespoons cake flour, or 1¾ cups all-purpose flour
2 teaspoons baking powder
½ teaspoon salt

½ cup butter
1 cup sugar
2 eggs, separated
½ cup milk
1 teaspoon vanilla extract

Sift together the flour, baking powder, and salt. In a separate bowl, cream the butter until soft. Gradually beat in the sugar, 2 tablespoons at a time, beating well after each addition. Beat in flour and milk alternately, beginning and ending with flour. Beat in vanilla extract. Turn into two buttered and floured 8-inch layer-cake pans or into an 8-inch-square buttered and floured baking pan. Bake in a preheated moderate oven (350°) for about 25–35 minutes or until cake tests done. Cool upright in pans for 5 minutes; then invert on wire racks and cool completely.

2 ROUND 8-INCH LAYERS

BOSTON CREAM PIE

From Massachusetts

In spite of its name, this is not a pie but a simple cream-filled cake, which may or may not be frosted with a plain chocolate glaze.

1 One-Egg or 1 Two-Egg Cake (pages 242, 243)
Vanilla Cream Filling (see following recipe)
Chocolate Glaze (page 245)

Make the cake according to directions; cool. Place one layer on cake plate. Spoon Vanilla Cream Filling over this layer. Top with second layer. Frost top layer only with Chocolate Glaze, or sprinkle with sifted confectioners' sugar, preferably through a lace-paper doily.

1 8-INCH TWO-LAYER CAKE

VANILLA CREAM FILLING

This can be used in cakes other than Boston Cream Pie; the recipe makes enough to fill any 8- or 9-inch two-layer cake.

    2 tablespoons cornstarch
    ⅓ cup sugar
    ¾ cup light cream or milk
    1 egg yolk
    ¼ cup milk
  1½ teaspoons vanilla extract

In a small heavy saucepan, mix together the cornstarch and sugar. Gradually stir in ¾ cup cream or milk, stirring until mixture is smooth. Cook over low heat, stirring constantly, until smooth and thickened. Remove from heat. Beat the egg yolk with ¼ cup milk. Beat 1–2 tablespoons of the hot mixture into egg yolk. Stirring constantly, add egg mixture to hot sauce in pan. Over low heat, cook for 1–2 minutes, beating constantly. Do not cook any longer, as cornstarch mixtures have a tendency to thin out with too much cooking. Remove from heat and stir in the vanilla extract. Cool, stirring frequently to prevent a skin from forming over the vanilla filling. Make sure filling is thoroughly cooled before spreading on cake.

MAKES ABOUT 1 CUP

CHOCOLATE GLAZE

This is enough to glaze any 8- or 9-inch two-layer cake. The butter gives the glaze a shine.

    2 squares (2 ounces) unsweetened baking chocolate
    1 tablespoon butter
    1 cup sifted confectioners' sugar
  2–3 tablespoons hot water
    ¾ teaspoon vanilla extract

In a small heavy saucepan, over low heat, melt the chocolate and butter. Stir until smooth. Remove from heat. Add ½ cup of the confectioners' sugar and 1 tablespoon hot water. Beat until smooth. Beat in the remaining sugar and the additional hot water, *1 tea- spoon* at a time, beating all the while, until mixture reaches a spreading consistency. Beat in the vanilla extract and beat until glossy.

Note:

More often than I care to think I have unduly thinned my glazes by adding too much water at once. Be forewarned!

MAKES ABOUT ⅔ CUP

WASHINGTON PIE

All-American

This, like Boston Cream Pie, is not a pie, but a cake.

1 recipe One-Egg Cake or Two-Egg Cake (pages
  242, 243)
  raspberry jam
  sifted confectioners' sugar

Make cake according to directions and let cool. When cake is cooled, spread one layer generously with raspberry jam and top with the other layer. Sprinkle top with confectioners' sugar. Better still, lay a lace-paper doily on top of cake and sprinkle sugar through it to form a nice pattern.

1 8-INCH TWO-LAYER CAKE

SWEET-CREAM TWO-EGG CAKE

From Maine

Cakes made with sweet cream rather than butter are for obvious reasons old American farm cakes, found throughout the country. These are tender, homey cakes, well suited for children's birthday parties or as a base for fruit toppings.

2 large or 3 small eggs, separated
1 cup sugar
1 teaspoon vanilla extract
2 cups flour
2 teaspoons cream of tartar
1 teaspoon baking soda
¼ teaspoon salt
1 cup heavy cream
  Cocoa Frosting or Blueberry Topping
  (see following recipes)

Beat the egg yolks until lemon-colored. Gradually beat in the sugar, 2 tablespoons at a time, beating well after each addition. Stir in the vanilla extract. Sift together flour, cream of tartar, baking soda, and salt. Stir flour mixture and cream alternately into egg mixture, beginning and ending with flour. Beat egg whites until stiff. Fold into batter. Spoon batter in equal amounts into two greased and floured 8-inch layer-cake pans. Bake in a preheated moderate oven (350°) for about 25–30 minutes or until cake shrinks away from sides of pans and tests done. Cool for 2–3 minutes in pans, then turn out on racks and cool. Spread Cocoa Frosting or Blueberry Topping between the layers. If using Cocoa Frosting, swirl remaining frosting over top and sides of cake; if using Blueberry Topping, spoon some over the top of the cake but not over the sides, and serve with whipped cream on the side.

Note:
Any other desired frosting and filling may be used.

1 8-INCH TWO-LAYER CAKE, OR 8 SERVINGS

COCOA FROSTING

All-American

More chocolatey when made with Dutch-type cocoa. The reason for heating the milk is that it partly cooks the corn-starch in the confectioners' sugar, removing its somewhat raw flavor. Rum, brandy, or any favorite liqueur can be substituted for the vanilla extract.

> 4 tablespoons butter
> 6 tablespoons cocoa
> 4 cups confectioners' sugar
> 4–5 tablespoons scalding-hot milk
> 2 teaspoons vanilla extract

In the top of a small double boiler, melt the butter without browning it; the butter must be barely melted. Stir in the cocoa. Cook over hot water until mixture is smooth. Remove pan from heat but leave frosting over hot water. Sift the confectioners' sugar into a bowl. Stir in 4 tablespoons of the hot milk and beat until mixture is smooth. Stir in the vanilla extract and the hot cocoa mixture. Beat until thick enough to spread; if too thick, stir in remaining tablespoon of hot milk. Use while still lukewarm; the frosting will set on the cake.

MAKES ABOUT 2½ CUPS

BLUEBERRY TOPPING

From Maine

> ½ cup sugar
> 1 tablespoon cornstarch
> ½ cup water
> 1 pint (2 cups) fresh blueberries, picked over and washed
>   grated rind of 1 lemon
> 1 tablespoon lemon juice

In a heavy saucepan, mix the sugar, cornstarch, and water to a smooth paste. Add the blueberries and bring to boiling point. Cook over medium heat, stirring constantly, for about 3–4 minutes or until clear and thickened. Remove from heat and stir in the lemon rind and juice. Chill. Use on ice cream, cake, puddings, pancakes, and so on.

Note:
You may substitute rum (or brandy or other liqueur) to taste for the lemon juice, but use the lemon rind.

MAKES ABOUT 2 CUPS

REAL OLD-FASHIONED POUND CAKE

All-American

People say that real pound cake, which must be made with butter, is too expensive and that it is too hard to make because it requires a lot of beating. To the first objection I say, no more, but much less, expensive than a boughten cake (even a mediocre one); and to the second, that we are in the age of electric beaters. The recipe may be halved, but it is worth making the whole amount, since the cake keeps and freezes well. Note that the cake contains no baking powder, since its texture must be fine and firm and moist. Some people use cake flour for pound cakes, but I don't think this necessary. However, ordinary all-purpose flour is better than unbleached flour, which makes for a heavier cake.

  2 cups (1 pound) butter
  2 cups (1 pound) sugar
 10 eggs, separated
  1 teaspoon ground mace
  3 tablespoons brandy
  4 cups (1 pound) all-purpose flour

Generously butter a deep large 10-inch-diameter or 10-cup ring mold if you are baking one cake; a ring mold will help a heavy cake of this kind to bake evenly. Flour the ring mold properly on all surfaces. Or butter and flour two 9×5×3-inch loaf pans and line bottoms with waxed paper. Butter the waxed paper. Cream the butter until light and fluffy. Gradually beat in the sugar, 4 tablespoons (¼ cup) at a time, beating well after each addition. Beat in the egg yolks, one at a time, beating very well after each addition (or beat all the egg yolks together until light and thick, then beat them gradually into the butter mixture). Beat in the mace and brandy. Beat in the flour gradually and beat until just smooth; do not overbeat. Beat the egg whites until stiff and fold gently into batter. Turn into mold or pans. Bake in a preheated slow oven (325°) for about 1¼ to 1½ hours for ring mold, or 60–75 minutes for loaf pans, or until cake tests done and pulls away from sides of pans. Stand the mold or pans on wire racks and cool for about 15 minutes before unmolding. Cool completely before slicing.

1 10-INCH RING-MOLD CAKE

GINGERBREAD

Legacy of the English colonists.

½ cup butter
¾ cup light-brown or dark-brown sugar, or white sugar
½ cup molasses
1 cup milk
1 egg
2½ cups flour
½ teaspoon ground cinnamon
½ teaspoon ground mace
½ teaspoon ground allspice
½ teaspoon ground cloves
1 teaspoon ground ginger
¼ teaspoon salt
1 teaspoon baking powder
1 teaspoon baking soda

Cream the butter until soft. Gradually add the sugar, beating well after each addition. Stir in the molasses, milk, and egg. Beat until smooth. Combine the remaining ingredients. Sift them, a little at a time, into the batter, beating well after each addition. Turn into a generously buttered and floured 8×8-inch baking pan. Bake in a preheated moderate oven (350°) for about 30 minutes or until cake tests done and shrinks away from the sides of the pan. Serve hot or cold with whipped cream or hard sauce.

6–8 SERVINGS

BLUEBERRY GINGERBREAD

From Maine

½ cup butter
1 cup sugar plus 3 tablespoons
1 egg
2–3 tablespoons molasses
2 cups flour
2 teaspoons ground cinnamon
2 teaspoons ground ginger
½ teaspoon salt
1 teaspoon baking soda
1 cup buttermilk
1½ cups fresh blueberries

Cream the butter until soft. Gradually beat in 1 cup of the sugar, beating well after each addition. Beat in the egg and molasses and beat thoroughly to blend. Sift together the flour, cinnamon, ginger, and salt. Stir the baking soda into the buttermilk. Add flour to butter mixture alternately with buttermilk, beginning and ending with flour. Stir in the blueberries. Turn batter into a buttered and floured 9-inch square pan. Sprinkle with remaining 3 tablespoons sugar for a crusty topping. Bake in a preheated moderate oven (350°) for 50–60 minutes or until cake tests done and shrinks from sides of pan. Serve as is, or with Blueberry Topping (page 248).

8 SERVINGS

SCHWENKFELDER
SAFFRON CAKE

From Pennsylvania

The Schwenkfelder are a Protestant sect from Silesia, Germany, who came to Pennsylvania in 1734. They brought with them this coffee cake, interesting because of its use of saffron. A prominent Schwenkfelder family operated a saffron warehouse in Holland before coming to America, which may account for the use of this unusual herb in this and other Schwenkfelder cooking. The cakes are usually mixed in the evening and set to rise overnight for breakfast baking. This is also a traditional Schwenkfelder wedding cake. It is a good plain cake, livened up by the crumb topping, which must be richer than the cake. But it takes a certain amount of time to make.

STEP 1

    2 medium white potatoes, peeled and quartered, to make
      1 cup mashed
  ½ cup sugar
    1 cup reserved potato water
    1 package granulated dry yeast

Cook the potatoes in salted water until soft. Drain, reserving 1 cup potato water. In a bowl, mash the potatoes and combine with the sugar; mix thoroughly. Heat the reserved potato water to lukewarm, add the yeast, and stir until dissolved. Add to potato and sugar mixture and mix. Cover bowl and set in a warm place to rise for 3 hours.

STEP 2

  ½–¾ teaspoon saffron
    ¼ cup boiling water
      1 cup milk
    ½ cup lard or other shortening
      2 eggs, beaten
      1 cup sugar
    ½ teaspoon salt
      9 cups flour, approximately

Sprinkle the saffron over the boiling water and stir; reserve. Bring the milk to boiling point and pour into a large bowl. Stir in the lard, eggs, sugar, and salt, beating well after each addition. Strain saffron water into milk mixture, reserving the threads for later use. Cool to lukewarm. Then add yeast mixture and 4 cups of the flour, beating well after each addition. Cover and let rise in a place that is warm (about 75°) and free from drafts for about 1 to 1½ hours or until bubbly. Add remaining flour, beginning with 4 cups to make a dough that can be handled for kneading. As flours absorb liquids differently, add remaining flour if necessary. Knead until smooth and satiny, shape into a ball and turn into a greased bowl. Turn dough in bowl to grease on all sides. Cover and let rise again in a warm place for about 4 hours or until doubled in bulk and light. Punch down and let rest 10 minutes before rolling out.

While dough is rising prepare the crumbs.

CRUMB TOPPING

2 cups flour
2 cups light-brown sugar
1 teaspoon ground cinnamon
1 cup butter, at room temperature
   saffron threads from cake water

Combine the flour, sugar, and cinnamon. Cut in the butter and, with hands, rub mixture together to make crumbs. Add reserved saffron threads.

TO PUT TOGETHER

¼–⅓ cup cream or ¼ cup melted butter
   crumbs

Divide the dough into three parts, or two parts if preferred. Roll out each part to a thickness of ⅓ inch. Place on greased cookie sheets. Let rise for about 1 hour. Then brush cakes with cream or melted butter and top with crumbs. Bake in a preheated slow oven (325°) for 25 to 30 minutes.

Note:

This is the original recipe, which was given to me by a Schwenkfelder lady at the Kutztown Folk Fair in Pennsylvania.

3 10×13-INCH CAKES

CHOCOLATE THREE-HOLE CAKE

All-American

This cake, which a child can make easily, is surprisingly pleasant.

1½ cups flour
  1 cup sugar
  1 teaspoon baking soda
½ teaspoon salt
  4 tablespoons cocoa
  6 tablespoons salad oil
  1 tablespoon white or cider vinegar
  1 teaspoon vanilla extract
  1 cup cold water
    confectioners' sugar

Grease and flour an 8×8-inch square baking pan. Sift together directly into baking pan the flour, sugar, baking soda, salt, and cocoa. Stir with a fork to mix. With a finger, make three holes in the flour mixture, spacing them at regular intervals. Pour the salad oil into the first hole, the vinegar into the second, and the vanilla extract into the third. Pour the water over the whole. Stir vigorously with a fork to blend thoroughly. Bake in a preheated moderate oven (350°) for 35–40 minutes or until cake shrinks from sides of pan and tests done. Cool in pan. Turn out on a cake plate and sprinkle with confectioners' sugar through a small sieve.

1 8-INCH SQUARE CAKE

CHOCOLATE SOUR-CREAM
FROSTING

From California

This frosting, which appeals more to grown-ups than to children, was invented by the late Helen Brown, one of the nation's most creative cooks and a very nice lady besides. It is good on any kind of cake.

    5 squares (5 ounces) semisweet chocolate
    ⅛ teaspoon salt
    ½ cup sour cream

Melt the chocolate in the top of a double boiler over hot water. Stir in the salt. Cool; then beat in the sour cream until mixture is smooth.

MAKES ABOUT ¾ CUP; ENOUGH TO FROST TOP AND SIDES OF AN 8-INCH SQUARE CAKE.

WALDORF CHOCOLATE CAKE

American, but of unknown origin

You'd never know this cake is made with mayonnaise instead of eggs and shortening unless you were told; the chocolate flavor covers the mayonnaise's tartness. I've fooled many people with this cake, which is extremely easy and good.

    2 cups flour
    1 cup sugar
    ¼ teaspoon salt
    ⅓ cup cocoa, preferably Dutch type
    1 teaspoon baking soda
    1 cup cold water

    1½ teaspoons vanilla extract
    ⅔   cup mayonnaise
    1   cup heavy cream, whipped, or ½ cup sifted
        confectioners' sugar

Sift the flour, sugar, salt, cocoa, and baking soda into a bowl.
Beat in the water, vanilla, and mayonnaise. Blend and then beat
75–100 strokes or until smooth. Grease two 8-inch layer-cake pans
and line bottoms with waxed paper. Turn an equal amount of batter into each pan. Bake in a preheated moderate oven (350°) for
about 25–35 minutes or until cakes shrink away from sides of pans
and test done. Cool in pans for 5 minutes. Turn out on racks and
peel off waxed paper. Or bake in a greased and floured 9×9×2-inch
baking pan for 45–50 minutes. If baked in layers, put half of the
whipped cream between the two layers and spread remaining
whipped cream over top. If baked in one pan, use a small sieve to
sprinkle top of cake with confectioners' sugar.

1 8-INCH TWO-LAYER CAKE, 1 9×9-INCH CAKE

WELLESLEY FUDGE CAKE

From New England

*This is one of the traditional cakes that I get asked for.
Cake flour makes for lighter cakes, but all-purpose flour
can be substituted. I prefer to use butter in my cakes
because it tastes better, but a shortening such as Crisco
may be used here, since the chocolate dominates the flavor
of the cake.*

    ½   cup shortening
    1½ cups sugar
    2   eggs, beaten
    1   teaspoon vanilla extract
    4   squares unsweetened baking chocolate, melted

    2 cups cake flour, or 1¾ cups all-purpose flour
    2 teaspoons baking powder
    ½ teaspoon salt
 1½ cups milk
    1 cup finely chopped nuts
       Wellesley Fudge Frosting (see following recipe)

Grease two 8- or 9-inch layer-cake pans and line bottoms
with waxed paper. Cream the shortening until soft. Gradually beat
in the sugar, beating well after each addition. Beat in the beaten
eggs and vanilla extract, beating well. Stir in the melted chocolate
and blend thoroughly. Sift together the flour, baking powder, and
salt. Beginning and ending with flour, alternately add flour and
milk to batter, beating well after each addition. Fold in chopped
nuts. Turn an equal amount of batter into each pan. Bang pans
once or twice on kitchen table to remove air pockets. Bake in a
preheated moderate oven (350°) for about 25–35 minutes or until
layers shrink from sides of pans and test done. Cool in pans for 5
minutes. Then turn out on a rack and peel off waxed paper. Cool
completely before frosting with Wellesley Fudge Frosting between
layers and on sides and top of cake.

1 8- OR 9-INCH TWO-LAYER CAKE

WELLESLEY FUDGE FROSTING

    2 squares unsweetened baking chocolate
    ½ cup butter (it must be butter), softened
    1 egg
    1 pound sifted confectioners' sugar
    1 teaspoon lemon juice
    1 teaspoon vanilla extract
    1 cup chopped nuts

Melt chocolate in the top of a double boiler over hot water.
Stir in the butter and stir until completely blended into chocolate.
Remove from heat. Beat the egg until thick. Gradually beat in the
sugar. Beat in chocolate mixture, lemon juice, and vanilla extract.
Beat until creamy and fold in the nuts.

INEZ KUBLY'S SUPER
DEVIL'S FOOD

From a cheesemaker's wife in Wisconsin

Dutch-type cocoa is infinitely the best.

¾ cup cocoa
1¾ cups sugar
3 eggs, separated
1 whole egg
½ cup milk
½ cup butter
2 cups sifted flour
1 teaspoon baking powder
1 teaspoon baking soda
½ teaspoon salt
1 cup sour cream
1 teaspoon vanilla extract
Double recipe of Seven-Minute Coconut Frosting
(page 261) or any favorite frosting

Generously grease three 8-inch layer-cake pans and line bottoms with waxed paper. In the top of a double boiler, over hot, not boiling water, cook the cocoa, ¾ cup of the sugar, 1 egg yolk, and the milk together until thick. Stir constantly to prevent lumping and sticking. Cool. Cream the butter until soft. Gradually add the remaining sugar to the butter, a little at a time, beating well after each addition. Beat in the whole egg and the remaining 2 yolks and mix well. Sift the flour with the baking powder, baking soda, and salt. Beat flour mixture gradually into egg mixture, alternating with the sour cream. Beat in the cocoa mixture and beat until well mixed. Beat the egg whites until stiff and fold into batter. Turn into pans. Bake in a preheated moderate oven (350°) for about 30 minutes or until layers shrink from side of pans and test done. Do not overbake; this cake must be moist. Cool upright in pans on wire racks for 5 minutes. Invert pans on racks, peel off waxed paper, and turn right side up again. Cool completely before filling and frosting.

8 SERVINGS

ANGEL FOOD CAKE

All-American

The snowy-white cake that graced the tables of elegant hostesses of the past, and well worth making today, if only for show—and taste. Serve it with strawberries, peaches, or other fruit, and whipped cream. Or hollow out the cake and use the shell for creams or fruit; use the crumbs from the hollowing out to mix with the filling. Top with whipped cream. Be sure to use cake flour and superfine sugar sifted, for best results. Remember that the tube pan must be absolutely free from grease or detergent or the egg whites won't expand. Be sure to preheat the oven.

```
  1     cup sifted cake flour (be sure it is sifted)
1½     cups sifted superfine sugar (be sure it is sifted)
1½     cups egg whites (whites of 10–12 medium-large
          eggs), at room temperature
  ¼     teaspoon salt
1½     teaspoons cream of tartar
1½     teaspoons vanilla extract
  ½     teaspoon almond extract
```

Sift the flour and ¾ cup of the sugar together three times. Put the egg whites into a large bowl; with an electric beater beat gently until foamy. Add the salt and cream of tartar and beat, increasing speed gradually. At high speed, start beating in the remaining sugar, 2 tablespoons at a time, beating well after each addition. Continue beating until stiff peaks form. Fold in vanilla and almond extracts. Sift 2 tablespoons of flour mixture over egg whites and fold in gently, briefly but thoroughly with a wire whip or a rubber spatula. Repeat until all flour is used. Pour batter into an ungreased, very clean, and dry 10×4-inch tube pan. Cut gently through batter to remove large air bubbles. Bake in a preheated moderate oven (350°) 40–50 minutes or until top is golden brown and lightly cracked, cracks are dry, and cake shrinks from pan. Invert pan immediately and hang from a funnel or bottle; the cake must cool from all sides. Let cake hang for at least 1 to 1½ hours to cool thoroughly and to set. Cut around all edges of cake with a sharp knife and turn out. Do not cut cake with a knife but use a wire cake cutter or pull apart with two forks inserted side by side.

10–12 SERVINGS

FRESH COCONUT CAKE

From the South

Fresh coconut makes all the difference to this cake, and it is worth the time it takes to prepare it. The cake, a standard 5-egg cake, can be frosted in any desired manner. Since I think a fresh coconut cake needs lots of frosting, I make up two batches of Seven-Minute Coconut Frosting for the three 9-inch layers and use about 3–4 cups grated or finely shredded coconut.

      3 cups sifted cake flour
      2 teaspoons baking powder
    ½ teaspoon salt
      1 cup butter
      2 cups sugar
      2 teaspoons vanilla extract
    ½ teaspoon almond extract
      5 eggs, separated
    1½ cups fresh coconut milk (page 262)
         Seven-Minute Coconut Frosting (see following
         recipe)
    2–3 cups grated fresh coconut (page 262)

Butter three 9-inch layer-cake pans and line the bottoms with rounds of waxed paper. Butter the waxed paper. Sift together the flour, baking powder, and salt. Cream the butter until soft and fluffy. Gradually beat in the sugar, about ¼ cup at a time, beating well after each addition. Beat in the vanilla and almond extracts. Beat in the egg yolks, one at a time, beating well after each addition. Beat in the flour alternately with 1 cup of the coconut milk. Beat egg whites until stiff and fold into batter. Divide batter evenly into the three pans. Bake in a preheated moderate oven (375°) for about 35 minutes, or until cake shrinks from sides of pan and tests done. Cool for 3–4 minutes, then turn out layers on racks and peel off waxed paper. Cool. When cake is ready for frosting, sprinkle each layer with some of the remaining ½ cup coconut milk. Spread frosting on two layers and sprinkle about ½ cup grated coconut on each layer. Top with third layer. Frost top and sides of the cake and sprinkle remaining coconut on top and sides.

10–12 SERVINGS

SEVEN-MINUTE COCONUT FROSTING

Depending on the beater, the frosting may take less or more than 7 minutes. It is ready when it stands in stiff peaks.

    2 egg whites
 1½ cups sugar, preferably superfine sugar
    1 tablespoon light corn syrup, or ¼ teaspoon cream
       of tartar
  ⅓ cup cold water
    1 teaspoon vanilla extract
  ½ cup grated or finely shredded coconut

Put the egg whites, sugar, corn syrup, and water in the top of a double boiler. Set over gently boiling water. Beat constantly with electric or rotary beater or with wire whisk for about 7 minutes or until frosting stands in stiff peaks. Remove double boiler from heat and top of double boiler from bottom. Beat in vanilla extract. Continue beating until frosting is of spreading consistency. Then beat in the coconut.

MAKES ENOUGH TO FILL AND FROST MODERATELY AN 8- OR 9-INCH TWO-LAYER CAKE.

HOW TO MAKE COCONUT MILK

Coconut water and coconut milk are not the same. The first is the clear liquid which sloshes around in the nut when it is shaken. The second is made from the grated stiff white meat of the mature coconut.

To open a coconut easily, place it in a preheated slow oven (325°) for 15–20 minutes. Do not overbake or the coconut will lose flavor. Remove from oven and cool the coconut until it is possible to handle it. Put the coconut on a deep pie plate. Insert a thick skewer or ice pick in each of the three "eyes" at the peak and hammer it in. Drain the liquid through these holes into a container; the pie plate prevents the liquid from splashing about. Then wrap the nut in a piece of cloth (to prevent scattering) and whack it with a hammer, meat mallet, or anything heavy. Remove the heavy shell. Cut the meat into pieces and grate in a food processor or, a few pieces at a time, in a blender. Or grate by hand. Place the grated meat in a bowl and cover with hot milk—about 1 cup hot milk for each 1 cup grated coconut. (For a more diluted coconut milk, use 1½ to 2 cups milk.) Let stand for 30 minutes. Drain through a strainer, pushing the meat to the sides with the back of a spoon to extract every drop. Or place in a kitchen towel and twist into a bowl. Refrigerate. When the liquid has been thoroughly refrigerated, the "cream" will rise and can be skimmed off like any cream.

HOW TO GRATE COCONUT

The easiest way to grate coconut is in a food processor or blender. The meat must be peeled or the brown skin will mar the whiteness of the meat which is essential to the effect in the dish it's used for. The easiest way to peel is to use a vegetable peeler or a small paring knife. Cut the peeled meat into smallish pieces before adding to food processor or into very small pieces for blender. If the meat is grated by hand, it need not be peeled. Use the fine side of the grater (as in grating cheese). Do not grate the skin.

DAFFODIL CAKE

Midwestern

*This sponge cake can be frosted in any desired manner.
Sponge cakes need very accurate measurements, and since
even eggs of the same category (large, medium, and so on)
may contain different amounts of white and yolk, I have
listed the eggs needed by volume rather than unit. An
electric beater or mixer is needed for this cake, as is cake
flour.*

1¼ cups cake flour, sifted
1½ cups sugar, preferably superfine sugar
½ teaspoon salt
½ teaspoon baking powder
¾ cup egg whites (from about 6 medium eggs)
1 teaspoon cream of tartar
½ cup egg yolks (from about 6 medium eggs)
¼ cup water (must be cold)
1 teaspoon vanilla extract
grated rind of 1 lemon or ½ teaspoon almond extract
Daffodil Soft-Sugar Frosting (see following recipe)

In a bowl, sift together the flour, 1 cup of the sugar, the salt,
and the baking powder. Put the egg whites into large bowl. Beat
with electric mixer until frothy. Add the cream of tartar. Beat at
high speed until egg whites stand in soft mounds. Beat in remaining ½ cup of sugar, 1 tablespoon at a time. Beat until egg whites
stand in stiff, shiny peaks. Lightly beat together the egg yolks,
water, vanilla extract, and grated lemon rind or almond extract. Stir
into sifted dry ingredients. Beat with an electric beater at medium
speed for 1 minute. Fold egg mixture, one quarter at a time, into
beaten egg whites, using a spatula or a wire whip. Fold gently until
mixture is thoroughly blended. *Do not stir.* Turn into an *ungreased*
10-inch tube pan or angel food pan. Bang very gently on kitchen
counter once to remove large air bubbles. Bake in a preheated
moderate oven (350°) for about 40–50 minutes or until cake is
golden and pulls away from the sides of the pan. Invert pan on a

rack and cool cake in pan for 1 hour. Then loosen edges with a spatula and turn out. Frost with Daffodil Soft-Sugar Frosting or serve as is.

1 10-INCH TUBE-PAN CAKE

DAFFODIL SOFT-SUGAR FROSTING

Also good on gingerbread.

½ cup butter, at room temperature
4 cups sifted confectioners' sugar
4–5 tablespoons lemon juice
grated rind of 1 lemon

Cream the butter until very soft. Beat in gradually and alternately the confectioners' sugar and 4 tablespoons lemon juice. If too thick, add remaining lemon juice, 1 teaspoon at a time. Beat in the grated lemon rind.

MAKES ABOUT 1¾ CUPS

BEGGAR'S CAKE

This is the Pennsylvania Dutch version of the famous egg-less, butterless, and milkless cake of olden days; I've seen a similar recipe in an early-nineteenth-century New England cookbook. Considering the modesty of the ingredients, it is a surprisingly palatable cake—a sustaining one, which owes nothing to nobody.

1 cup lard
1 cup dark-brown sugar, without lumps
1 cup white sugar
½ pound seedless raisins
3 teaspoons baking soda
1 cup hot water
4 cups flour
1 tablespoon ground cinnamon
1 teaspoon ground nutmeg
½ teaspoon ground cloves
½ teaspoon ground ginger
   grated rind of 1 lemon

Cream the lard until soft. Gradually stir in the brown and white sugars, beating well after each addition. Beat until the mixture is very creamy. Stir in the raisins. Put the baking soda into a measuring cup and pour the hot water over it; it will foam. Stir the baking soda–water mixture into the lard-and-raisin mixture and blend as well as possible; some of the mixture will float on top but will be absorbed later by the flour. Sift together the flour, cinnamon, nutmeg, cloves, ginger, and lemon rind. Beat into the lard mixture by half-cupfuls, beating well after each addition; the batter should be smooth. Turn into a greased, floured 10½×6½×3-inch loaf pan. Bake in a preheated slow oven (325°) for about 1½ hours or until the cake tests done in the middle. It will sink a little in the middle. Cool in the pan for 5 minutes, then turn out and cool completely.

1 10½×6½×3-INCH CAKE

LIGHT FRUIT CAKE

From the South

The secret of moist, flavorful fruit cake is to let the fruits soak in the spirits for days before they are put in the cake. Using separate glacé fruits, rather than the bright glacé

*mixtures found in supermarkets, means that you can con-
trol the amounts of each so that there's not too much of
one or another.*

       1 pound glacé lemon peel
       1 pound glacé orange peel
       1 pound red and green glacé cherries
       1 pound golden raisins
       2 cups dry white wine
       2 cups good-quality brandy or bourbon
       6 cups flour
       4 teaspoons baking powder
       1 teaspoon ground cinnamon
       1 teaspoon ground nutmeg
       1 teaspoon ground mace
       1 teaspoon ground cardamom
       1 pound butter, at room temperature
       2 cups sugar
       8 eggs, well beaten
       1 tablespoon rose water (see note)
       ½ teaspoon almond extract

First prepare the glacéed fruits. If peels and cherries are
very sugary, wash off sugar under running cold water and dry fruit
well. Cut—do not grind or process—into very small dice, about ¼- by
¼-inch. (Cut fruit looks and tastes better than ground or chopped
fruit.) Put glacéed fruits and raisins into a deep bowl and mix well
with hands. Combine wine and brandy or bourbon, pour over fruit,
and let stand, covered, at room temperature for at least 3 days. Stir
twice daily.

On baking day, prepare pans first. You will need four
8½×4½×2½-inch loaf pans. Using unglazed brown paper (such as
paper bags), cut four pieces the size of the pans' bottoms and strips
to fit the sides of the pans—sixteen strips in all. Generously butter
or grease bottoms and sides of pans. Line with brown paper pieces
and grease the paper. Turn oven on to slow (300°).

Sift together flour, baking powder, and spices. In a bowl
large enough to hold all the ingredients, cream butter with an electric beater until very soft. Beat in sugar, ¼ cup at a time, beating
well after each addition. Beat in eggs, 2 at a time, rose water, and
almond extract. Beat well to mix. Gradually beat in flour mixture

and stir until thoroughly blended. Add prepared fruit and its liquid and mix again thoroughly. It is easiest to do this with (clean) hands. Spoon batter evenly into the pans, filling no more than three-quarters full.

Place a shallow baking pan containing about 2 inches water on oven bottom. Place cake pans on middle rack. Bake about 2¾ hours. Remove pan with water during the last 30 minutes of baking. Test cakes with skewers; they should test done but not be overbaked. Cool cakes in pans for about 3–4 minutes. Then turn out on cake rack. Cool completely. When completely cooled but not before, peel off bottom and side paper strips. Either wrap cakes in clean kitchen towels wetted with brandy or bourbon, or dribble more liquor on cakes and wrap tightly in foil. Store in airtight containers for at least 2 weeks before cutting. The cakes can be kept this way for months but should be moistened with more liquor when they look dry, about once every 10 days at first and then at longer intervals.

Note:

The cakes can be baked in other kinds of pans, but pans must always be greased and lined with greased paper. Baking times will have to be adjusted according to size of pans.

French rose water to be used in cooking can be bought in any good gourmet shop. There is also a rose water of Lebanese origin which can be had in Arab or other Middle Eastern shops, as well as in some gourmet shops, but it is not as good as the French.

MAKES ABOUT 10 POUNDS

A DIFFERENT FRUIT CAKE

From North Carolina

This is a cake served in ante-bellum days with eggnog.
It is not very sweet and it stays fresh for a long time.

       1 cup butter
       2 cups sugar
       4 eggs
    1 ½ teaspoons baking soda
       1 cup buttermilk
      ⅔ cup dark molasses
       4 ounces (4 squares) unsweetened chocolate, melted
       1 cup mashed potatoes
       2 cups flour
       1 teaspoon ground cinnamon
       1 teaspoon ground cloves
       1 teaspoon ground nutmeg
       1 teaspoon ground ginger
      ½ teaspoon ground mace
       1 tablespoon lemon juice, or 2 tablespoons bourbon
       1 cup chopped walnuts
       1 cup seedless raisins, plumped in hot water and drained

Cream the butter until soft. Gradually beat in the sugar, beating well after each addition. Beat in the eggs, one at a time. Dissolve the baking soda in the buttermilk and beat into the batter. Beat in the molasses, melted chocolate, and mashed potatoes. Sift together the flour and spices. Add gradually to batter, beating well after each addition. Stir in the lemon juice or bourbon, walnuts, and raisins and mix well. Turn into a well-buttered and well-floured 10-inch tube pan (angel food pan). Place pan in a baking pan containing 2 inches water. Bake in a preheated slow oven (275°) for about 2½–3 hours or until cake tests clean. Remove from baking pan and cool a little before turning out of tube pan.

        1 10-INCH TUBE-PAN CAKE

KENTUCKY BOURBON CAKE

From Kentucky and Tennessee

Pecan and bourbon cakes, descendants of the old English fruit cakes, abound in the bourbon states. This is a particularly good one, developed by Peggy Gaines.

1½ cups sifted flour
. 1 teaspoon baking powder
  1 pound shelled pecans
  1 cup seeded raisins, preferably golden raisins
  2 teaspoons ground nutmeg or, preferably, freshly
     grated nutmeg
 ½ cup bourbon
 ½ cup butter
  1 cup sugar
  3 eggs, separated
     pecan halves
     candied cherries

Cut brown paper to line bottom and sides of an 8- or 9-inch spring-form pan or a 10-cup tube pan. I prefer the 9-inch spring-form pan, which makes a flatter cake but one better baked through than does the 8-inch pan. Generously grease the bottom and sides of pan. Line with brown paper (the kind used for parcels, or from a paper bag) and grease the paper. Set aside ½ cup of flour. Sift together remaining 1 cup flour and the baking powder. Break pecans into pieces with fingers and combine with the raisins in a bowl. Stir reserved ½ cup flour into mixture. Mix well, making sure that raisins and nuts are thoroughly coated with flour; this flouring will prevent them from sinking to bottom of the cake. Combine the nutmeg and bourbon; reserve. Beat the butter until soft. Gradually beat in the sugar, beating well after each addition. Beat in the egg yolks, one at a time. Stir the sifted 1 cup flour and the bourbon alternately into egg mixture, beginning and ending with flour. With a heavy wooden or metal spoon, stir raisin mixture into batter. Stir until mixture is well distributed throughout the batter, scooping up batter from bottom of bowl as you stir. Beat the egg whites until stiff and glossy. Carefully fold into batter. Turn mixture into the prepared pan. Let stand at room temperature for 10 minutes. Meanwhile, decorate top of cake with pecan halves and candied cherries. Bake in a preheated slow oven (325°) for about 1¼ hours or until top of cake is firm. Do not overbake; cake should be on the moist side. Cool cake in pan for 30 minutes. Turn out, holding cake decorated side up, and peel off bottom and side paper. Cool completely on a rack, decorated side up. Preferably, let stand for 1 day before cutting. Store in airtight container.

ABOUT A 3-POUND CAKE

PECAN TORTE

From a Kentucky hostess

The torte may also be made with walnuts. There is a difference in the volume of eggs, depending on how they are beaten. Large electric beaters, such as Kitchen Aid, beat more air more energetically into them (as into all things). This increases the volume, which in its turn affects the volume of the cake and the size of pan in which it is baked. You may have to adjust cake pans according to the beater you use.

    bread crumbs
  6 large eggs, separated
  ¾ cup sugar
    grated rind of 1 orange
    grated rind of 1 lemon
  3 tablespoons lemon juice
  1 tablespoon bourbon or brandy
  ⅓ cup fine dry breadcrumbs, sifted
1½ cups shelled pecans, finely ground
  ½ teaspoon cream of tartar
    whipped cream

Generously butter an 8- or 9-inch spring-form mold (the size depends on your beater) and sprinkle it on bottom and sides with fine dry breadcrumbs. Shake off excess crumbs. Beat the egg yolks until light. Gradually beat in the sugar, 2 tablespoons at a time, beating well after each addition. Continue beating for 3 more minutes; the eggs should be high and fluffy. Beat in the orange and lemon rinds, lemon juice, and bourbon or brandy, mixing well. Fold in sifted breadcrumbs and ground pecans. Beat the egg whites until foamy. Add the cream of tartar. Beat until egg whites stand in peaks. Fold gently into batter. Turn batter into spring-form pan.

Bake in a preheated slow oven (325°) for 30–40 minutes or until cake tests done and shrinks from sides of pan. Turn off heat, open oven door very slightly, and cool in oven for 15 minutes. To serve, cover top with whipped cream.

8–10 SERVINGS

CARROT TORTE

From New York

Carrot cake has become popular during the last few years, one of the reasons being that it keeps well. I cannot trace its origin, but I imagine that somebody brought it from Europe, since carrot cakes are popular in Switzerland and Germany. Since there is no leavening in this version, a great deal of air must be beaten into both egg yolks and egg whites to achieve volume. It's a matter of taste, but I think it is more interesting to bake the cake in layers and put them together with apricot jam or whipped cream, topped by Lemon Frosting or whipped cream, to make it into a nice dessert.

  6 large eggs, separated
  1 cup minus 2 tablespoons sugar
    grated rind of 2 lemons
  1 tablespoon rum, or 2 tablespoons Kirsch
1⅔ cups finely grated raw carrots (about 6 medium
    carrots)
  2 cups finely ground blanched almonds (about
    1⅓ cups whole blanched almonds)
  1 teaspoon ground cardamom or mace
 ¼ teaspoon ground cinnamon
 ⅛ teaspoon ground cloves
 ⅓ cup unflavored fine dry breadcrumbs or
    zwieback crumbs
    apricot jam
    whipped cream
    Lemon Frosting (see following recipe)

Generously butter and flour two or three 9-inch layer-cake

pans, depending on thickness of layers desired. Or butter and flour a 13×9×2-inch baking pan. Beat the egg yolks until very thick. Beat in the sugar, 2 tablespoons at a time. When all the sugar has been beaten in, beat for 5 more minutes. Beat in the lemon rind and rum or Kirsch. Fold in the carrots, almonds, cardamom or mace, cinnamon, cloves, and breadcrumbs. If making layers, spoon equal amount of batter into each pan. Or put the batter into the large baking pan. Bang pans gently on kitchen table once or twice to remove any air pockets. Bake in a preheated moderate oven (350°) for 35–45 minutes or until cake shrinks away from sides of pan and tests done. Layers bake in less time than whole cake. Cool upright for 5 minutes, then invert pan on rack and cool completely. If making layers, sandwich them together with apricot jam or whipped cream and top with whipped cream or Lemon Frosting.

1 9-INCH TWO- OR THREE-LAYER CAKE, OR 1 13× 9×2-INCH CAKE

LEMON FROSTING

  1 cup confectioners' sugar, sifted
2–3 tablespoons fresh lemon juice

Sift the confectioners' sugar into a small bowl. Stir in 2–3 tablespoons fresh lemon juice, 1 teaspoon at a time, beating to desired consistency. Be careful not to beat in too much lemon juice at a time, or frosting will be too thin.

ABOUT ⅔ CUP

ETHEL BLOCK'S
SUPERIOR CHEESECAKE

From New York

*This, according to all who've eaten it, is one of the out-
standing cheesecakes. The recipe has remained unchanged*

*for forty years. The cake is easy to make and keeps well.
The lady who gave me the recipe says that the secret is to
allow the cream cheese to get very soft (she advises letting
it stand at room temperature for 6–8 hours) and to bake
the cake for 55 minutes only. Since the cake is moist, it is
best cut with a knife with a serrated edge. You will need a
9-inch spring-form pan.*

CRUST
about 1 ½ cups zwieback crumbs or graham
cracker crumbs
2 teaspoons sugar

Combine crumbs and sugar. Generously grease a 9-inch
spring-form pan. Cover bottom with 1 cup of the crumbs, pressing
them down with the back of a spoon. Reserve remaining crumbs.

FILLING
2½ pounds cream cheese, very soft
2½ cups sugar, preferably superfine sugar
6 large eggs
juice of 1 lemon
1 teaspoon vanilla extract
1 cup (½ pint) heavy cream

Preheat oven to very hot (450°). Cream the cream cheese
until very soft and fluffy; this is best done with an electric beater or
in an electric mixer. Gradually beat in the sugar, ¼ cup at a time,
beating well after each addition. Beat in the eggs, 2 at a time, beating well after each addition. Beat in the lemon juice and vanilla extract, mix well. Stir in the heavy cream. Turn into the prepared
spring-form pan and top with the remaining ½ cup crumbs. Bake
cake in the preheated hot oven *for 10 minutes only.* Turn heat
down to low (325°) and bake for 45 minutes more. Turn off oven
and let cake stand in oven for 1 hour or until almost completely
cooled. Remove from oven and cool completely. Slide a knife
around edges of cake to loosen from pan sides. Leaving cake on
pan bottom, chill overnight. Serve as is or carefully remove to a
serving plate, using a spatula to loosen cake.

1 9-INCH CHEESECAKE   •

Pies

———◆◆◆———

PASTRY FOR ONE 9-INCH
TWO-CRUST PIE

I like putting lard into my pastry, just as our grandmothers did, because it makes it flaky.

2¼ cups flour
½ teaspoon salt
8 tablespoons unsalted butter and 4 tablespoons lard,
or ¾ cup (12 tablespoons) butter
⅓ cup ice water

Sift the flour and salt together into a bowl. With two knives or a pastry blender cut in the butter and lard only until pieces of mixture are about pea-sized. (Bits of unincorporated fat make a flakier crust.) Add the water all at once. With a fork, stir only until mixture forms a loose ball. Place two thirds of the dough on a large piece of waxed paper. Cover with a matching piece of waxed paper. Pat dough into a flat round. With a rolling pin or a bottle, roll out dough into a circle from center of dough. Circle should be about 1½ to 2 inches larger than the 9-inch pie pan you are using. Peel off top piece of waxed paper and turn dough into pie pan; there should be an overlapping edge of 1½ to 2 inches. Peel off waxed paper. For the top crust, roll out remaining dough in the same manner. Refrigerate the pie pan and bottom crust dough, and the top crust dough between the pieces of waxed paper, until ready to use.

Note:
For recipes calling for a single pie shell, you will only need to roll out the bottom crust.

NONA'S APPLE PIE

All-American

One of the best apple pies ever.

5–6 medium-sized tart apples (about 2 pounds)
 5 tablespoons butter
 1 cup sugar, white or brown, or mixed (if apples are
      not tart, use about ⅔ cup)
 ¼ cup applejack, Calvados, or other apple brandy
 1 teaspoon ground cinnamon
 ½ teaspoon ground nutmeg
 2 tablespoons flour
      (If apples are not tart, add 2 tablespoons lemon juice
      and 1 teaspoon grated lemon rind)
1–2 tablespoons fine dry breadcrumbs
      Pastry for 1 9-inch Two-Crust Pie, unbaked
      (see preceding recipe)

Peel the apples, cut into quarters, and core. Cut each quarter
into 3 slices. Heat the butter in a heavy frying pan. Stir in sugar
and cook, stirring, until melted. If white sugar is used, cook until it
turns golden. Add apple slices. Cook over medium heat, lifting
apple slices gently with a spatula, until all slices are coated with
the butter-sugar mixture and are about one-quarter to one-half
cooked. Cooking time depends on apples, but do not overcook,
since pie will be baked later. Pour the apple brandy into a ladle,
warm and ignite it, and pour over apples. Mix the cinnamon, nutmeg, and flour; reserve. Sprinkle breadcrumbs over bottom of the
pie shell; this will keep it from getting soggy. Layer apples in pie
shell, sprinkling the flour-spice mixture between layers. (Sprinkle
lemon juice and rind, if used, between apple layers.) Pour any
apple syrup remaining in frying pan over apples. Cover with the
top crust, crimping the edges by pinching with fingers or tines of a
fork, and make a few slits to allow steam to escape while baking.
Bake in a preheated hot oven (400°) for about 30 minutes or until
crust is golden brown. Do not overbake since apples were partially
precooked.

1 9-INCH TWO-CRUST PIE

SHREDDED-APPLE PIE

From South Dakota

A juicy pie in which apples are shredded rather than sliced.

     1 large lemon
 4–6 cooking apples, peeled and shredded to make
          3½–4 cups
     3 egg yolks
     ½ cup sugar
     2 tablespoons heavy cream
     ⅓ cup raisins, preferably golden raisins
     ⅓ cup slivered blanched almonds
     ⅛ teaspoon ground cloves
     ⅛ teaspoon ground cinnamon
     ⅛ teaspoon ground mace
     ⅛ teaspoon ground ginger
     ⅓ to ½ cup ground almonds
     1 unbaked 9-inch pie shell (see page 274)

     TOPPING
     ¼ cup melted butter
     ⅓ cup flour
     ½ cup firmly packed light-brown sugar

Grate yellow rind off the lemon and reserve. Squeeze the lemon into a bowl. Add the shredded apples, and using your hands, mix so that the apples are moistened with lemon throughout; this keeps them white. If the apples are very juicy, drain off lemon juice; if they are dry, keep them in the juice. Beat together the egg yolks, sugar, and cream. Stir in the raisins, slivered almonds, and spices and mix well. Turn the apples into the egg mixture and mix thoroughly. Sprinkle the ground almonds over the bottom of pie shell; they will absorb moisture from the filling and keep the crust dry. Turn filling into crust and smooth top. Bake in a preheated hot oven (400°) for 25 minutes. While pie is baking, combine the topping ingredients (butter, flour, and sugar) to make a crumble. Remove pie from oven and spread topping evenly over apples. Return to oven and bake for about 20 more minutes or until topping is golden brown and filling set. Cool for about 20 minutes before serving. Good warm or cold.

8–10 SERVINGS

BANANA CREAM PIE IN MERINGUE SHELL

All-American

I think any cream pie is improved by the crisp texture of a meringue shell, plain or nut.

FILLING

- 2 tablespoons flour
- 2 tablespoons cornstarch
- 1/3 cup sugar, preferably superfine sugar
- 3/4 cup milk
- 1 cup heavy cream
- 3 egg yolks, well beaten
- 1 tablespoon butter, at room temperature
- 1/8 teaspoon ground nutmeg
- 1 recipe Meringue Shell (page 291)
- 4 ripe but firm bananas
- 1 cup heavy cream, whipped stiff

Combine the flour, cornstarch, and sugar in a saucepan. Stir in the milk to make a smooth paste and stir in the cream. (Or use 1¾ cups milk.) Cook over low heat, stirring constantly, until mixture is smooth and thickened; cook for 2 more minutes, stirring all the time. Remove from heat and stir 2 tablespoons of the sauce into the egg yolks and mix well. Add the egg mixture to the sauce and blend thoroughly. Return to very low heat and cook for about 12 minutes. Do not boil or mixture will curdle. Remove from heat and stir in the butter and nutmeg. Put a piece of waxed paper over the saucepan and cool the filling to room temperature, stirring occasionally. (The waxed paper keeps mixture from forming a skin.) When thoroughly cooled, spoon half of the filling into the meringue shell. Slice three of the bananas and arrange them in circles on the filling. Top with remaining filling. Chill. At serving time, slice remaining banana. Using a spoon or pastry tube, spread the cream in a lattice pattern over pie top. Place a banana slice in each lattice square. Serve immediately.

6–8 SERVINGS

LATTICED BLUEBERRY PIE

All-American

Blueberry pies can be flavored with any favorite spices. But I like the pristine flavor of the berries, pointed up by the lemon rind and juice, and the nonobligatory dash of gin.

  pastry for 1 9-inch Two-Crust Pie, unbaked
    (page 274)
  2 pints (about 4 cups) fresh blueberries, picked over,
    washed, and well drained
  ¾ cup sugar
  ¼ cup flour
    grated rind of 1 lemon
  2 teaspoons lemon juice
  1 tablespoon gin (optional)
  2 tablespoons butter

Divide the pastry dough into halves. Roll out one half. Line a deep 9-inch pie pan with pastry and trim pastry about ½-inch larger than rim. Fill with blueberries. Mix together sugar and flour and sprinkle over berries. Sprinkle with lemon rind, lemon juice, and gin (if used). Dot with the butter. Roll out remaining dough and cut with a knife or a pastry cutter with crimped edges into ½-inch strips. Moisten edge of bottom crust with water. Criss-cross the pastry strips over the blueberries to make a lattice pattern. Fold the ½-inch overhang of the bottom crust over the ends of the strips. Press together and flute with fingers or a fork. Bake in a preheated hot oven (425°) for about 35–45 minutes or until crust is golden and the filling begins to bubble. Cool before serving.

Note:
When baking berry pies it is wise to line the shelf below with foil to catch any overflow.

1 9-INCH PIE

CHOCOLATE ANGEL PIE

Midwestern

    3 squares (3 ounces) unsweetened chocolate
    4 egg yolks
    2 tablespoons water
    ½ cup sugar, preferably superfine sugar
    1 teaspoon vanilla extract, or 2 tablespoons rum, brandy,
      or Grand Marnier, or 1 tablespoon Crème de Menthe
 1½ cups heavy cream, whipped
    1 baked Meringue Shell (page 291)
      candied violets

Melt the chocolate in covered top of a double boiler over boiling water. Remove cover when chocolate is melted. Beat together egg yolks, water, and sugar, blending very thoroughly. Gradually stir mixture into chocolate. Cook over boiling water, stirring constantly, until very thick, almost the consistency of soft fudge. Cool, stirring frequently to prevent lumping. Beat in vanilla extract or other flavoring. Reserve about ½ cup of whipped cream and fold remaining cream into the cooled chocolate mixture, blending thoroughly. Turn into Meringue Shell, smoothing top. Drop teaspoonfuls of remaining whipped cream in a decorative pattern over pie top. Decorate with candied violets. Chill well before serving.

6–8 SERVINGS

FRESH FIG PIE

From California

    2 tablespoons unflavored gelatin
    ¼ cup water
    2 eggs, separated
    6 tablespoons sugar
    ⅛ teaspoon salt
    ¾ cup milk
    1 tablespoon grated orange rind
    2 tablespoons orange liqueur or concentrated
       orange juice (it must be concentrated)
    2 cups unpeeled diced (¼-inch dice) ripe fresh figs
    ½ cup heavy cream, whipped
    1 9-inch graham-cracker pie shell

Sprinkle the gelatin on the water and stir to blend. Beat egg yolks with 4 tablespoons of the sugar and the salt. Scald the milk in a heavy saucepan or the top of double boiler. Add 2 tablespoons of the scalded milk to the egg yolks and blend; then stir egg mixture into scalded milk and blend thoroughly. Cook over very low heat or over hot water, stirring constantly, until mixture thickens and coats the spoon. Add gelatin and stir until it is dissolved. Remove from heat and stir in the orange rind and liqueur or concentrated juice. Cool custard until it has the consistency of thick egg whites or until it is beginning to jell. Beat the egg whites with remaining 2 tablespoons sugar until stiff. Fold figs, whipped cream, and egg whites into cooled custard. Turn into the pie shell and chill until set.

1 9-INCH PIE

GRASSHOPPER PIE

A Texas version of a Southern favorite. Best made the day before it is served.

CHOCOLATE COOKIE SHELL

1½ cups chocolate cookie crumbs
¼ cup melted butter
⅛ teaspoon ground cinnamon

Cookie crumbs must be fine; if necessary, press through a sieve. Place crumbs in a bowl and stir in the melted butter and cinnamon. Press crumbs on bottom and sides of a generously buttered deep 9-inch pie pan; the shell should be thin.

FILLING

1½ teaspoons unflavored gelatin
⅓ cup milk
4 egg yolks
¼ cup sugar, preferably superfine sugar
¼ cup green or white Crème de Menthe
¼ cup Crème de Cacao
1 cup heavy cream, whipped
⅓ cup shaved chocolate curls (see note)

In a small bowl sprinkle the gelatin over the milk and mix. Stand bowl in a saucepan with boiling water and heat until gelatin is completely dissolved; keep it dissolved. Beat the egg yolks until thick. Gradually beat in the sugar, the Crème de Menthe, and the Crème de Cacao, beating well after each addition. The sugar must be completely assimilated in the mixture. Stir in the gelatin and mix well. Chill until mixture begins to thicken. Fold in the whipped cream. Turn into the cookie crumb shell, smooth, and chill overnight. At serving time, sprinkle top with chocolate curls.

Note:

To make chocolate curls, have chocolate at room temperature. Use a vegetable peeler with a long narrow blade. Draw peeler along smooth surface of a square or a block of chocolate. For large curls, pull peeler over wide surface; for small ones, pull blade along narrow side. Refrigerate curls until ready to use.

1 9-INCH PIE

KEY LIME PIE

There are several versions of this famous pie, which is based on the juice of the so-called Key lime, a small, seedy lime which grows on the Keys from Miami, Florida, around to Fort Myers. Though the most flavorful of limes, it is not widely grown because of its sensitivity to cold and because it doesn't do well in the citrus regions of mainland Florida. Many of the Key lime trees are in home gardens. The following recipe differs from others because it is made with sweet condensed milk; the recipe is famous. The crust can be pastry, zwieback, graham cracker crumb, or even a nut crust. The pie may be topped with meringue or whipped cream.

- 3 egg yolks, lightly beaten
- 1 14-ounce can sweetened condensed milk
- ⅔ cup freshly squeezed lime juice
- ½ teaspoon grated lime rind
  few drops of green food coloring (optional)
- 1 baked 9-inch pie shell (see note above)
- 1 cup heavy cream, whipped with 2 tablespoons
  sugar, preferably superfine sugar, or 3 egg whites
  and 4 tablespoons sugar

Combine the beaten egg yolks and the condensed milk and beat just enough to blend. Add the lime juice and rind and mix well; filling will be soft. Color if you wish with a few drops of green food coloring and turn into a baked pie shell. Spread whipped cream over the filling, touching the pastry edges and covering the filling completely. The pie topped with whipped cream needs no further baking. But chill it at least 4 hours or overnight before serving. If pie is to be topped with meringue, chill, then beat egg whites until stiff and beat in sugar, 1 tablespoon at a time, beating well after each addition. Spread the meringue over the filling, touching pastry edges all around. Bake in a preheated slow oven (325°) for 10 minutes or until golden.

1 9-INCH SINGLE-CRUST PIE

LEMON CHESS PIE

From the South

The origin of the name of these very Southern custardy pies is moot. But the pies (like many Southern settlers) seem to be of English origin and to have been known as "cheese" pies. It must be remembered that in old English usage the word cheese included not only the foods we now call cheese but also concoctions resembling the consistency of cheese, such as Lemon Cheese, made from sugar, eggs, butter, and lemon, and in this case, cheese or "chess" pies. There are many versions of this favorite Southern delicacy, as pies and also as tartlets.

    1½ cups sugar
     2 tablespoons white stone-ground cornmeal
     1 tablespoon flour
     4 eggs
     4 tablespoons melted butter
    ¼   cup milk
     1 tablespoon grated lemon rind
    ¼   cup lemon juice
     1 unbaked 9-inch pie shell (see page 274)

Sift together the sugar, cornmeal, and flour. Beat in the eggs, one at a time, beating well after each addition. Beat in the butter, milk, grated lemon rind, and lemon juice. Mix thoroughly. Turn mixture into unbaked pastry shell. Bake in a preheated low oven (325°) for about 45 minutes or until browned on top and testing done. Cool before cutting. The pie, puffed up during baking, will level during cooling.

1 9-INCH SINGLE-CRUST PIE

OHIO LEMON PIE

This is an old Shaker recipe. Though the lemons are very thinly sliced (best done with a serrated knife), the rind does not soften in baking but remains chewy; I think this makes a pleasant texture contrast. I have tried modern adaptations of the recipe in which the lemons are peeled but the pie is not nearly as flavorful and gets mushier, since the rind holds the pulp in. I give this recipe (which works) exactly as it came to me. But I have found that using 3 small thin-skinned lemons (weighing about 10 ounces altogether) works better because there is more juice and less pithy white membrane.

2 large lemons, weighing about 10 ounces
2 cups sugar
   pastry for 9-inch Two-Crust Pie (page 274)
4 eggs

"Slice two [or three] lemons as thin as paper, rind and all. [I remove seeds.] Place them in a yellow bowl and pour over them 2 cups of sugar. Mix well and let stand 2 hours or better. Then go about making your best pastry to 2 crusts. Line a [deep 9-inch] pie dish with same. Beat 4 eggs together and pour over lemons. [Mix well.] Fill unbaked pie shell with this and add top crust with small vents cut to let out steam. Place in a [preheated] hot oven at 450° for 15 minutes and then cut down heat [to 350°] and bake [for 20–30 minutes, until lightly browned] until a silver knife inserted into custard comes out clean."

1 9-INCH TWO-CRUST PIE

PEACH CREAM PIE

From Georgia

4 cups peeled, sliced fresh peaches
⅔ cup sugar, or to taste
¼ teaspoon ground nutmeg
¼ cup flour
½ cup ground almonds
1 9-inch unbaked pie shell (see page 274); use a
 deep pie pan
1 egg yolk
1 cup heavy cream
¼ cup blanched sliced almonds

Put the peaches into a bowl. Sprinkle with the sugar, nutmeg, and flour. Toss peaches gently to blend. Distribute the ground almonds on the pie shell; this will prevent the crust from getting soggy. Turn peaches into pie shell. Beat the egg yolk with the cream and pour over peaches. Bake in a preheated hot oven (400°) for 35 minutes. Remove from oven and sprinkle with the sliced almonds. Return to oven and bake about 5 more minutes or until filling is set and almonds are golden brown. Cool before cutting.

Note:
If you do not have a deep pie pan, put a piece of foil on oven rack below pie to catch drippings. Or place pie pan on a flat cookie sheet.

1 9-INCH PIE

"UTTERLY DEADLY"
SOUTHERN PECAN PIE

Southern

This splendid version of the filling comes from Marjorie Kinnan Rawlings, author of The Yearling, *who also wrote a marvelous cookbook,* Cross Creek Cookery. *This book is now out-of-print, but well worth searching for. There are pecan pies made with white sugar, and even some flavored with maple syrup, which make Southern purists shudder. Be sure to use a deep 9- or 10-inch pie pan.*

1 unbaked 9- or 10-inch pie shell (see page 274), in pie pan
4 eggs
1¼ cup Southern corn syrup or dark Karo syrup
1 cup sugar (author Rawlings does not specify which kind, but I use dark-brown sugar)
4 tablespoons butter, at room temperature
1 teaspoon vanilla extract
1½ cups coarsely broken pecans
1 cup cream, whipped (my addition)
pecan halves (my addition)

Preheat oven to 425°. Line the pie shell with a sheet of buttered foil and place on top of it another pie pan of the same size, buttered on the underside. This is to keep the shell from buckling; do not prick shell or filling will run out during later baking. Bake shell for 5 minutes and cool. (This short first baking helps keep the crust from getting soggy from a wet filling.) Beat the eggs in a bowl until well mixed but not thickened. Combine the syrup and sugar in a small heavy saucepan. Cook over low-to-medium heat, stirring constantly, for about 2–3 minutes or until sugar has dissolved and mixture is smooth. Pour the hot syrup gradually into the eggs, stirring all the time. Stir in the butter and when it is melted stir in vanilla extract and broken pecans. Turn mixture into the cooled pie shell. Bake in a preheated hot oven (400°) for 10 minutes. Reduce heat to low (325°) and bake for 30 minutes or until set. Cool before serving. At serving time, decorate with rosettes of whipped cream (piped through a pastry tube or dropped from a teaspoon) and top each rosette with a pecan half.

Note:
If you don't like chopped nuts, omit from filling mixture, and arrange pecan halves flat sides down, in concentric circles on bottom of pie shell. Pour the filling mixture over pecans; they will rise to the top during baking.

1 9-INCH PIE

CRUSTLESS PUMPKIN PIE

New England

So many people leave pie crust (over which I've slaved) on the plate after a good dinner that I am apt to make crustless pies—just bake the filling in a pie pan. This amount of filling, however, will fill a deep 10-inch pie pan.

1 ½   cups fresh or canned pumpkin purée
2   tablespoons melted butter
¾   cup light-brown or dark-brown sugar
1   teaspoon ground cinnamon
½   teaspoon ground nutmeg
¼   teaspoon ground mace
4   eggs, separated
¾   cup heavy cream

Combine the pumpkin purée, butter, sugar, cinnamon, nutmeg, and mace and mix well. Beat the egg yolks; then beat into pumpkin mixture. Beat in the cream and mix well. Beat the egg whites until stiff and fold gently into pumpkin mixture. Turn into a generously buttered deep 10-inch pie pan. Bake in a preheated moderate oven (350°) for about 40–50 minutes or until pie tests done. Serve warm or cool, with heavy cream on the side.

8 SERVINGS

SOUR-CREAM RAISIN PIE

From Wisconsin

    1 cup light-brown or dark-brown sugar
    2 tablespoons flour
    ½ teaspoon ground cinnamon
    ½ teaspoon ground nutmeg
    ½ teaspoon ground allspice
    ¾ cup sour cream
    3 eggs, separated
1⅓ cups seedless raisins
    ¼ teaspoon cream of tartar
    4 tablespoons white sugar, preferably superfine sugar
    1 deep 9-inch pie shell, baked (see page 274)

In the top of a double boiler, combine the brown sugar, flour, cinnamon, nutmeg, allspice, and sour cream. Cook over boiling water, stirring constantly, for about 5 minutes, or until mixture is smooth and thickened. Remove from heat but let stand over hot water. Beat the egg yolks until thick. Beat about 2–3 tablespoons of sugar mixture into egg yolks. Add egg yolks to sugar mixture. Return to heat and cook, stirring constantly, for about 5 minutes or until thickened. Stir in the raisins and cool completely. Meanwhile, beat the egg whites until frothy and beat in the cream of tartar. Beat in the white sugar, 1 tablespoon at a time, beating well after each addition. Beat until the meringue is stiff and shiny but not dry. Turn the cooled filling into the baked pie shell. Spread meringue over filling in swirls; it must touch the pastry or meringue will shrink away from edges. Bake in a preheated moderate oven (350°) for 10 minutes or until lightly browned. Cool for at least 15 minutes before cutting.

1 9-INCH PIE

SPRING RHUBARB PIE

All-American

    pastry for 9-inch Two-Crust Pie (page 274)
1 tablespoon seedless raspberry or blackberry
    preserve, melted
5 cups fresh young rhubarb cut into ½-inch pieces
1½ cups sugar
⅓ cup flour
¼ teaspoon almond extract
1 tablespoon butter
    vanilla ice cream

Roll out dough for bottom and top crusts. Line a 9-inch deep
pie pan with bottom crust. Prick with fork. Bake on lowest shelf of
a preheated hot oven (425°) for 6 minutes. Remove from oven and
brush with the melted preserve. Return to oven and bake for 2
more minutes; time accurately. Remove from oven and cool. Lower
oven heat to 400°. In a large bowl, combine the rhubarb, sugar,
flour, and almond extract. Toss thoroughly; it is easiest to do this
with the hands. Turn mixture into pie pan. Dot with butter. Cover
with top crust, sealing edges with a fork. Prick top two or three
times with fork. Place pan on a baking sheet, as juices will run over
during baking. Bake on middle shelf of oven for 40 minutes or until
browned and bubbling. Serve warm with vanilla ice cream.

Note:
Prebaking the bottom crust and brushing it with the melted
preserve prevents later sogginess.

1 9-INCH PIE

FRESH STRAWBERRY PIE

From Kansas

1 quart large firm ripe strawberries
3 tablespoons cornstarch
½ cup water
1 tablespoon lemon juice
⅛ teaspoon salt
1 cup sugar
1 baked 9-inch pie shell (see page 274), or
   Meringue Shell (see following recipe)
1 cup heavy cream, whipped, flavored with
   ⅛ teaspoon ground mace

Hull and wash the berries. Drain. Divide berries into two parts, picking out best berries for one part. Reserve best berries. In a saucepan, crush remaining berries with a fork. Combine the cornstarch, water, and lemon juice to a smooth paste and stir into crushed berries. Stir in the salt and sugar. Cook over low heat, stirring constantly, for about 5 minutes or until mixture thickens and is clear. Cool. Place the reserved berries in the pie shell and top with the cooked mixture, spreading it evenly. Decorate with whipped cream. Refrigerate until serving time.

Note:
The pie can be made a day ahead and refrigerated, but the whipped cream must not be added until just before serving time.

1 9-INCH PIE

MERINGUE SHELL

Midwestern

The volume of egg whites varies depending on the way they are beaten. A hand beater gives the least volume, an electric one good volume, and a large Kitchen-Aid type beater a very large volume. Make sure there are no specks of yolks in the whites and that bowl and beater are immaculately clean and free of grease. Add sugar very slowly, by the tablespoonful, beating well after each addition to dissolve the sugar fully. If it is not fully dissolved, the baked meringue will "weep" with beads of sugar syrup. Do not overbeat, especially with a large electric beater. Beat until meringue is glossy and very stiff but not dry; it should spread smoothly and not lump. Be sure to preheat the oven to low (250°). It really is not hard to make meringues.

    4 egg whites
  ¼ teaspoon salt
  ½ teaspoon cream of tartar
    1 cup sugar, preferably superfine sugar
  ½ teaspoon vanilla extract
  ½ cup whole blanched almonds, ground very fine
      to make about ¾ cup (optional)

Lightly butter a deep 9- or 10-inch pie pan (size depends on your beater). Beat egg whites and salt until foamy. Beat in cream of tartar. Continue beating, gradually adding sugar 1 tablespoon at a time, beating well after each addition. Beat in vanilla. Fold in almonds, 2 tablespoons at a time (if used). Spread a 1-inch layer of egg white on bottom of pan. Pile remaining egg white on sides of pan, building it up to about ½ inch above edge of pan. Smooth lightly with a spatula dipped in water. Bake in preheated 250° oven for 1 hour. Turn off oven and let meringue shell dry in closed oven until oven is cooled. Do not open oven door while meringue is drying.

1 9- OR 10-INCH SHELL

FRIED FRUIT PIES

From North Carolina

Schoolchildren took these to school as snacks.

   1 8-ounce package dried fruit (apples, peaches, or
     apricots, or mixed)
   2 cups water
   ½ cup sugar or to taste
   1 recipe 9-inch Two-Crust Pie pastry (see page 274)
     shortening or oil for deep-frying

In a heavy saucepan, combine the fruit and water. Simmer covered over low heat for 20 minutes. Add the sugar and continue cooking for 10–15 more minutes. Mash fruit (do not purée it) to a thick consistency. If fruit is still too moist, return to heat and cook, stirring constantly to avoid scorching, for 3–6 more minutes or until dried out. Cool and reserve. Roll out pastry to a thickness of ⅛-inch. Cut into rounds about 4 to 4½ inches in diameter. Place about 1 tablespoon cooked fruit in center of each round. Wet edges with water and fold over to completely enclose the filling, making a halfmoon shape. Seal edges by pressing down with the tines of a fork. Heat shortening in deep-fryer to a temperature of 375° on the frying thermometer. Fry a few pies at a time (they must not touch) for 3–4 minutes. Turn and fry on other side for 3–4 minutes or until golden. Drain on paper towels and serve hot or cold.

ABOUT 1 DOZEN 4½-INCH PIES

Cookies

RICH BROWNIES

All-American

    4 squares (4 ounces) unsweetened baking chocolate
    1 cup butter, cut into pieces
    2 cups sugar
    4 eggs
    1½ cups flour
    ¼ teaspoon salt
    1½ teaspoons vanilla extract
    1½ cups coarsely chopped walnuts or pecans

Over lowest possible heat or in top of a double boiler over (not in) boiling water, melt the chocolate. Stir in the butter gradually, stirring well after each addition. Stir in the sugar and stir until completely melted. Beat in the eggs, one at a time, beating after each addition. Beat in the flour, salt, vanilla extract, and nuts. Butter and flour a square 9×9×2-inch baking pan. Turn batter into it. Bake in a preheated moderate oven (375°) for 40 minutes or until brownies begin to shrink away from sides of pan. Do not overbake; brownies should be moist. Cool in pan, then cut into 16 or 20 squares.

ABOUT 16–20 BROWNIES

HERMITS

All-American

1¾ cups flour sifted before measuring
 2 teaspoons ground cinnamon
 ½ teaspoon ground nutmeg
 ½ teaspoon ground cardamom
 ¼ teaspoon ground cloves
 ¼ teaspoon salt
 ⅔ cup butter
 1 cup dark-brown sugar
 2 eggs, well beaten
 ¼ teaspoon baking soda
 3 tablespoons sour cream
 1 cup chopped pecans or walnuts
 ½ cup chopped raisins or dates
 ½ cup chopped glacé fruit mix
   Vanilla Icing, if desired (see following recipe)

Sift together the flour, cinnamon, nutmeg, cardamom, cloves, and salt. Cream the butter until light. Gradually beat in the sugar, ¼ cup at a time. Beat in the beaten eggs and mix thoroughly. Stir the baking soda into the sour cream and stir into batter, mixing well. Stir in flour-spice mixture and beat well. Stir in nuts, raisins or dates, and glacé fruit, mixing well after each addition. Grease and flour two or three large cookie sheets. Drop batter from a tablespoon onto cookie sheets, leaving about 2 inches between cookies to allow for spreading. Bake in a preheated moderate oven (350°) for 10–15 minutes or until browned and set. If desired, glaze with Vanilla Icing while still hot. This is best done by letting the cookies cool on cookie sheets for 3–4 minutes, and then glazing them while still on cookie sheets. Have a bowl of Vanilla Icing and a pastry brush ready and dab about ½ teaspoonful on each hot cookie. It will form a glaze when cool.

ABOUT 50 COOKIES

VANILLA ICING

This can be used for any cookies.

    2 tablespoons butter, at room temperature
 1½ teaspoons vanilla extract
    2 tablespoons light or heavy cream, or more
      dash salt
 1½ cups sifted confectioners' sugar

Cream the butter until soft and beat in vanilla extract, cream, and salt. Gradually beat in the sugar and beat until mixture is of spreading consistency and creamy. If necessary, beat in a little more cream, ½ teaspoon at a time. (It is extremely easy to beat too much liquid into an icing that will then run.)

FOR ABOUT 50 COOKIES

ELLA ELVIN'S PEANUT-BUTTER COOKIES

All-American

 ½ cup butter
 ½ cup smooth or chunky peanut butter
 ¾ cup sugar
  1 egg
  1 teaspoon vanilla extract
 1¼ cups flour, sifted before measuring
 ¼ teaspoon baking powder
 ½ teaspoon salt
    shelled peanuts

Cream the butter until soft and fluffy. Blend in the peanut butter. Gradually beat in the sugar, egg, and vanilla extract. Sift together the flour, baking powder, and salt. Beat into the creamed mixture. Drop by teaspoonfuls on greased cookie sheets. Flatten each cookie with a fork dipped in cold water. Press 1 or more peanuts into the center of each cookie. Bake in a preheated moderate oven (350°) for about 10–12 minutes. Cool on racks.

ABOUT 5 DOZEN SMALL COOKIES

ROCKS

From Michigan

This is from a handwritten recipe of my husband's mother.

2⅔ cups flour
  1 teaspoon ground nutmeg
  1 teaspoon ground allspice
  1 teaspoon ground mace
  ½ teaspoon ground cinnamon
  1 teaspoon baking soda
  1 cup butter
1½ cups dark-brown sugar
  3 eggs, well beaten
  2 cups chopped raisins
  1 cup chopped walnuts
  2 teaspoons vanilla extract
  2 tablespoons strong cold coffee

Sift together the flour, nutmeg, allspice, mace, cinnamon, and baking soda. Cream butter until soft. Gradually beat in sugar, beating well after each addition. Beat in beaten eggs, beating well. Put about ½ cup flour into a paper bag and add raisins and walnuts. Shake to coat well. Add raisins and walnuts, with the flour in which they were shaken, to batter. Stir in all remaining flour, the vanilla extract, and the coffee and mix very thoroughly to distribute fruit through the batter. If necessary, add a little more flour, 2 tablespoons at a time, but not more than 6 tablespoons. The batter should be very stiff. Drop by teaspoonfuls 2 inches apart onto buttered and floured cookie sheets. Bake in a moderate preheated oven (350°) for about 8–10 minutes or until golden and almost firm. Cool on racks.

ABOUT 65 COOKIES

TOLL HOUSE COOKIES

From the inn of the same name
in Massachusetts

½ cup butter
½ cup white sugar
¼ cup firmly packed light-brown sugar
 1 egg, beaten
 1 teaspoon vanilla extract
 1 cup flour
½ teaspoon baking soda
½ cup chopped walnuts or pecans
 1 6-ounce package semisweet chocolate bits

Cream the butter until soft. Gradually beat in the sugars, beating well after each addition. Beat in beaten egg and vanilla extract. Sift the flour and baking soda into the batter. Stir until smooth. Stir in nuts and chocolate bits, making sure they are well distributed throughout the batter. Drop by scant teaspoonfuls on lightly greased baking sheets, leaving a 2-inch space between cookies. Bake in a preheated moderate oven (375°) for about 8–10 minutes or until edges are beginning to brown. Transfer to wire racks and cool.

ABOUT 4 DOZEN

SOMEMORES

All-American

This treat, which brings nostalgia to many of my female friends, is pronounced "smores" and comes from the Junior Girl Scout Handbook, which says that this food is so good that you are certain to want "some more."

    one-third of a 1½-ounce bar milk chocolate
2   graham crackers
1   marshmallow

1. Make a sandwich of the chocolate and the 2 crackers.
2. Toast marshmallow to a golden brown.
3. Put it into sandwich between chocolate and crackers.
4. Press gently together and eat.

You can make other Smores:
* Use peanut butter or toasted peanuts instead of chocolate. (These are sometimes called "Robinson Crusoes.")
* Use slices of apples instead of crackers.
* Use chocolate-covered crackers and no chocolate bars.
* Use chocolate peppermints instead of chocolate bars.

Index